High public debt: the Italian experience

The Italian Macroeconomic Policy Group

The Italian Macroeconomic Policy Group first met in 1986. It consists of a small group of Italian economists who wish to promote discussion of economic policy issues that are relevant not only to Italy, but also of more general interest. The Group periodically commissions papers from economists based in Italy and elsewhere. Subsequently these papers are discussed by an international panel at meetings convened by the Group.

Current members of the Group are:

Giorgio Basevi
Mario Draghi
Francesco Giavazzi
Alberto Giovannini
Mario Monti
Paolo Onofri
Antonio Pedone
Luigi Spaventa

Centre for Economic Policy Research

The Centre for Economic Policy Research is a registered charity with educational purposes. It was established in 1983 to promote independent analysis and public discussion of open economies and the relations among them. Institutional (core) finance for the Centre has been provided through major grants from the Economic and Social Research Council, the Leverhulme Trust, the Esmée Fairbairn Trust and the Bank of England. None of these organizations gives prior review to the Centre's publications nor do they necessarily endorse the views expressed therein.

The Centre is pluralist and non-partisan, bringing economic research to bear on the analysis of medium- and long-run policy questions. The research work which it disseminates may include views on policy, but the Board of Governors of the Centre does not give prior review to such publications, and the Centre itself takes no institutional policy positions. The opinions expressed in this volume are those of the authors and not those of the Centre for Economic Policy Research.

High public debt: the Italian experience

Edited by

FRANCESCO GIAVAZZI

and

LUIGI SPAVENTA

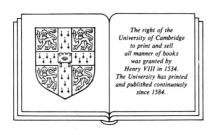

The right of the
University of Cambridge
to print and sell
all manner of books
was granted by
Henry VIII in 1534.
The University has printed
and published continuously
since 1584.

CAMBRIDGE UNIVERSITY PRESS

Cambridge
New York   New Rochelle   Melbourne   Sydney

Published by the Press Syndicate of the University of Cambridge
The Pitt Building, Trumpington Street, Cambridge CB2 1RP
32 East 57th Street, New York, NY 10022, USA
10 Stamford Road, Oakleigh, Melbourne 3166, Australia

© Cambridge University Press 1988

First published 1988

Printed in Great Britain by the University Press, Cambridge

British Library cataloguing in publication data
High public debt: the Italian experience.
1. Debts, Public – Italy
I. Giavazzi, Francesco   II. Spaventa, Luigi
336.3'433'0945   HJ8675

Library of Congress cataloguing in publication data
Surviving with a high public debt: lessons from the Italian
experience / edited by Francesco Giavazzi and Luigi Spaventa.
    p. cm.
Proceedings of a conference sponsored by the International
Center for Monetary and Banking Studies
Includes index.
1. Debts. Public – Italy – Congresses.   2. Fiscal policy – Italy – Congresses.
3.Monetary policy – Italy – Congresses.   4. Budget deficits – Italy – Congresses.
I. Giavazzi, Francesco.
II. Spaventa, L. (Luigi).
III. International Center for Monetary and Banking Studies.
HJ8678.S87 1988
336.3'4'0945 – dc 19   87-33394   CIP

ISBN 0 521 35635 0

CE

Contents

Figures

Tables

Preface

This volume contains the proceedings of the conference "Surviving with High Public Debt: Lessons from the Italian Experience", held on 15–16 June 1987 in Castelgandolfo, Italy. The conference is the first in a series to be held annually on issues of economic policy which are at the same time relevant for Italy and also of more general interest.

Members of the programme committee for this conference series were Antonio Pedone and Luigi Spaventa of the University of Rome, Mario Monti of Bocconi University in Milan, Giorgio Basevi, Francesco Giavazzi and Paolo Onofri of the University of Bologna, Alberto Giovannini of Columbia University and Mario Draghi of the World Bank.

Publication arrangements for this volume were handled by the Centre for Economic Policy Research. The Centre's involvement arose naturally from its close associations with Italian economists such as Marco Pagano, Alberto Alesina, Guido Tabellini and Francesco Giavazzi, who are represented in this volume and are members of CEPR's international network of Research Fellows. The growth of this network is a natural result of the Centre's emphasis on the international dimensions of economic policy and the importance of international collaboration in economic policy research.

We are grateful to Euromobiliare S.p.A., Centro Europa Ricerche and Prometeia, who provide financial support for this series of conferences, and to E.N.I., who hosted the first meeting at Villa Montecucco in Castelgandolfo. Thanks are also due to Stephen Yeo of CEPR for arranging this publication and to Carol Dasgupta, the Production Editor. Their painstaking work was essential to the book's swift publication. Finally, our principal debt is to the contributors, discussants and all the conference participants whose insights and hard work have ensured that this volume is both authoritative and timely.

FRANCESCO GIAVAZZI
RICHARD PORTES
LUIGI SPAVENTA

Conference participants

Alberto Alesina, *Carnegie Mellon University*
Mario Arcelli, *Università di Roma*
Giorgio Basevi, *Università di Bologna*
Andrea Bollino, *Banca d'Italia*
Remy Cohen, *Euromobiliare SpA*
Carlo D'Adda, *Università di Bologna*
Marcello de Cecco, *Università di Roma*
Rudiger Dornbusch, *MIT*
Mario Draghi, *World Bank*
Barry Eichengreen, *University of California, Berkeley, and CEPR*
Renato Filosa, *Ente Nazionale Idrocarburi*
Stanley Fischer, *MIT*
John Flemming, *Bank of England*
Francesco Frasca, *Banca d'Italia*
Jeffrey Frankel, *University of California, Berkeley*
Gianpaolo Galli, *Banca d'Italia*
Francesco Giavazzi, *Università di Venezia and CEPR*
Alberto Giovannini, *Columbia University*
Piero Gottardi, *Università di Venezia*
Vittorio Grilli, *Yale University*
Tullio Jappelli, *Università di Palermo*
Patrick Minford, *University of Liverpool and CEPR*
Giuseppe Nicoletti, *OECD*
Maurice Obstfeld, *University of Pennsylvania*
Paolo Onofri, *Università di Bologna*
Marco Pagano, *Università di Roma and CEPR*
Ruggero Paladini, *Università di Roma*
Antonio Pedone, *Università di Roma*
Edmund Phelps, *Columbia University*
Richard Portes, *CEPR and Birkbeck College, London*

Pietro Reichlin, *Istituto Universitario Europeo*
Nicola Rossi, *IMF*
Luigi Spaventa, *Università di Roma*
Franco Spinelli, *Università Cattolica, Milano*
Guido Tabellini, *University of California, Los Angeles, and Università Bocconi, Milano*
Theresa Ter-Minassian, *IMF*
Ignazio Visco, *Banca d'Italia*
Charles Wyplosz, *Institut Européen d'Administration des Affaires and CEPR*
Stephen Yeo, *CEPR*

1 Introduction: is there a public debt problem in Italy?

LUIGI SPAVENTA

The purpose of this introductory chapter is firstly, to provide common factual background to the essays on various aspects of the Italian experience of debt growth collected in this volume and secondly, to discuss briefly some issues of analysis and policy which, though immediately relevant for Italy, are perhaps of more than local interest. The summary review of facts and figures in the first part, and the discussion of issues in the second, have no ambition to provide accomplished theoretical or empirical answers, this task being left to other essays in the volume or to further research.

1 A review of the facts and figures

1.1 A preliminary word of warning on the situation of the data base is in order. Italy's national accounts were recently subjected to a very thorough revision. The results of the revision were to increase the estimates of GDP by as much as 15–18 percent, to change the composition of both demand and output and to alter the growth profile. For the moment, however, new series are only available from 1980. Furthermore, the revised sectoral accounts for households, enterprises and financial institutions are not yet available. There is thus a break in the series for all the ratios to GDP, and there are no data for sectoral disposable income, savings and expenditure.[1]

1.2 What is so special about Italian public debt? Figure 1.1 (where the break in the relevant lines corresponds to the break in the GDP series) provides the trivial answer: the high level reached by the ratio of debt to GDP (0.86 for overall debt and 0.72 for non-monetary debt in 1986),[2] its almost uninterrupted rise in the past 11 years, and the steady speed of its rise in the past six years. The climb is expected to continue at more or less the same pace for the next two or three years, while levels well above 1

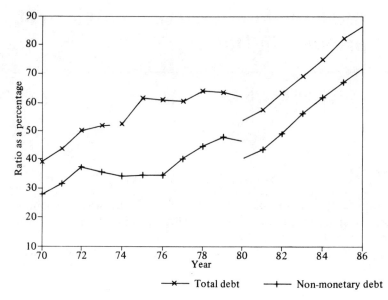

Figure 1.1   Ratio of total and non-monetary debt to GDP.
Sources:
1 Bank of Italy.
2 Camera dei deputati, *L'indebitamento pubblico in Italia*, 1985.

for the overall ratio are considered plausible in the not too distant future, by longer-run projections.[3]

We may be suitably impressed by such high figures. But we also know that neither economic theory nor economic history provide us with any cogent criterion by which we can decide that a particular level of the ratio is "too high." We have the uneasy feeling that something at some stage may happen: what and when, however, we hardly know in sufficiently general terms (though any individual episode of debt crisis can of course be modeled by introducing specific assumptions as to agents' behavior and expectations). The transversality condition imposing an intertemporal budget constraint upon the government does not by itself set any limit to the level of the ratio. We can say at most that, if irrelevance theorems do not hold, an optimal plan would require the ratio to be kept constant at mid-cycle, with "tax smoothing" over the cycle: but constant at which level?[4]

What we *can* say, at this stage, is that the Italian figures are very high, both in terms of contemporary international comparisons and, with due qualifications, historically.

We should of course treat international comparisons with the greatest

Table 1.1 Gross public debt: ratios to GDP

	Changes		Levels[1]
	1970–80	1980–86	1986
USA	− 7.5	+ 12.8	50.5
Japan	+ 39.9	+ 17.2	69.1
Germany, FR	+ 14.1	+ 9.9	42.4
France	− 4.4	+ 11.4	36.4
UK	− 31.0	− 1.2	53.8
Italy	+ 23.2[2]	+ 30.2[3]	88.6[3]
Canada	− 9.2	+ 22.8	67.4
Belgium	+ 4.2	+ 47.5	132.5
Ireland	+ 22.1	+ 40.1	127.8

Notes:
1 Data for 1986 are partly estimated.
2 Old national accounts.
3 New national accounts.
Sources: For Italy, Bank of Italy; for other countries, OECD.

caution, especially because of the differences in the definition of the "public sector." In Italy the latter includes general government, some public boards (like the railways and the post office – but not electricity), social security and public health (which are not included in some countries). But it does not include the (vast) State holdings in companies in the productive sector (which are included in other countries). Attempts to compare net, rather than gross, debt ratios, though justified in principle, are somewhat arbitrary, because it is difficult to find uniform criteria for the choice and the valuation of the assets to be netted out. I shall stick to gross figures, with one proviso: the Italian debt figures I use have been netted out for the Public Sector's liquid assets, which consists of deposits with the banking system.

Still, whatever caution has to be used in international comparisons, there is little doubt that Italy's position is somewhat anomalous in the league of industrialized countries (see Table 1.1). This is obviously so, if we consider only the major countries; while in a wider set, a higher debt ratio than in Italy (even after the revaluation of Italy's GDP) can only be found in two far smaller economies – Belgium and Ireland.[5] The comparison of levels is confirmed by a comparison of the recent *dynamics* of the debt ratio, which is perhaps more meaningful from an economic and less arbitrary from a statistical point of view. On this score, Italy lags behind other countries (notably Japan) in the 1970s; but since 1980 the

Table 1.2 Economic indicators

	Italy			EEC		
	1980–84	1985	1986	1980–84	1985	1986
Rates of change						
Real GDP	1.3	2.7	2.7	1.1	2.5	2.6
Gross fixed						
capital form	− 1.4	3.3	1.2	− 1.2	2.3	3.4
Id. equipment	− 3.1	7.4	3.1	..	9.2	4.2
GDP deflator	15.0	8.9	8.0	9.1	6.1	5.6
Consumption deflator	15.9	9.3	6.3	9.5	5.9	3.7
Ratios to GDP						
Gross private						
investment		17.2	16.0		16.3	16.5
Net borrowing of						
general govt		− 12.2	− 11.2		− 5.2	− 4.8
Current balance		− 0.8	0.7		0.6	1.5
Gross private savings		28.6	27.9		22.1	22.5

Source: Instituto Centrale di Statistica and Commission of the European Communities.

rise of the Italian gross debt ratios (3 percentage points for overall debt, 29 for non-monetary debt) is surpassed only by Belgium and Ireland.

The Italian debt ratio, though undoubtedly high by contemporary international standards, may not seem exceptionally so by historical standards. For long periods of her history, Britain exhibited levels of the debt ratio higher than one, and sometimes near two: this happened after the Napoleonic wars, in the 1920s and the 1930s, and again for a few years after the Second World War. In France the ratio peaked at above 1.8 in 1922 and then kept well above 1 until 1928. It remained above 1 in the US in the postwar period, until 1950. In Italy, we find levels similar to the current ones in the period 1933–36 and during the Second World War. In all these diverse episodes, however, the peak levels of the ratio could properly be considered as "abnormally" high, insofar as they were the result either of an overhang of debt due to a previous war effort or of an uncommonly severe recession. As the budget situation was restored to normal after wars, or as growth resumed, the debt ratio would gradually climb down from its peak.[6] In contemporary Italy, on the contrary, debt accumulation started in earnest in peace-time years. Cyclical factors may cause a jump, as in 1975, but the ratio never reverts to former levels and also keeps rising in more prosperous years of faster growth. It is thus legitimate to conclude that both the current level and the speed of the recent rise of the Italian debt ratio are uncommonly high in the light of past experience.

Italy's anomaly in the size of public deficits and debt is not matched by comparable anomalies in the recent overall economic performance, as appears from Table 1.2 which provides some summary comparisons with EEC aggregates. Italy's real growth rate has been on the whole slightly above the European average. Inflation was considerably higher, but the gap has narrowed in the past two years. The growth of private investment was slightly more sluggish, but the investment share in GDP is at about the European level. The gross savings ratio is, as we would expect, far higher than elsewhere, and the difference would be even more marked if we compared households' savings.[7]

This sketchy information on economic performances serves to complete the comparative picture, but cannot of course be even casually suggestive of any inference as to the effects, or lack thereof, of mounting public debt. I therefore abandon comparisons and turn to a brief consideration of the factors responsible for debt growth.

1.3 The path of primary deficits is one of the factors affecting the behavior of the debt ratio. Other variables, such as the growth rate of the economy or the real interest cost of debt may at times acquire greater importance, as witnessed by the British experience in the interwar period examined in the paper by Alesina. In the Italian case, a succession of primary deficits is the original cause of debt growth; the effect of these is later compounded by that of a mounting real interest burden.

Table 1.3 reports the ratios to GDP and the compound growth rates of revenues and expenditures, as well as the primary and total deficits and the Public Sector Borrowing Requirements (PSBR) for some selected years.[8] Starting with a primary surplus, a very low borrowing requirement and a low debt ratio in 1960, a deterioration of the situation already occurs in the late 60s, with the pace of non-interest expenditure outstripping that of revenues. This trend becomes more marked in the first half of the 70s. Later, the remarkable increase in the share of revenues (also due to the increase in real tax rates caused by inflation) was matched by a parallel rise in the share of expenditures, with the ratio of primary deficits to GDP stabilizing in the 3–4 percent range. (It is too early to know whether the 1986 decline is more than an ephemeral phenomenon.)

Between the ratios of primary PSBRs to GDP and the yearly *changes* of the total gross debt ratio there is not, nor would we expect there to be, any particular relationship. The path of the debt ratio also depends on

Table 1.3 Revenues, expenditures and deficits

Ratios to GDP	Revenues			Expenditure net of interest			Deficit			PSBR
	Taxes	Contrib.	Total	Current	Capital	Total	Interest	Net of interest	Total	
1960	17.6	8.3	31.4	26.2	4.7	30.9	1.6	−0.6	1.0	1.7
1970	16.8	10.7	32.4	29.7	4.8	34.4	2.0	2.0	4.0	6.3
1976	17.5	14.0	35.6	35.6	5.0	40.6	4.7	5.0	9.7	11.3
1980	21.3	14.5	39.9	37.2	5.2	42.5	6.3	2.6	8.9	11.1
1980	18.2	12.7	34.6	32.1	5.9	38.0	5.5	3.4	8.9	9.7
1983	22.7	14.1	40.8	39.0	5.3	44.3	7.8	3.4	11.2	14.4
1984	22.4	13.7	40.2	38.4	5.2	43.6	8.3	3.4	11.7	14.1
1985	22.2	13.7	40.6	39.0	5.9	44.9	8.3	4.3	12.6	14.9
1986	22.1	14.0	41.2	38.5	5.2	43.8	8.7	2.6	11.3	12.3
Compound growth rates										
1960–70	10.0	13.3	10.8	11.9	10.5	11.7	12.8			
1970–80	21.2	22.0	20.8	21.1	13.5	20.8	32.7			
1980–86	18.6	16.6	18.2	17.6	17.3	17.5	23.9			

Note: For the period 1960–80, old national accounts; for the period 1980–86, new national accounts.
Source: Bank of Italy.

the effects of the real interest cost of debt and of the GDP growth rate. Table 1.4 provides a more detailed account of the determinants of changes in the ratio to GDP of the sum of public sector securities (bonds and bills) on the market plus Post Office savings, which, after 1976 (see Table 1.5), represent around 95 percent of non-monetary debt.[9] The change in the ratio (line 11) is equal, as shown by the note to the table, to the primary PSBR (net of changes of deposits with the banks, line 2) *minus* monetary financing by the Bank of Italy (line 9) and other financing (line 8) *plus* the real interest burden (line 5) *minus* the effect of GDP growth (line 6). The loss in the real value of assets due to inflation (subtracted from nominal interest payments to obtain the real interest burden) is computed so as to allow also for the losses on new debt, while preserving stock consistency.[10] The interest burden is somewhat overstated, because interest payments also include interest on other forms of financing and net interest to the Bank of Italy: the error is not, however, very relevant nor does it affect the trend.[11]

Notwithstanding the difficulties of comparison due to the change in national accounts, Table 1.4 provides some relevant information. Note that the behavior of the primary PSBR does not follow closely that of the primary deficit as the difference between the two variables tends to increase in recent years.[12] The primary PSBR ratio rises on average in the second period, especially considering the likely upward revision of GDP with the new estimates for the earlier period. Also, the ratio of PSBR net financing from the Bank of Italy rises on average. Financing by the Bank of Italy becomes steadier, but does not change much, either as a ratio to GDP or as a fraction of the borrowing requirement.

A remarkable development is the steady rise in the real interest burden (as a ratio to GDP). More important, since 1982, the latter has always exceeded the GDP growth effect. Furthermore, notwithstanding the return to higher and more stable growth, this difference has increased over time, accounting for between one third and one half of the rise in the debt ratio. With a given real interest rate exceeding a given real growth rate, we would of course expect such a difference (line 7 in Table 1.4) to increase over time, as long as the increase in the debt ratio is not curbed by a matching primary surplus. But the difference between the real interest rate and the real growth rate has itself increased in the 1980s: the average ex-post real cost of the debt aggregate considered in the table (the real interest burden divided by the average of the debt ratios in the corresponding and the previous period) has increased in the 1980s relative to the real growth rate.

The rise of real interest rates in the 1980s was of course a worldwide phenomenon, and not an Italian peculiarity. If anything, Italy at the

Table 1.4 Determinants of changes in the debt ratio: 1976–80; 1981–86
Marketable securities and PO savings: ratios to GDP

	1976	1977	1978	1979	1980	1981	1982	1983	1984	1985	1986
			(Old nat. accounts)					(New nat. accounts)			
1 Ratio of real value of securities and PO savings to real GDP	24.8	34.4	41.8	44.0	42.3	38.0	42.8	50.2	55.5	60.9	66.2
2 Primary PSBR[1]	5.7	4.2	6.1	5.3	4.6	6.1	6.4	5.9	5.8	6.3	3.8
3 Interest payments	4.7	5.1	6.0	5.9	6.3	6.3	7.4	7.8	8.3	8.3	8.7
4 Correction for loss of real value of assets	5.0	4.0	4.6	6.6	7.7	6.2	5.7	5.7	3.9	4.8	4.3
5 Real interest burden: (3–4)	− 0.3	1.1	1.4	− 0.7	− 1.4	0.1	1.7	2.1	4.4	3.5	4.4
6 Effect of real GDP growth on debt growth	− 1.6	− 0.5	− 0.9	− 1.9	− 1.6	− 0.4	− 0.1	− 0.2	− 1.7	− 1.5	− 1.6
7 (5–6)	− 1.9	0.6	0.5	− 2.6	− 3.0	− 0.3	1.6	1.9	2.7	2.0	2.8
8 Other forms of financing[2]	− 0.5	2.4	3.0	− 0.4	− 0.8	− 1.7	− 1.2	− 0.5	− 1.6	0.1	− 0.4
9 Bank of Italy financing	− 6.3	2.1	− 2.3	− 0.1	− 2.5	− 2.9	− 2.3	− 0.2	− 1.9	− 3.4	− 1.2
10 (2 + 7 + 8 + 9)	− 3.0	9.3	7.3	2.2	− 1.7	1.2	4.5	7.1	5.0	5.0	5.0
11 Discrepancies	− 0.2	0.3	0.1	0.0	0.0	0.1	0.3	0.3	0.3	0.4	0.3
12 Changes of 1	− 3.2	9.6	7.4	2.2	− 1.7	1.3	4.8	7.4	5.3	5.4	5.3

Explanatory note to the table on the factors of growth of the ratio of real debt to real GDP

The assets considered are: bonds and bills on the market and Post Office savings.

Let:

B_t: the nominal value of outstanding assets at the end of year t

A_t: the borrowing requirement net of change of public sector deposits with banks and net of interest payments in year t

I_t: interest payments in year t

BIF_t: Bank of Italy financing of the borrowing requirement in year t

AF_t: other forms of financing net of changes of public sector deposits with banks

Y_t: nominal GDP in year t

y_t: real GDP in year t

$\bar{p}_t$: the average GDP deflator for year t

p_t': the GDP deflator for the last quarter of year t

C_t: the correction for the loss in real value of assets

g_t: the GDP real growth rate for year t

Then:

$$\frac{B_t/p_t'}{y_t} - \frac{B_{t-1}/p_{t-1}'}{y_{t-1}} = \frac{A_t}{Y_t} + \left(\frac{I_t}{Y_t} - \frac{C_t}{Y_t} \right) - \left(\frac{BIF_t}{Y_t} + \frac{AF_t}{Y_t} \right) - \frac{g_t}{1 + g5.5t} \frac{B_{t-1}/p_{t-1}'}{y_{t-1}} + \frac{\delta t}{Y_t}$$

where:

$$C_t = \frac{\bar{p}_t - p_{t-1}'}{p_{t-1}'} B_{t-1} + \frac{p_t' - \bar{p}_t}{p_t'} B_t$$

and δ is a discrepancy, largely due to the differences between the redemption value of bonds and their issue price.

Notes:
1 Net of changes of public sector's deposits with banks.
2 Includes banks' financing of public sector net of changes of public sector's deposits.
Source: Bank of Italy.

beginning lagged behind other countries, as real rates were still negative in 1980. Later, however, real rates increased steadily, often exceeding corresponding rates elsewhere. Further, the average ex-post real cost of debt appears at times to have increased more than the real yield on new issues. This leads me to consider the relationships between monetary policy and debt management.

1.4   I can be brief on the developments of monetary policy, which, together with the institutional setting of the relationships between the Bank of Italy and the Treasury, are examined in the paper by Guido Tabellini.

In the early 1970s the authorities all but lost control of the situation, as after a succession of domestic and external shocks, there occurred a sudden rise in inflation and a balance of payments crisis. Outstanding debt being all medium-term and with low fixed interest, bondholders suffered heavy losses. Owing to this and to the fact that the rise in nominal rates was insufficient to compensate for current and expected inflation, the market was unwilling to absorb new debt issues and monetary financing of the deficit increased steeply. Monetization reached a peak in 1976, with over 55 percent of the borrowing requirement and with debt to the Bank of Italy at 43 percent of the total. The return to a more normal type of Treasury financing began soon after, with the transition to a more orthodox course of monetary policy, only interrupted by a renewed inflationary outburst (not due this time to deficit monetization) in 1979–80.

In the course of this process, which found firmer grounds as a result of stricter adherence to the European Monetary System (EMS) discipline, the strategy of monetary policy also changed. There was a movement away from domestic credit expansion towards monetary aggregates (M2 and bank reserves) as the main intermediate target; and away from administrative controls, which also served the purpose of placing public debt with the banks.

To regain control over money creation with a high and rising public borrowing requirement, it was necessary again to attract the non-banking public into investing in government paper. This obviously required an adequate (and therefore sizeable, considering the starting point) rise in real yields. It further required innovations in debt management, since the issue of fixed nominal interest medium-term securities was out of the question in a situation of persistent high inflation and high inflationary expectations. Two such innovations, in succession, served the purpose of reconciling the needs of the Treasury with the inclinations of the public. First, short-term (from three months to one

Table 1.5 Composition of total public sector debt[1]

	Bonds		Treasury bills	PO savings	Foreign debt	Other[1]	Bank of Italy
	CCT	Other					
1976	—	17.3	10.1	16.9	1.5	11.0	43.2
1977	3.1	18.6	21.6	16.8	1.4	5.3	33.2
1978	7.5	20.3	23.9	17.0	1.4	− 0.5	30.4
1979	12.0	18.2	25.5	17.9	1.4	− 0.1	25.1
1980	9.6	14.1	33.5	15.8	1.6	0.1	25.3
1981	8.6	12.1	36.7	13.3	2.4	2.0	24.8
1982	14.0	9.4	36.9	11.3	2.8	2.8	22.8
1983	26.1	8.3	31.7	10.1	2.9	2.6	18.3
1984	30.9	7.6	28.3	9.3	3.0	3.7	17.2
1985	35.7	8.9	22.9	9.0	2.8	2.5	18.2
1986	36.9	11.6	20.6	9.2	2.2	2.5	17.0

Note:
1 Net of Public Sector deposits with Banks.
Source: Bank of Italy.

year) bills, previously issued only to smooth the Treasury's cash requirements and reserved only for banks, became a major debt instrument and were made available to general investors. Second, longer term variable-rate Treasury certificates were introduced, with a yield set equal to that of the six-months (one-year more recently) Treasury bills, plus a substantial spread.

The objective of luring savers back into purchasing public debt was no doubt successfully achieved with the help also of a regime of total tax exemption of interest on public securities, allied to a frequent increase in the withholding tax on bank deposits – which are near substitutes of Treasury bills and certificates. Table 1.5 (on the composition of total debt) shows the steep rise of the share of short-term bills and variable-rate securities (CCT): from some 10 percent in 1976 to almost 60 percent of total debt, and from 18 to 72 percent of non monetary debt, with the increase occurring mostly at the expense of fixed-rate debt (including PO savings). Table 1.6 shows the extent of the process of disintermediation with reference to public securities on the market, with an uninterrupted decline of the share held by banks and a parallel increase of that held by households.

Granted the success of the innovations in debt management aimed at a return to stricter monetary discipline, there is little doubt that they also involved some important costs. These costs have arisen from two

Table 1.6 Distribution of marketable debt by category of holders

	Treasury bills			Bonds			Total		
	Banks	House-holds	Others	Banks	House-holds	Others[1]	Banks	House-holds	Others[1]
1976	72.2	24.0	4.0	66.7	31.8	1.5	68.7	28.9	2.4
1977	74.2	22.1	3.7	72.5	25.0	2.5	73.3	23.6	3.1
1978	70.4	25.9	3.7	67.5	29.7	2.8	68.8	28.0	3.2
1979	57.2	36.9	5.9	66.1	30.5	3.4	62.0	33.4	4.6
1980	44.8	43.3	11.9	64.5	32.8	3.7	55.9	39.0	5.1
1981	39.7	53.1	7.2	58.1	37.7	4.2	46.4	47.6	6.0
1982	44.4	48.9	6.7	59.2	31.8	9.0	50.1	41.3	8.6
1983	37.2	58.5	4.3	54.1	39.7	6.2	46.0	48.7	5.3
1984	29.3	66.3	4.4	46.3	44.7	9.0	39.1	53.8	7.1
1985	17.6	76.2	6.2	43.3	43.4	13.3	34.6	54.2	11.2
1986	19.2	75.1	5.7	34.4	43.8	21.8	29.8	53.1	17.1

Note: The growth in the share of "others" in 1985 and 1986 is accounted for by the operation of mutual funds, which started in 1984. The share of mutual funds was the following:

	Total
1985	2.5
1986	6.7

Source: Bank of Italy.

consequences of the way chosen to place public debt on the market: the shortening of the average maturity of the debt, and, no less important, the effective collapse of the term structure of interest rates into the six-months (and, more recently, the one-year) rate, owing to the financial indexation to short rates of longer term certificates.

The average life of debt reached a minimum of 11 months at some stage in 1981; owing to the diffusion of medium-term, financially indexed certificates, it has gradually lengthened since, to reach some four years. As John Flemming points out in his discussion on Marco Pagano's paper in this volume, the arguments for preferring a longer to a shorter maturity of debt are not in principle obvious, or at least not clear-cut, without further specifications. In a system beset by political instability and where the investors' confidence is more likely to be unsettled by political factors and by the inordinate amount of noise generated at times from political quarters, the argument that a shorter maturity and a greater turn-over of the debt can cause fragility and may destabilize monetary policy, carries more weight. More relevant, the shortening of debt maturity occurred while real interest rates were rising steeply. An increase in the rate of turn over of debt magnifies the effect of the increase in real interest rates on the average real cost of the outstanding debt stock; the time profile of gross issues and of interest rates over the year may even be such as to cause an increase in the cost of the stock greater than the increase in interest rates, as we noted in the last section.

The virtual disappearance of long rates has limited the effectiveness and the freedom of monetary policy on at least two counts.[13] First, the high liquidity of debt instruments increases the substitutability between loans and bonds in banks' assets, thereby dampening the effects of monetary impulses on credit. Second, any change in the short (six-month) rate affects the cost of a very large share of the outstanding stock of debt: this inevitably constrains the extent to which the interest rate is allowed to vary and increases the number of occasions of conflict between the monetary and the fiscal authorities.

It is not obvious that these costs were entirely inevitable. They would be, if we take it for granted that the only other option was longer-term securities with fixed nominal interest. With high though declining inflation, but with inflationary expectations lagging behind the actual decline, the inflation premium would have to be such as to greatly increase the real cost of debt. (Actually, as expectations more recently adapted to the decline in inflation, issues of fixed-interest medium-term securities were resumed while the one-year replaced the six-months rate as the reference for new financially indexed certificates.) But it is an open issue, to which I shall briefly return later, whether this was the only available alternative or whether other innovations in the menu of debt instruments were (and still are) conceivable.

1.5   As we have seen, the outcome of the developments which I have briefly described, has been a remarkable increase in the share of debt owned by households, at the expense of that owned by banks: from some 26 percent in 1976–77, to almost 60 percent (allowing also for the share indirectly owned through the newly created mutual funds) in 1986. There occurred, as a result, equal profound changes in the composition of households' wealth.

Table 1.7 shows the compositions of households' financial savings and financial wealth. In recent years almost half of new savings has been invested in public securities;[14] the share of the latter in (gross) financial wealth rose by over 20 points in the decade. The substitution mostly took place at the expense of monetary assets. This development, which reflects the peculiar role of bank deposits as the once preferred (and more accessible) instrument for holding households' financial wealth, is examined in the paper by Bollino and Rossi, who analyze the house-

Table 1.7 Households: financial savings and wealth

	Savings				Wealth			
	1983	1984	1985	1986	1976	1981	1985	1986
1 Monetary assets	34.4	38.7	35.2	30.7	63.1	56.8	45.7	41.0
2 Public bonds and bills	50.3	47.4	38.9	29.1	4.3	17.3	26.7	25.4
3 Other MLT securities	4.7	3.2	2.1	1.6	6.6	2.5	2.7	2.5
4 Mutual funds of which:	—	0.9	12.2	26.6	—	—	2.2	5.8
4.1 Public bonds and bills	—	0.7	8.7	17.4	—	—	1.2	3.2
4.2 Shares	—	0.2	2.7	5.9	—	—	0.6	1.6
5 Shares	0.2	0.1	1.1	2.8	5.1	7.2	10.1	13.5
6 Others	10.4	9.6	10.5	9.2	20.9	16.2	12.6	11.8
Total	100.0	100.0	100.0	100.0	100.0	100.0	100.0	100.0
7 (2 + 4.1)	50.3	48.1	47.6	46.5	4.3	17.3	27.9	28.6
Memorandum item: ratio of total to GDP	15.3	15.6	15.5	15.7	..	108.4	112.5	124.6

Source: Banca d'Italia, Bollettino Economico, number 6 and Annual Reports.

holds' demand function for more liquid forms of wealth and the degree of substitutability between deposits, on the one hand, and Government bills and floating-rate bonds, on the other.

The reshuffle in the composition of households' wealth, however, goes beyond the substitution of Government securities for monetary assets. First, the introduction of capital controls in the early 1970s (now dismantled for the purchase of securities) caused a considerable decline in the share of foreign assets. The extent to which controls have been instrumental to the need to insure orderly domestic financing of persistently high deficits is far from obvious. The issue of capital controls is treated in the paper by Alberto Giovannini, and I shall briefly touch on it later from the viewpoint of the effects of liberalization on debt management, and, indirectly, on fiscal discipline. Let me only note here that controls may have restricted the choice of alternative assets in periods of high inflation and negative interest rates, as in the 1970s and again around 1980; later, controls have not prevented real rates from rising at, and above, international levels.[15]

Second, other changes have occurred in the composition of total (and not only financial) households' wealth. The ratio of total wealth to disposable income exhibits a remarkable constancy, at levels in line with those of other industrialized countries. The rise in real interest rates in the 1980s has, however, been accompanied by a decline in the share of the real component, due both to falling values of, and reduced investment in, real property and especially land.[16]

The analysis of past changes in the composition of wealth and of its determinants is important, if the outlook is one of continuing growth of the debt ratio. This leads me to a brief discussion of some issues of analysis and policy as may be suggested by the Italian experience of high and growing public debt.

2   A discussion of the issues

2.1   Given the size reached by the debt ratio and the prospect of further rises in the near future, is there, or is there going to be, a public debt problem in Italy? Let me adopt a loose and somewhat elusive specification of this question. A problem arises when the agents begin to lose some of their earlier confidence in the ability of the State to service its debt: when, in other words, there occurs some change in the agents' perception of the regime they are in.[17]

No such problem need arise if expectations are for a return to a stable norm of excess of the growth rate over the interest rate: debt service would then be taken care of by growth, without any particular commitment on the part of the authorities. This is not, however, the present reality. More important, the widespread conviction is that relatively high interest rates and relatively low growth rates are there to stay.

Ruling out this possibility, confidence in the State's ability to service the debt must rest on the belief that fiscal policy will at some stage generate surpluses for this purpose: in more formal terms, on the belief that the government meets an intertemporal budget constraint. In its general formulation, however, such a constraint provides a rather loose criterion to assess, in practice, the action and the credibility of finitely lived governments. Besides being compatible with cases of indefinite growth[18] of the debt ratio, the constraint spans over an infinite horizon: it thus provides the greatest freedom as to when primary surpluses will eventually replace deficits in order to service the accumulated debt. The underlying assumption is that any fiscal program meeting the intertemporal constraint is accepted as credible evidence that debt will not be serviced entirely by borrowing, no matter how far ahead in the future the achievement of primary surpluses is deferred. This in turn implies that credibility as to the debtor's ability to service the debt is unaffected by the size of the debt ratio.[19]

There are at least two reasons why this assumption is not likely to be fulfilled in practice. First, when the accumulation of debt has not been the result of "wars" or depressions and has lasted long enough, a commitment to generating primary surpluses *in the future* may lose credibility: the public is bound to wonder whether the constraint is ever going to bite and may become suspicious that Ponzi games are being played. Second, and more important, there is a problem of feasibility.[20] The higher the level the debt ratio is allowed to attain, the greater the size of primary surpluses which will eventually be required to meet the constraint and to service the debt. If there are perceived social and political limits to the government's ability to reduce expenditure and to increase taxation net of transfers, or, more generally, to enforce a growing redistribution of income from earnings and income from capital towards unearned income from interests on public debt, there are also limits to the level of the debt ratio which is compatible with a credible commitment on the part of the government to meet the intertemporal constraint and insure that the debt will not be always serviced by further borrowing.[21]

Supposing that at some stage the public's confidence begins to crack, what shape will a debt problem take? The symptoms of debt pathology may vary, depending on the history, politics and institutions of the specific case. Risk premia may raise the cost of new issues and alter the term structure of interest rates: the resulting increase in the cost of debt would make the problem even more intractable. Alternatively, the authorities may suddenly find it necessary to increase the monetary financing of the deficit. We must distinguish here between a long-run strategic decision to finance steadily, with money creation, a higher fraction of the deficit, taken because debt stabilization appears more feasible with a mix of lower explicit taxation and higher inflation tax,[22] and a sudden spurt of monetization, which is the unplanned but unavoidable result of a negative reaction of the market to new issues. Both in this latter case and when there is an incipient demand for risk premia, the emergence of a problem is likely to be accompanied by a shortening of the average duration of the debt, as in either case the expectations of higher nominal rates keeps the market away from longer-term bonds. The problem becomes more complex in a small open economy with free capital movements and only limited freedom to move the exchange rate, owing to the wider choice of alternative assets available to investors and to the loss of freedom in the conduct of monetary policy.

2.2   Is Italy anywhere near to facing this kind of problem, caused by a loss of confidence on the part of the public? Neither theory nor empirical analysis can help us much in providing convincing answers to questions concerning the formation, in a specific context, of agents' beliefs as to the regime they are in. This is so whether it be one of credible and feasible commitment on the part of governments to future primary surpluses (net of a constant seignorage) within the agents' horizon, or one of persistent but unsustainable deficits. I shall therefore confine myself to considering some aspects of the Italian case which are or may become relevant in shaping agents' expectations.

We saw that the record of the decade 1977–86 is one of a growing popularity of government debt enhanced by the initial concentration of households' wealth in bank deposits, the relatively primitive state of Italian financial markets and the poverty of the menu of alternative financial assets available to the public, the imposition of capital controls, a discriminatory tax treatment and a decline in the relative price of real assets. Considering the demand for monetary assets and for government securities, Bollino and Rossi, in their contribution to this volume, conclude that "the present (end 1986) level of total financial wealth and the structure of rate of return differentials would imply" further long-run substitution of public (floating rate) bonds for bank deposits "far beyond the one already taking place". Thus, from what we know of assets demand, the danger of a debt problem may seem remote; and all the more so, considering the debtor's power to use discriminatory tax treatment in order to reduce the attractiveness of alternative assets.[23]

Other considerations, however, may cast some doubts on, or at least suggest some qualifications to, this conclusion. First, the expression of good intentions on fiscal policy has lost credibility. A Treasury four-year plan to slow down and eventually halt debt growth was neither accompanied by operational targets regarding specific items of revenues or expenditures, nor otherwise followed by action. Nominal PSBR targets yearly set by governments have hardly ever been met.[24] Whatever improvements have occurred in the budget situation have been due more to faster growth of revenues rather than to reductions in the growth of expenditures and have proved inadequate to offset the rise in real interest costs and to check debt growth. More important, in view of the public's perception of future developments, increases in the tax burden meet with growing social and political resistance.

The opposition to higher taxes finds an explanation not only as a common symptom of the *Zeitgeist* of the 1980s, but also, to a greater extent, in the inequitable distribution of the tax burden in a country where tax evasion is so pervasive and tax avoidance so easy for personal incomes other than wages and salaries. What is less understandable is that governments, sensitive to this tendency but unable to remove its causes, have lately committed themselves not to increase further the ratio of tax revenues to GDP. This is a rash promise. Since it is unthinkable that expenditures can be cut by an amount sufficient to meet the rising real interest burden, either the promise will not be kept, at high political cost, or it will be realized that an intertemporal constraint cannot be respected. ("Who is going to pay for it?" is the oft repeated question of the non-technical press, which has recently discovered the debt issue for the benefit of its public.)

A fuller understanding of the alternative and of its implications may conceivably cause some damage, especially considering the medium-term effects of the recent measures of liberalization of capital movements.[25] A structural process of diversification into foreign denominated assets will gradually occur after the removal of existing limitations to investment in foreign non-monetary assets. Even marginal effects on the share of financial wealth invested in public debt may affect the cost of new issues and, *via* financial indexation, that of a large part of the outstanding stock. Greater freedom of capital movement requires further greater variability of interest rates, especially at an initial stage when the end of restrictions may feed expectations of parity changes within the EMS. (The effects of diversification, of expectations of rising interest rates and of anticipations of a realignment were felt in the summer of 1987. The demand for public bonds of longer duration collapsed; as only very short-term bills could be placed, the policy of gradual lengthening of the average life of debt had to be reversed *and* interest rates had to be raised substantially.)

Italy has not faced a true debt problem up to now; it is however possible that the conditions for a problem to emerge are building up. Greater instability of assets demand would make the system more fragile and compel the authorities into making awkward choices. The nature of these choices is illustrated, first, by the measures of September 1987, when temporary administrative controls on bank loans and on short-term capital movements were re-introduced, and second, by a recent statement of the Governor of the Bank of Italy, who, after pointing out that gross issues of public debt will exceed 40 percent of GDP in 1988, warned that even a slight difference between actual market behavior and that implied by the authorities' estimates "would jeopardize the control of bank reserves and the respect of the targets of monetary policy."[26]

2.3   Finally, I will turn briefly to some policy issues.

When the debt ratio is high and its growth becomes self-generating, owing to mounting interest payments, there always looms the temptation to take a short-cut to solve the problem – to find a way to get rid of at least part of the accumulated debt. Alesina, in this volume, after examining past experiences, concludes that drastic remedies of this nature (ranging from repudiation to a wealth tax) are not applicable to today's Italy: a view with which I concur, and for the same reasons, as I agree with his qualification that, once primary deficits have been eliminated, some form of "extraordinary" measure may be of help.

In the domestic debate, it is also sometimes suggested that recourse be made to "administrative debt management" – in short, to compel banks to invest a predetermined share of their assets in public debt instruments. This remedy would probably have positive effects on the level and the variability of the cost of debt; but the basic fiscal problem would remain unsolved, while there would be high costs in terms of resource allocation and of efficiency of the banking system.

Easy alternatives to greater fiscal discipline do not, therefore, exist. This obvious conclusion, however, by no means exhausts the list of the policy issues which deserve consideration. Some concern the timing and the mix of the re-entry policy which ought to be pursued. Should the authorities pursue a gradual elimination of the deficit, or should they do it all at once? Should they only cut expenditure or should they also raise taxes?

These are important questions, which, however, can only be answered in reference to a specific policy context, and not in general terms. Considering the Italian case, I surmise that credible gradualism may be a better and more practicable alternative, especially if deficit cuts are made to coincide with periods of high growth in world demand and are accompanied by measures to increase Italian competitiveness. With a structural primary PSBR net of seignorage at around 3 percent, the task of attaining a modest surplus does not appear so difficult, at least on paper, but it no doubt requires a moderate permanent increase in the tax burden.

A more general policy issue regards whether more constraints should be imposed on the behavior of governments and parliaments and if so, how it should be done. A well represented view, to which Guido Tabellini provides rigorous foundations in his contribution, is that fiscal authorities will only feel compelled to follow the straight and narrow path if life is made hard enough for them. Monetary authorities should thus set, and adhere to, rigid and non-permissive rules, while liberalization of capital movements should be enforced not only for its intrinsic merits, but also because it increases the costs of fiscal profligacy.

This is an intellectually attractive view, because it yields simple and unambiguous policy prescriptions. Changes of assumptions and of model specifications in theory, as well as the consideration of the peculiarities of individual policy cases may, however, lead to less drastic conclusions. It may thus be the case that, when the initial stock of debt, and hence interest payments, are very high, some degree of cooperation between the fiscal and the monetary authorities is appropriate, to avoid an incipient debt problem getting out of hand and becoming a full-fledged financial crisis. More relevantly, suppose that a credible program of gradual elimination of the primary deficit has been agreed upon by the fiscal authorities. Its political feasibility and its eventual success may depend on the possibility of achieving some parallel reduction in the real cost of debt – hence on a somewhat more pragmatic attitude also regarding the speed and the extent of liberalization of capital movements.

A related issue is that of debt management, which is discussed in the contribution by Marco Pagano. Is it possible to reduce the cost of debt (and also to alleviate the burden which debt management imposes upon monetary policy) by introducing suitable innovations in the working of the markets and especially in the menu of assets offered to the public? I neglect here institutional problems regarding the auction systems, the very imperfect functioning of the secondary market, and the role of financial intermediaries and the central bank in such a market.[27] It is perhaps more interesting to note that very little change has occurred in the composition of marketable debt in recent years (Table 1.5): short-term bills and floating-rate bonds indexed to the short rate still represent the largest share, while the share of foreign denominated debt in the total is particularly low in comparison with other countries. The disadvantages of this debt structure both for the cost of debt and for the conduct of monetary policy were briefly sketched in section 1.4, above. Considering the level and the variability of the inflation rate in Italy, issuing long-term securities with fixed nominal interest would have been far too costly. But then why not issue long-term real bonds, with a fixed real yield in terms of a price index? Pagano reminds us that debt indexed to inflation would probably sell at a premium. More important, sizeable issues of long-term indexed bonds would help to lengthen not only the average duration of debt, but also the term structure of interest rates (which was instead unaffected by the issue of longer term, but financially indexed bonds). This in turn would reduce the liquidity of debt instruments and increase the short-term freedom of monetary policy.

There are further arguments for an increase in the issue of long-term foreign denominated bonds. There has been in recent years, as pointed out by Jeffrey Frankel in his comment to the paper by Bollino and Rossi, a negative Euro-domestic differential. Foreign borrowing would not alter Italy's net position as it would only (and partially) offset the structural increase in Italian investment in foreign assets after the liberalization. Given the conditions of pent-up demand for currency diversification, foreign denominated public bonds tradable in the domestic market could be successfully placed (probably at a premium, as happened with some private issue) in domestic portfolios.

It is not easy to understand why the Italian authorities have not so far pursued a more imaginative and diversified policy of debt management which may have reduced the cost of debt. The "practical view," that the State should endeavour to minimize such cost, does not seem to have more general counter-indications, at least in the case of indexed or foreign denominated bonds. As I mention in my discussion of Pagano's paper, however, one reason for the monetary authorities' hostility to these applications of the practical view may be their aversion to all forms of indexation; another may be their fear that lower *nominal* interest payments would induce a more relaxed attitude on the part of governments, beset by money illusion. One obvious counter-argument is that, especially at times of uncertain expectations and diminishing confidence, the issue of indexed and foreign denominated bonds would represent an implicit and binding commitment by the government not to allow an inflationary outcome of the debt problem.

Italy has so far survived with uncommonly high levels and rates of accumulation of public debt: not much better than other more disciplined countries, but not much worse either. The original title of this conference and of the planned conference volume was "Surviving with a high public debt: the Italian experience". It was soon realized however that there was still much to explore of the ways of past survival, while that title may be interpreted as a forecast (or, worse, a program) for the future. One purpose of this introductory chapter was to help to explain why the editors chose to shorten the title.

NOTES

1 Data on sectoral *financial* savings are however available, being provided, and intermittently revised, by the Bank of Italy. Such data have not been affected by the revision of national accounts. The sectoral definitions of financial statistics do not wholly coincide with those of the national accounts: see Ministero del Tesoro (1987).

2 With the old national accounts the two ratios would have been approximately 1.02 and 0.85.

3 See, among others, Cividini, Galli and Masera (1987).

4 On the possibility of debt growth under an intertemporal budget constraint, see McCallum (1984) and, for a discussion, Spaventa (1987). On the irrelevance of the initial debt level for optimal plans see Pagano, in this volume.

5 Unlike the case in the latter two countries, the share of foreign public debt is negligible in Italy (see Table 1.5), so that the domestic debt ratio is highest in Italy.

6 In the British case both factors were present. The fact that the debt ratio did not undergo a process of gradual reduction after the First World War was not due to fiscal profligacy, but, as shown by Alesina's paper in this volume, to deflationary policies, which raised the real interest burden while keeping real growth low. For a summary of past experiences, see Alesina (1987), and Chouraqui, Jones and Montador (1986). The data on Italy are drawn from Confalonieri and Gatti (1986).

7 This has been a permanent feature of the Italian economy in periods, such as the 1950s and 60s, of low and about constant debt ratio.

8 There is, as usual, a break in the series due to the revision of national accounts. Consider that for 1980 the revaluation of GDP was slightly above 15 percent. Note that the revision has also affected the Public Sector accounts, as some items formerly included in the PSBR but not treated as expenditures have been transferred to the latter. Note further that the PSBR of Table 1.3 is, unlike the primary PSBR of Table 1.4, gross of the changes of the public sector's deposits with the banks.

9 The items of non-monetary debt not included in the ratio and included instead under "other forms of financing" (line 8) are foreign debt, bank loans net of deposits and some other minor items.

10 For the method of correction, see the note to the table and Cotula and Masera (1980).

11 The overestimation does not probably exceed 0.5–0.7 percent of GDP, considering the small share of non-monetary debt other than that included in the ratio and considering that a large part of the interests paid to the Bank of Italy are refunded to the Treasury and netted out from interest payments.

12 The difference between the borrowing requirement and the deficit is given by the net acquisition of financial assets: e.g. the increase in/capital conferred to State holding enterprises or acquisition of assets of special credit institutions.

13 See Ministero del Tesoro (1987).

14 The apparent decline in the share of savings invested in public bonds in 1985 and 1986 is due to the introduction of mutual funds at the end of 1984. Public securities, however, represent the most important component of mutual funds' assets; further, the majority of mutual funds is specialized, or semi-specialized in bonds, and hence in public securities.

15 Jeffrey Frankel, in his discussion of Bollino and Rossi's paper, in this volume, provides evidence in this sense.

16 See Fazio (1986).

17 See Sargent (1982).

18 Examples of indefinite growth of the ratio compatible with the intertemporal constraint are: constant total borrowing requirement and zero nominal growth rate of the economy, or a borrowing requirement growing at a rate lower than the interest rate but higher than the nominal growth rate of GDP. In either case the primary surplus must also grow indefinitely.

19 At any given point of time, with a given stock of debt, policies causing further non-temporary increases in the stock of debt are not optimal, as Pagano shows in his contribution to this volume. Such policies may, however, be consistent with the intertemporal constraint, in a long-term fiscal plan envisaging that they will be reversed at some stage in the future.

20 I take up this point in my discussion of Pagano's paper.

21 The consequences of, and the limits to, rising taxation are discussed in Spaventa (1987).

22 This is not "debt monetization," intended as the depreciation of the nominally denominated outstanding debt by means of a sudden burst of inflation. Assuming full indexation of the debt, to a steadily higher rate of monetary financing and of inflation, there corresponds a lower steady-state level of the debt ratio, and hence, under normal conditions of demand for money, lower taxation; if the size of debt affects the interest rate, the latter will also be lower, as shown in Spaventa (1987).

23 Soon after the introduction of a 12.5 percent withholding tax on interest from public debt, the withholding tax rate on interest from bank deposits was raised from 25 to 30 percent.

24 Setting targets in terms of the ratio of nominal PSBR to GDP may later cause bitter surprises in periods of declining inflation; a decrease in the ratio which is only due to a decrease in nominal interest has obviously no effect on the growth of the debt ratio.

25 In May 1987 an interest-free deposit on the purchase of foreign non-monetary assets was abolished and restrictions on the length and modes of financing of trade credits were removed. The latter restrictions were temporarily reintroduced three months after.

26 Audizione del Governatore della Banca d'Italia Carlo A. Ciampi innanzi alle Commissioni Riunite V del Senato della Repubblica e V della Camera dei Deputati, October 6, 1987.

27 See Ministero del Tesoro (1987).

REFERENCES

Alesina, A. (1987), "The End of Large Public Debts," this volume.

Camera dei deputati (1985), *L'indebitamento pubblico in Italia*. Roma.

Chouraqui, Jean-Claude, B. Jones and R.B. Montador (1986), "Public Debt in a Medium-Term Perspective," *OECD Economic Studies*, no. 7, Autumn.

Cividini, Andrea, G. Galli and R.S. Masera (1987), "Debito pubblico e politica monetaria – Vincoli di bilancio e sostenibilità del debito: analisi e prospettive," *Debito pubblico e politica economica in Italia*, edited by Franco Bruni, Roma.

Confalonieri, Antonio and E. Gatti (1986), *La politica del debito pubblico in Italia, 1919–1943*, Roma–Bari.

Cotula, Franco and R.S. Masera (1980), "Private Savings, Public Deficits and the Inflation Tax," *Review of Economic Conditions in Italy*, no. 3.

Fazio, Antonio (1986), "Debito pubblico, ricchezza e sviluppo dell'economia," Banca d'Italia, *Bollettino Economico*, February, no. 6.

McCallum, Bennett T. (1984), "Are Bond-Financed Deficits Inflationary? A Ricardian Analysis," *Journal of Political Economy*, vol. 92.

Ministerio del Tesoro (1987), *Ricchezza finanziaria, debito pubblico e politica monetaria nella prospettiva dell'integrazione internazionale*, Rapporto della Commissione di studio nominata dal Ministro del Tesoro, Roma.

Sargent, Thomas J. (1982), "Beyond Demand and Supply Curves in Macroeconomics," *American Economic Review*, May.

Spaventa, Luigi (1987), "The Growth of Public Debt: Sustainability, Fiscal Rules, and Monetary Rules," *Staff Papers*, International Monetary Fund, vol. 34, no. 2.

Discussion

RUDIGER DORNBUSCH

National Debt is like a toothache; it is best not to have one, but if you have got one it is next best to get rid of it as soon as you can. (E.H. Young, 1915)

There is nothing worse that a moderate evil! If wasps and rats were hornets and tigers we should have exterminated them before now. So with Great Britain's obligations to her *rentiers* arising out of the war. (J.M. Keynes, 1929)

When is public debt too high, and what happens when it becomes too high? Spaventa provides an excellent introduction to the issues raised by Italian debt and leaves us with these basic questions. There are few usable answers, in part because the question is so new. The old tradition in public finance allowed that debts be created during wars, national emergencies or major upheavals and that they should be retired during peacetime. A newer tradition requires that they be inflated away during peacetime. Yet another places primary emphasis on tax smoothing rather than debt management so that debt levels are allowed to drift indefinitely.

The peacetime (non-depression) growth of national debt which we witness today is something new; for a while it could be rationalized on cyclical grounds. Moreover, transitory and moderate growth of debt (relative to nominal income) could be defended any time. But steady growth in the ratio of debt to income, as shown for the Italian case in Figure 1.2, requires fresh thinking. It suggests that debt might grow without limits, raising questions about what happens at the end of the rainbow. In older literature this is called *Staatsbankrott*. Is this something of the past which somehow can no longer happen?

We do not really have many models of debt management that characterize debt problems.[1] There are plenty of models of the hyper-inflation process, including explosive paths of deficit finance. But surprisingly little has been done on what happens when debt is excessive. Work

25

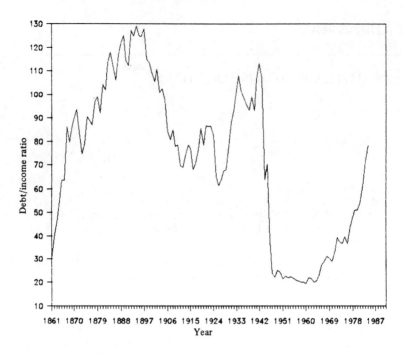

Figure 1.2   The Italian debt/income ratio

by Dornbusch (1978) and Sargent and Wallace (1981) showed that a shift from money to debt finance may ultimately be inflationary: when the government can no longer roll over the debt, recourse to inflationary finance generates the seignorage with which to service the interest on public debt. But the integrity of the debt is fully respected and inflation taxes (rather than income taxes) are the accepted solution to the problem of deficits and the inability to cut taxes or raise outright taxes. The literature on tax smoothing as a debt management rule is even further removed from a satisfactory answer to these problems.

1   Debt dynamics

The starting point is to identify exactly where the debt problem lies. When the real interest rate exceeds the growth rate of output the debt ratio rises automatically unless there is an offsetting non-interest surplus. The point is apparent from the familiar debt-dynamics equation:

$$x_t = \alpha_t x_{t-1} - \beta_t \tag{1}$$

Table 1.8 Debt determinants

	1960–69	1970–75	1976–80	1980–85	1986
Primary deficit	2.0	2.6	5.2	6.1	3.8
Seignorage	1.6	3.6	3.1	2.0	1.1
Real interest less GDP growth	− 5.4	− 6.5	− 8.3	− 2.3	0.5

Source: Spaventa (this volume), Masera (1987) and IMF.

where

α is the real interest rate less the growth rate of output

β is the non-interest surplus as a ratio of GNP net of seignorage

x is the debt income ratio

Table 1.8 shows averages for the main determinants of changes in the debt/income ratio.[2]

The table (allowing for possible data problems) helps us understand the broad determinants of the increasing debt/income ratio. In the 1960s the debt ratio was small, nominal income growth exceeded the interest rate, the deficit was small and seignorage paid most of the bill. Hence there was a stable debt/income ratio as seen in Figure 1.2. The stable debt/income ratio held up for a while into the 1970s because seignorage increased significantly more than the primary (or non-interest) deficit. By comparison, in the 1980s seignorage is down, the primary deficit is up and the growth rate of nominal income does not exceed interest rates by much.

2 Debt problems and solutions

By 1986 the problem is stark because now both the primary deficit and the high level of real interest rates relative to growth contribute to debt growth. The slowing of real income growth and the deliberate reduction in inflation dramatically reduce seignorage. When a situation has come to that point one can ask the following questions:

Is there a plausible reason to expect the interest rate/growth relationship to revert to the previous negative pattern?
Is there a possibility of a near term decline in the non-interest deficit?
Is there reason to believe that (non-inflationary) seignorage revenue might increase?

If the answer to each of these is firmly negative then, quite unquestionably, there is a debt problem. The debt/income ratio will continue rising sharply and without bound. And here is the problem: when the debt rises relative to income this brings about crowding out unless agents are suitably Ricardian. Interest rates must rise and capital formation is displaced or else external debt is being accumulated which leads to a reduction in long-run disposable income. There is also the certainty that at some point financial instability and foreign exchange crises result.

But, in fact, there is no definitive answer to the above questions. It may be the case that real interest rates are only transitorily high relative to growth, and policy possibilities and preferences might raise seignorage by a more relaxed attitude toward inflation, and the non-interest budget could improve because of greater ease of taxation or budget cuts.

2.1   Stark remedies

But supposing, tentatively, that none of the above are expected to emerge, what could the government do and when is the time to take action? To stop the debt accumulation and its crowding out effects, and rising financial instability, the government has essentially three remedies: The first is to break with the pattern of primary deficits by raising taxes or improving tax collection and by reducing outlays. Italy has already experienced such a shift in tax collection, albeit without an improvement in the primary surplus. Bringing about a shift in the primary surplus has political and/or economic costs which recent governments have found themselves unable to accept.

The shift in the non-interest budget is not only a political issue. It also involves economic costs among which one would certainly include the resource allocation effects of distortive taxes. The more the extra taxes required to improve the budget stem from taxation under high marginal rates applicable to factor supplies, the more welfare costs and underground effects will be important and must be included in the cost/benefit analysis.

The second method of improving the budget is a shift to higher inflation. This policy option comes in two variants. A moderate one is to opt for a stable and higher rate of inflation so as to raise seignorage and enjoy an erosion of that part of debt which is medium-term. The option is made very difficult by the campaign to reduce inflation to German levels and might bring about a loss in confidence and funding problems for the short-term debt.[3]

The alternative of using inflationary money creation to finance the deficit is also costly since, beyond a certain level, the inflation involves undesirable resource allocation effects. Moreover, without effective exchange controls, a rapid inflationary erosion of debt may be difficult to achieve. The traditional remedy of inflation is therefore limited and may, at best, help to stabilize the debt/income ratio.

The traditional way of liquidating debt by inflation is more drastic in that it involves a fast and large increase in the price level brought about by currency depreciation. Historically when debt becomes excessive, inflationary liquidation of debt is the normal route. The overriding experience is that the bond holder loses out. Colin Clark (1945) has given the political economy explanation:

> But excessive taxation, levied for payment of interest on public debt, and capable therefore of being relieved (in real terms) by a general rise in prices, may cause a temporary allegiance from the deflationary to the inflationary side in the part of politicians, bankers, economists and others, sufficient to alter the balance of power. The parliamentarian, banker or administrator, confronted with what he considers excessive taxation (or with a large deficit which holds out the prospects of higher taxation in the near future) becomes, consciously or unconsciously, more reluctant to erect those barriers which in more normal times, he would erect against rising wages and prices ... When the value of money has been reduced sufficiently to make the burden of the budget bearable, there will be a retransfer of allegiances: government authorities and bankers will resume their normal opposition to all proposals which they think would have an unduly expansionist effect.

An alternative to inflationary erosion of debts is to repay debts by recourse to a once and for all wealth tax or the capital levy. Such a procedure was used (along with inflation) in the aftermath of the First World War in various European countries.[4] In the United Kingdom it was advocated by Keynes, Pigou, Hicks, and Edgeworth among others. Keynes (1929, 174–175) noted later that failure to use a capital levy was a critical error in British debt management:

> Indeed, instead of abating these claims by a capital levy in 1919, we spent the subsequent years up to 1925 in riveting them in our necks still more heavily by raising the value of the currency in terms of which they had been contracted.
>
> The war-finance of other European currencies was far less "virtuous." But such is the duplicity of Fate that these "vicious" courses worked out better in the end than British moderation. For the result was to make the burdens so intolerable that they had, by mere force of events, to be entirely or largely obliterated through a depreciation of the currency in which they were contracted.

The basic argument for a capital levy is that this helps avoid the highly distortionary costs or high marginal taxes otherwise needed to gain the growth of debt. In the 1927 Report on National Debt and Taxation in the UK the opposition to a capital levy is argued as follows:[5]

We conclude that, even if there were a prospect of a Capital Levy being well received, the relief from debt which it offers would be insufficient to justify an experiment, so large, difficult and full of hazard; this would hold good in any circumstances not differing widely from those of the present time. Further, unless a levy were accepted with more goodwill than it would be possible to anticipate under present conditions, it would be highly injurious to the social and industrial life of the community.

The Report reflected a clear awareness of the time consistency issue: it is recommended that should a levy be undertaken, it should be large enough so that a repetition would not be anticipated for a very long time!

2.2   Solvency

An increasing debt/income ratio raises the question where the process leads ultimately, whether the government is obeying the budget constraint and, if not, when the resulting default (via inflation or capital levies) will be administered.

Even though debt may be high and growing rapidly, in an apparently unsustainable fashion, in an expected value sense the government may actually be solvent. The explanation is that there are other states of the world to which the system might move and in which the output growth rate exceeds the real interest rate, or the primary budget shows significant surpluses. There is some probability of a transition to these states and hence the expected value of debt service in these favorable states compensates for the apparent insolvency observed from extrapolating the current bad state as if it were to persist forever with certainty.

Specifically, following Cohen (1987), suppose there are two states denoted by the subscripts $k = 1$ and 2 with transition probabilities p_{12} and p_{21} from state 1 to state 2 and p_{21} for the reverse transition. Let $v_{jk} = (1 + y_{jk})/(1 + i_{jk})$ denote the ratio of the growth factor to the interest rate factor in period j and state k. Suppose for simplicity the primary surplus ratio β is a constant. Given a debt income ratio x_0 solvency requires that the debt income ratio be smaller than or equal to the expected value of debt service payments:

$$x_0 < \beta E \, \Sigma \pi v_{jk} = \beta \Phi_k \quad k = 1, 2 \tag{2}$$

where the right hand side denotes the expected present value of the primary surplus β expressed as a fraction of output.

There is no debt problem if the long-run expected value of growth exceeds the interest rate. In that situation the economy can expect to grow out of any debt. A debt problem can exist only if the long-run expected value of the real interest rate exceeds the growth rate. But the good/bad state distinction matters because extrapolating bad states may lead to an unjustified inference of insolvency. The good states in which the economy will find itself part of the time (in the expectation sense) may compensate at least when debt is sufficiently low.

Alternatively, we can think of different primary surplus ratios in the two states. In the favorable states the growth rate exceeds the real interest rate, for example, and the primary budget shows a surplus. In the adverse state growth falls short of the real interest rate and the primary budget shows a deficit. Thus instead of a constant we now have state dependent primary surplus ratios and the solvency condition in (2) becomes:[6]

$$x_0 < E \Sigma \pi \beta_k v_{jk} = \theta_k \qquad (3)$$

The point of this exercise is to show that solvency depends not only on the current situation (in the sense of $\beta_k v_{0k}$) but also on the transition probabilities and the description of alternative states. To believe that there is a state of near insolvency one must believe that the alternative states are not much better and/or the transition is not very likely.

What happens when the government becomes insolvent? Now the price per dollar debt falls to a discount determined by the equation:

$$P_k = \theta_k / x_0 < 1 \qquad (4)$$

As the government finances itself at least in part by rolling over debt the implicit interest rate paid increases over time as the insolvent state persists. Debt is being accumulated, insolvency increases and the implicit interest rate paid on debt rises relative to that on safe assets. Is there a natural end to the process? The process certainly must come to a threshold when the debt becomes so large that even in a good state there is insolvency. Thus the transition to that debt level will imply an increasing probability that the government cannot meet its payments fully in an expected value sense. That is *Staatsbankrott* and as that debt level is approached the interest rate at which the government lends may be extreme, but the government can borrow even if the bonds increasingly become state lottery tickets.

Thus governments cannot in fact let this process of deficit finance run its way to eternity. But the financial instability emerges often much before the state of insolvency. One reason is that the government may be reluctant to allow an increase in interest rates sufficient for the public to absorb the increasing size of the debt. In that case, run off of the short-term debt by monetization finances capital flight and brings about an exchange crisis. This is the "floating debt problem."

The other possibility is that government bond pricing becomes a central activity: the debt is large and the sensitivity of the bond price (or interest rates) to shifts in the state of the world (and in politics) becomes extreme. These shifts in turn affect the growth rate of debt and hence the evolution of the bond price over time. The instability of the high debt process is enhanced by speculation not only on the states of the world but also, after a while, on the question of how long the government is willing to accept that debt should be at the center of attention. In these circumstances there is a temptation to shift to normalcy: just as a government might fix the exchange rate because volatility is too much, so they might attempt to liquidate excessive debt by inflation or capital levies simply to establish normalcy.

Since there is no possibility of precommitment on debt service (except with state contingent bonds and perfect foresight) debt problems of the kind described cannot be avoided with total certainty. The important new fact is that they should occur in peacetime. In part this is a result of disaster myopia: the run of low growth and high real interest rates was simply not anticipated. In part it is a reflection of a new society where intertemporal public sector planning is no longer Victorian but rather very shortsighted. Institutionally the maturity of the debt adjusts, and crises need not be thought of until they occur, at which time it is too late to bring a gradualist solution.

NOTES

1 See, for example, Blanchard (1984) and Blanchard, Buiter and Dornbusch (1983).
2 The adjustment factor "real interest less real GDP growth" is calculated as the rate on government debt less the rate of increase of nominal GDP. Up to 1980 the interest rate is the government medium term bond rate and afterwards the average of this rate and the Treasury bill rate. Seignorage is calculated as the change in high powered money as a fraction of GDP.
3 On the history of funding crises for floating debt see League of Nations (1946).
4 See Rostas (1940) and Gottlieb (1952), the Report of the Royal Commission on Taxation (1928) as well as Alesina's contribution in this volume.
5 See Colwyn Report (1927) p. 296.
6 Again we assume that the expected long-run real interest rate exceeds the growth rate so that there is a potential for debt problems.

REFERENCES

Blanchard, O. (1984), "Anticipated and Unanticipated Deficits and Economic Activity," *European Economic Review*, August.

Blanchard, O., W. Buiter and R. Dornbusch (1983), "Public Debt and Fiscal Responsibility," CEPS Discussion Paper, reprinted in *Dollars, Debts and Deficits*, by R. Dornbusch, Cambridge, Mass: MIT Press, 1987.

Clark, C. (1945), "Public Finance and Changes in the Value of Money," *Economic Journal*, December.

Cohen, D. (1987), "External and Domestic Debt Constraints of LDCs. A Theory with Numerical Application to Brazil and Mexico." Unpublished manuscript, CEPREMAP, Paris.

Colwyn Report of Committee on National Debt and Taxation. (1927) London: HMSO.

Dornbusch, R. (1978), "Inflation, Capital and Deficit Finance," *Journal of Money, Credit and Banking*, February.

Flemming, J. S. (1987), "Debt and Taxes in War and Peace: The Case of A Small Open Economy," in *Private Saving and Public Debt*, edited by M. Boskin, J. S. Flemming and S. Gorini, Oxford: Basil Blackwell.

Gottlieb, M. (1952), "The Capital Levy After World War I," *Public Finance*.

Keynes, J. M. (1929), *A Treatise on Money*, vol. II. London: Macmillan.

League of Nations (1946), *The Course and Control of Inflation*. Geneva. Reprinted by Arno Press, New York, 1978.

Masera, R. (1987), "Four Arguments for Fiscal Recovery in Italy," in *Private Saving and Public Debt*, edited by M. Boskin, J.S. Flemming and S. Gorini, Oxford: Basil Blackwell.

Rostas, L. (1940), "The Capital Levy in Central Europe 1919–1924," *Review of Economic Studies*.

Sargent, T. and N. Wallace (1981), "Some Unpleasant Monetary Arithmetic," Federal Reserve Bank of St. Louis *Quarterly Review*, Fall.

Spaventa, L. (1987), "The Growth of Public Debt," *IMF Staff Papers*, June.

Young, E. H. (1915), *The System of National Finance*, London: Smith, Elder & Co.

2   The end of large public debts*

ALBERTO ALESINA

1   Introduction

Large government debts and deficits are not always "bad" nor always "good." Government deficits (and surpluses) can be used for optimally redistributing over time the burden of taxation. In particular, debt financing should be used in the downturn of the cycle (when tax revenues are low) and in cases of temporarily and exceptionally high government expenditures, such as during wars, natural calamities and so on.[1] This paper disregards cyclical fluctuations and concentrates on large accumulations of public debt.

The basic argument of this paper is that the choice of how to manage the debt is the result of a redistributive struggle between economic agents currently alive and, to a much lesser extent, between current and future generations. A redistributive problem is intrinsically a political problem; thus, the policies pursued by different countries at different points in time and their degrees of success cannot be understood without a reference to their political situation. To put it more strongly: theoretical models based upon the assumption of the "representative agent" (infinitely lived or finitely lived with heirs) cannot provide a convincing explanation of why one observes different solutions to the debt problem. On the contrary, it is only with reference to the political struggle over income and wealth distribution that one can account for these differences.

This paper examines from this perspective several examples of large public debts: specifically, Germany, France, Italy and Great Britain after the First World War and the United States after the Second World War. These examples have been chosen because they provide a vast array of different policies which could be chosen in an economy with large public debts.

Several points are emphasized in this paper. Let us first define as "stable" a political situation in which (a) one political side has a solid majority and controls economic policy decisions and/or (b) there is a low level of polarization between political parties. An "unstable" political situation is one in which neither of these characteristics applies.

In an "unstable" political situation, distributive disputes over which taxes to increase (or which type of transfers to reduce) generate fiscal deadlocks which undermine the government's ability to increase explicit tax revenues. This situation occurs if each group has enough power to "block" explicit taxes on itself but not enough political influence to impose explicit taxes on others. In this case public debt grows and the situation eventually resolves in an inflationary spiral because it forces the government to "monetize." In addition, the less independent the Central Bank, the more likely it is to observe this outcome. Furthermore, political uncertainty about the policies of future governments which could replace the current one may destabilize expectations, generate capital flight and exchange rate depreciation and add an additional channel of inflationary pressure. Germany and France in the first half of the 1920s and Italy in the period 1919–22 represent examples of these mechanisms.

In a "stable" political situation one political side imposes on the other the burden of the debt. If one political side or constituency has control over policymaking, it chooses the policies which maximize its own welfare. These policies in general may or may not coincide with those which would be chosen by a "social planner." This was the case in France in the second half of the 1920s, Great Britain in the entire inter-war period, and Italy under the Fascist regime. Relative to these, the United States since the Second World War has been an example of an approach to the debt problem involving less distributional struggle. This has been due to its fast growing economy.

Finally this paper attempts to evaluate the costs and benefits of different debt policies. In particular, non-defaulting, non-inflationary approaches (such as those followed in Great Britain, the United States, and France after 1926) are compared to defaulting approaches (such as those of Germany, Italy and France in the first half of the 1920s). These comparisons may shed some light on the choice between alternative policy options available in the current Italian situation.

The paper is organized as follows. Section 2 briefly reviews the theory of public debt with explicit references to problems of optimality and time-consistency; section 3 suggests a political approach to modelling the debt management problem; sections 4 to 9 illustrate the five historical cases; section 10 presents some normative observations which may be relevant for the current Italian experience.

2   The pure theory of public debt

Let us consider a "social planner" who supplies a public good financed by means of taxes, money creation or by borrowing against future tax revenues. The theory of optimal taxation prescribes the principle of tax-smoothening over time. Thus, debt financing should be used either in the case of temporary and exceptionally high government spending or when tax receipts are temporarily low, such as during recessions. (See Barro 1979, 1985a, b, 1987; Lucas and Stokey 1983.) This paper focuses exclusively on the second issue. In addition we refer to non-Ricardian models of debt, particularly to models in which income and consumption taxes are distortionary, as in Lucas and Stokey (1983), and lump sum taxes on accumulated stocks of financial or real wealth are not (as in Fischer 1980 or Calvo 1978). This difference between distortionary and non-distortionary taxes is crucial for the issue of dynamic consistency of optimal fiscal policy.

Consider, for example, the case of a "war" which is expected in the near future and is expected to be temporary. The ex-ante optimal budget policy is first to run surpluses, then to accumulate debt during the war when military expenditure is exceptionally high; after the war the government should run primary surpluses to service and reduce the outstanding debt.[2] Consider instead the case of a permanent increase in government spending. The optimal fiscal policy in this case is to increase taxes permanently and always balance the budget (apart from cyclical fluctuations). Additional examples of several alternative situations can be found in Lucas and Stokey (1983) and Lucas (1986).

However, these fiscal plans have many problems of time inconsistency, as shown, for example, by Calvo (1978), Fischer (1980), Lucas and Stokey (1983), Lucas (1986) and Rogers (1986) in various contexts. Namely, at some point in time the government has an incentive to deviate from the preannounced and ex-ante optimal policy. It is important to stress that this incentive arises even if the government maximizes the aggregate welfare of the country, which in these models coincides with the welfare of the representative agent. Consider, in fact, a "social planner" which after the "war" faces a large outstanding, nominally denominated, internal (and possibly external) debt. Suppose, also, that the "social planner" finds it in "his" interests to reduce the stock of outstanding debt. In order to achieve this goal, the planner has essentially four options: (a) to default; (b) to introduce an extraordinary tax on wealth (capital levy) "once and for all"; (c) to generate inflation to reduce the real value of the nominally denominated debt; (d) to create surpluses by reducing expenditure and transfers and/or by increasing income taxes and indirect taxes.

Let us briefly consider these four policies in the context of a "representative agent" model, i.e., abstracting from income distribution. The fourth policy is the ex-ante optimal policy, namely the optimal policy as viewed from before the "war." However, at the end of the "war," the first three policies may be superior to the fourth, in the sense that they may produce a higher aggregate standard of living (measured in terms of consumption level or of GNP). This is precisely the cause of the time-inconsistency problem that a "social planner" faces.

The advantage of an explicit debt repudiation or of an extraordinary tax on wealth is that they amount to a non-distortionary, possibly unexpected lump-sum capital levy which avoids the need for running budget surpluses for several years. More precisely, an unexpected non-distortionary capital levy is superior to a distortionary income tax on labor or to indirect taxes on consumption. The cost of this policy is the "loss of reputation," which occurs if the public thinks that such a policy will be repeated in the future. This may have three negative consequences: (a) it may discourage savings and investment for fear of future taxes on accumulated wealth; (b) it may discourage investment in government bonds; thus the government could be "liquidity constrained" for some time in the future; (c) it may produce capital flights out of the country.

There are theoretical and empirical arguments which question the dimensions of these problems in general. From a theoretical point of view, one has to distinguish between "excusable" and "non excusable" defaults. (See Grossman and Van Huick 1986a and Bental, Kantorovitz and Peled 1986.) The idea is that when the public decided to hold a government's debt it was expected that if a "bad" state of the world occurred (such as a defeat in a war) the government could default. Presumably, such a risk is in general well understood and is part of the "contract" between the government and the public. Thus an "excusable default" does not imply a loss of reputation. However, a "non-excusable" repudiation, namely a repudiation which is unexpected and unjustified by the clauses of the borrowing/lending agreement implies a loss of reputation for the government which breaks the "contract." This argument suggests that in some circumstances a partial default should not be seen as an unexpected and traumatic shock in the relationship between government and citizens, but simply as a plan for fiscal adjustment which was agreed upon, under the circumstances. In addition, it is unclear if a new government replacing the old one, which had issued the debt should feel bound by the clauses of the "contract." Thus, it is unclear if a new government damages its reputation by repudiating a "contract" which it did not sign. Empirically, there are several examples of countries which have defaulted on their internal or external debt and have been able to borrow again in the future, as emphasized for example by Dornbusch (1986).

The policy of inflating away the debt, if successful, has in many respects the same costs and benefits of an explicit default. There are two channels through which inflation can affect the debt burden: (a) An unexpected burst of inflation reduces the real value of outstanding nominally denominated debt. (This effect is stronger the longer is the maturity of the debt.) (b) Although anticipated inflation should not have an effect on the real value of the debt (see Barro 1979 for example), there is a strong empirical inverse relationship between real interest rates and expected inflation. Although "largely unexplained" this empirical relationship may be very important. (See Blanchard, Dornbusch and Buiter 1986.) If an inflationary shock has additional costs, besides the benefits of inflating the debt, it is unclear why it should be preferred to an explicit default.

The ex-ante optimal policy of running budget surpluses by increasing income and consumption taxes generates the deadweight losses of tax distortions which are avoided by a lump sum capital levy or by a repudiation. On the other hand this policy does not imply any loss of reputation for the government.

3   Towards a political theory of the debt

The economic models based upon the assumption of the "representative agent" and of the "social planner" fail to capture the crucial redistributive aspects connected with the problem of large public debts. The choice of "who should pay for the war" is essentially a problem of income redistribution between agents who are currently alive. To a lesser extent it also involves redistributive choices between current and future generations. In fact, large government debts have often been reduced (or at least dealt with) quite rapidly, certainly in the life cycle of a very large fraction of the population alive when the debt was issued. (This point is emphasized also by Poterba and Summers 1986.) Thus, in this paper we focus mostly on intra-generational redistributive flows.

There are three economic groups which have conflicting objectives in an economy with a large public debt:

(a)   the holders of the debt (labelled "rentiers");
(b)   the holders of physical capital, thus profit earners (labelled "businessmen"); in this group one has to include entrepreneurs and wealthy equity owners;

(c)   the holders of human capital, thus wage earners (labelled "workers").

Obviously there is a continuum between these three groups because each person may hold shares of the three different types of wealth. The basic argument of this paper is that the solution chosen by the government to the debt problem has very little to do with the criteria of optimality derived from a representative consumer/social planner model; instead it is the result of the political struggle between these three groups and their political representatives. In other words, actual policymakers do not compute costs and benefits of alternative debt policies as "social planners" would. On the contrary, the policymakers evaluate costs and benefits for their respective group or constituency and account for the possible reactions of their opponents. A given fiscal policy which may be very costly for society as a whole may be adopted if it is beneficial for the group which has political control. In game-theoretic parlance, the debt policy which is chosen results from a non-cooperative politico-economic game between players (i.e. these three constituencies) with conflicting economic interests.

The three groups favor different solutions to debt problems. The "rentiers" oppose explicit default or inflation and favor various forms of tax increases; and since they, in general, belong to the upper middle class, they tend to be averse to progressive taxation. The "businessmen" favor inflation, debt default and eventually non-progressive income taxes, or a combination of these three measures. They benefit from inflation as a means of reducing the debt burden, possibly as a means of reducing real wages and of stimulating exports via exchange depreciation. They oppose taxes on wealth and on physical capital. The "workers" favor taxes on wealth and on capital, progressive income taxes and debt default; they are hurt by inflation if real wages fall but they gain from it if employment increases. The "workers" oppose proportional income taxes and indirect taxes on necessary goods.

The debt policies followed in different historical episodes are determined by the results of this struggle over income distribution. The determinants of the solution of this political struggle are quite complex and go beyond the economic arena. In this paper there is no attempt to explain why, for example, communist revolutions did not overthrow Parliamentary institutions in Germany and Italy or why the Fascist regime took over in Italy. For the most part this paper examines the influence of political equilibrium on economic policy. The influence working in the opposite direction is only briefly explored.

When one political side gains enough political control, it imposes the burden of the debt on the other side(s). In an "unstable" political situation (the term "unstable" has been defined in the Introduction), this is not possible; each group has enough influence and "credible threats" to prevent the other side(s) from imposing a costly adjustment. This was the case in the Weimar Republic in Germany, of France in the first half of the 1920s, and of Italy in the period 1919–22. In all three cases the socialist "workers" were strong enough to represent a credible threat to the conservatives; the "rentiers" and the "businessmen" could not impose overly harsh measures on the working class for fear of communist insurrections. In some cases the socialists held office in left-wing coalitions, but they were not strong enough to impose expropriatory taxes on capital. The resulting fiscal deadlocks forced monetization of the debts. Thus, inflation is viewed in this paper as a residual outcome. This approach is consistent with Clark's (1945) observation that in several countries in the interwar period there seemed to be a limit to the tax/GNP ratio (which he estimates about 25 percent). Every time this limit was reached inflation increased.

In France the political uncertainty also had a destabilizing effect on expectations; thus it generated speculation against the franc which was a second channel of inflationary pressure, even when primary deficits were actually declining.

The lack of independence of the Central Bank eliminated one possible institutional obstacle to the monetization. In fact, both in France and Germany during the inflationary years the Central Banks were for all practical purposes agencies of the government. Non-inflationary fiscal adjustments were made much easier when institutional reforms made the Central Banks more independent, and strong and independent Central Bankers, such as Schacht and Moreau, were appointed.

A non-inflationary fiscal adjustment was achieved in France and Italy, when one side imposed its own regime: in 1926 the conservative coalition headed by Raymond Poincaré; and in Italy the Fascist regime.

Great Britain in the interwar period and, in particular, in the 1920s represents an example of a fiscal adjustment imposed by a solid coalition of "rentiers" and "businessmen." The political stability under a conservative coalition prevented inflation, explicit debt default and expropriatory taxes on capital. Instead, the Conservative governments followed deflationary monetary and fiscal policies, particularly in the 1920s. The United States represents an example of a consensus about how to distribute the burden of debt. The favorable economic conditions after the war relative to the interwar period made the policy of debt reduction particularly successful. Great Britain in the interwar period and the United States since the Second World War provide a remarkable

Table 2.1 The German public budget during the First World War
(in billions of marks)

Fiscal Year[1]	Expenditures	Taxes	Deficits covered by short-term borrowing	Deficits covered by long-term borrowing	Taxes over expenditures
1914	9.7	2.4	1.4	5.9	0.24
1915	26.7	1.8	2.7	22.2	0.06
1916	28.8	2.0	4.2	22.6	0.07
1917	53.3	7.7	16.2	29.4	0.14
1918	45.5	6.8	11.3	27.4	0.15

Note: 1 From April 1 to March 31.

Source: Computations from Graham (1930) and Mitchell (1975).

comparison, which highlights the different degrees of success of non-defaulting, non-inflationary debt policies as a function of different rates of growth of the economy relative to the real rate of interest.

4   Germany

Germany financed the extraordinary government expenditure during the First World War by issuing debt. Tax revenues were an almost negligible fraction of expenses for most of the war period. In addition, an increasing share of the war deficits was financed by short term borrowing (Table 2.1). Like all other countries, Germany was hoping to win the war and to make foreign taxpayers pay for it. However, Germany lost the war and at the end of it had about 50 billion marks of floating debt and about 58 billion marks of consolidated government debt. The servicing of the debt amounted to about half of the budget outlays (Bresciani-Turroni 1937).

4.1   Government debt, deficits and political conflicts

The political situation in postwar Germany was extremely unstable. The old aristocratic-militaristic regime collapsed with the German defeat. In the aftermath of the war, Germany was on the edge of a communist, Soviet-inspired revolution. Instead, a coalition of Parliamentarists and Social Democrats took office, prevented the communist revolution and proclaimed a Constitution in January 1919. The new democratic regime (Weimar Republic) was threatened on opposite sides by the forces of the old regime (aristocrats, nationalists, the army) and by the communist

Table 2.2 The German budget 1920–23
(in millions of gold marks)

Fiscal Years[1]	Taxes	Total expenditures	Taxes/ expenditures	Deficits	War reparations under Treaty of Versailles
1920	3,497	9,697	0.36	6,200	1,850.9
1921	3,924	8,936	0.44	5,012	2,810.3
1922	2,255	6,244	0.36	3,989	1,136.7
1923[2]	1,100	9,675	0.11	8,575	742.4
Total				23,776	6,540.3

Notes:
1. April 1 to March 31.
2. From April to December.

Source: Graham (1930) for taxes and expenditures and Bresciani-Turroni (1937) for war reparations.

movement, which retained its influence on the working class. Paxton (1975), for example, writes that "the Weimar Constitution was applied to the old society . . . and it came into being over the bodies of its natural supporters . . . The Nationalists, who hated the Weimar Republic . . . had plenty of leverage thereafter with which to fight it. Only the most successful operation would save the Weimar Republic from its internal enemies."

Large government deficits are shown in Table 2.2 even after the war (1919–23); in this period tax revenues were still well below one-half of the expenditures. The war reparations imposed upon Germany by the Allies aggravated the fiscal problem but they "were not the only cause and never the most important" (Bresciani-Turroni 1937). Several contemporary commentators (mostly Germans) claimed that the reparations sanctioned by the Treaty of Versailles were the sole cause of the German fiscal problem. Schacht (1931), in his memoirs, provides a passionate attempt to shift the responsibility of the German collapse to the Allies (particularly to France) for their "absurd" requests of reparations. In fact, the reparations can explain only about a third of the total German deficits in the period 1920–23 and they cannot explain the deficit of 1919 (since no reparations were paid that year). Table 2.2 demonstrates this point.[3]

The most important reason for the deficits of the 1919–23 period was the fiscal deadlock, which made it very difficult for the government to collect explicit taxes. In the summer of 1919 a tax reform was introduced. However the implementation and assessment of new taxes was so slow that it resembled a "comedy of inaction" (Maier 1975). This standstill was the result of the political struggle between the representatives of different constituencies which attempted to switch the tax burden away from their own group. Bresciani-Turroni (1937, chapter II, part 1) and Maier (1975) document in great detail precisely this fact. Bresciani-Turroni (1937) writes that "the revolutionary government had not the courage to resort to decisive fiscal measures because it feared that it would have given a great shock to that already weakened political situation." Sargent (1982) also notes that the political compromise between the new and the old regime in effect "undermined the willingness and capability of the government to meet its admittedly staggering revenue needs through explicit taxation."

A typical example of this fiscal deadlock was the attempt of the Social Democrats to introduce extraordinary taxes on wealth and industrial profits and/or directly to seize real assets sheltered from inflation. The Socialists proposed in 1919 a seizure of 20 percent of industry's stocks. This proposal was met with violent opposition from the Nationalists, the Democratic Party and, needless to say, from the spokesmen of the business community. Given this opposition, the Chancellor did not accept the Socialist plan and proposed a compromise: an extraordinary tax on wealth of about 4 per cent. Contemporary observers (surveyed by Maier 1975) acknowledged that this tax would have been fairly harmless for the wealthy; nevertheless, it was opposed. The "businessmen" proposed an advanced payment of regular income taxes instead of an extraordinary capital levy. This proposal was not accepted by the Socialists and the political debate continued and no new taxes were introduced in the years 1919–22.[4] Note that each of the "blocking coalitions" could appeal to a nationalistic chord in their refusal of accepting new taxes: they could always blame the Allies for "unreasonable" requests of war reparations.

In such a situation, the French occupation of the Ruhr was the "coup de grace" (Bresciani-Turroni 1937) to German public finances. Dornbusch (1987) notes that "the occupation was met by German 'passive resistance,' the financial costs of which completely outstripped any chance of price stability."

The struggle between France and Germany over war reparations can be characterized as an "internal fiscal deadlock" closely related to the difficulties that both countries experienced in raising tax revenues. In an attempt to place the cost of the war on the shoulders of the other country's taxpayers, the two countries paved the way for the last phase of

Table 2.3 Indices of nominal debt, real debt, inflation, money supply and seignorage in Germany (1919–23)

	Index of nominal debt	Index of CPI	Index of real debt	Index of real money balances	Index of nominal money supply	Seignorage $\frac{M_t - M_{t-1}}{P_{t-1}}$
1919						
Q1	104	100	104	104	104	3.9
Q2	120	100	120	117	117	4.9
Q3	133	133	104	91	121	2.4
Q4	144	233	63	58	135	4.0
1920						
Q1	153	523	30	31	161	1.6
Q2	176	490	36	39	190	1.8
Q3	221	490	45	44	213	1.6
Q4	250	490	51	47	230	1.0
1921						
Q1	275	457	60	51	233	1.0
Q2	304	443	68	55	242	1.1
Q3	344	600	59	45	266	1.6
Q4	393	1043	38	32	326	2.5
1922						
Q1	450	1466	31	27	385	1.0
Q2	492	2263	22	21	485	1.8
Q3	532	6433	10	13	773	2.2
Q4	1601	35503	5	7	2499	2.5
1923						
Q1	6972	147310	5	7	10909	2.8
Q2	23148	3640566	7	9	31028	2.6
Q3	N.A.	266125390	N.A.	8	29152838	6.7
Q4	N.A.	2.4E11	N.A.	5	1.5E+12	3.5

Source: Computations based upon Youal (1986).

the German hyperinflation. This non-cooperative game between the governments of France and Germany superimposed on the non-cooperative game between social groups in the two countries, led to even greater conflicts over income distribution.

4.2   Debt, deficits, the Reichsbank and the stabilization

The political and fiscal deadlock of the years 1919–23 forced the government to issue new debt and to monetize the deficits. An index of the money supply is presented in Table 2.3. In this political situation a strong and independent Central Bank, committed to a non-inflationary policy, might have played a role in influencing the events. However, in this period the Reichsbank was essentially an agency of the government; monetary policy decisions were directly influenced by the Reich.

At the beginning of the war, Germany abandoned the gold standard. During and after the war (until the stabilization) the German government had open access to the Reichsbank credit. At least until May 1922 the Reichsbank had no legal or practical independence from the government. The Reich's Chancellor had full authority to give "instructions" to the Bank. In May 1922 the Reichsbank became legally independent, but at that stage the Bank's President, Havenstein, could not in practice do much to resist the government's requests. (See Holtfrerich 1985 and Schacht 1931.) Schacht (1931) documents that Havenstein virtually never opposed resistance to any request from the government. Only in the spring of 1923, in the last stage of the hyperinflation, did he take a stand against the Reich and, as a result, was asked, but refused, to resign.

There are essentially three views (not necessarily conflicting) about the economic determinants of the stabilization. The first one (Keynes 1937 and Cagan 1959) emphasizes that the inflation was stopped when money creation was brought under control. Sargent (1982) emphasizes the role of a "credible" fiscal stabilization (i.e. the elimination of fiscal deficits) as the necessary and sufficient condition for fiscal stabilization. Dornbusch (1987) and Dornbusch and Fischer (1986) emphasize the stabilization of wages and of the exchange rate as a crucial additional element of the stabilization program. For instance, Dornbusch (1987) writes that the stabilization of the exchange rate "is the critical step that coordinates expectations . . . around a new trend of prices and thus gives a chance to fiscal stabilization."[5]

For the purpose of this paper it is interesting to notice that both Sargent (1982) and Dornbusch (1987) agree that the stabilization of the mark was made possible by the political stabilization, which in this respect was the necessary precondition. In fact, political stabilization was probably the crucial factor which made the program credible, unlike previous stabilization attempts. The Streseman government, which took office in August 1923, passed an "empowering law" which gave the government more power to implement quickly new laws and regulations and allowed a suspension of the Constitution whenever national economic interests required. The independence of the Reichsbank was reinforced by establishing that it would no longer be allowed to discount government bills. In addition, the sudden death of Havenstein in November 1923 provided the opportunity to appoint a stronger character, Schacht, President of the Reichsbank.[6] Schacht was a "self-

Table 2.4 The German budget after the stabilization
(in millions of marks)

Fiscal year	Tax revenues	Expenditure	Deficit
1924	4.7	5.0	0.4
1925	4.7	5.7	1.0
1926	5.3	6.6	1.3
1927	6.4	7.2	0.8
1928	6.6	8.6	2.0
1929	6.7	8.2	1.5

Source: Mitchell (1975).

confessed gold standard man" (Dornbusch 1987): this change of direction at the Reichsbank certainly added credibility to the stabilization program.[7]

4.3   Inflation and real debt devaluation: costs and benefits

One of the most spectacular effects of the inflationary process was the complete default of the outstanding debt at the end of the war, as Table 2.3 shows. By the fall of 1922 the real value of the outstanding debt was about 5 percent of its value in 1919: German government debt had essentially vanished. In the budget of 1924 the expenses for interest and amortization of the debt were estimated to be only 3 percent of total government expenditures (Bresciani-Turroni 1937). Table 2.4 reports the post-stabilization budgets.

The benefits of the default on the real debt are fairly evident: virtually all the burden of the debt and of interest payments had been eliminated.[8] In addition, at least during the 1919–22 period, the German economy was in a boom sustained by the price and exchange rate inflation. (See Table 2.5.) This economic expansion is particularly remarkable since most other countries were in a recession in 1920–21.

The costs of the inflationary default on the real debt were essentially three: (a) the economic costs associated with the last phase of the hyperinflation and with the stabilization of 1923–24; (b) the retaliation of France; (c) the political and economic effects of the redistribution of income and wealth. I will discuss these in turn.

(a)   In the last year of the hyperinflation, the effects of inflation on government finances turned clearly negative. It is well known that seignorage is not a monotonic function of the rate of money growth.

Real money balances fall during hyperinflations. Table 2.3 documents these facts. In addition, delays in tax collections automatically devalued government receipts, while nominal government purchases increased automatically with inflation. Table 2.2 in fact shows the drastic fall of real tax receipts over expenditures in 1923. (However, part of this fall is due to the French occupation of the Ruhr.) The fact that the inflation-devaluation process was in 1923 harmful for government revenues is well understood by Bresciani-Turroni (1937) who wrote that "[in 1923] various attempts to reduce the deficits . . . by new taxes would not have been successful if the exchange was not stabilized."[9] The German economy entered into a recession in 1923 which was dramatically aggravated after the stabilization (as shown in Table 2.5). The real costs of the stabilization were far from negligible and partly compensated for the earlier expansion. Nevertheless, the growth of the German economy in the period 1919–26 is clearly superior to all the other major European countries (as Table 2.6 shows).[10]

Thus, one may conclude that the beneficial effects of inflation on public finances occurred up to the summer of 1922 and then turned into costs in 1923. In some sense, there was "too much" inflation if the "goal" of the inflation was to eliminate the debt burden. This observation is consistent with the theory that German inflation was the sub-optimal result of distributional struggles rather than an explicit policy choice.[11]

(b)   The retaliation costs came from the French invasion of the Ruhr at the beginning of 1923. This desperate attempt of France to seize German assets as war reparations is a good example of a retaliatory act which imposes costs on both parties. The invasion accelerated the complete collapse of German finances and made it even less likely for France to receive reparations. (Obviously anti-French sentiments also reduced the willingness of Germany to pay.) The invasion was a highly suboptimal result of the non-cooperative game between France and Germany over war reparations, which generated the "international fiscal deadlock."

(c)   It is a fairly well established fact that the inflation and the default on the debt affected mostly the middle class. This was the group which held the largest fraction of government debt (Maier 1975) and had limited access to assets sheltered from inflation. Several authors have documented in great detail the annihilation of middle class wealth (see, for example, Paxton 1975). A second, perhaps less spectacular, channel of income distribution between social groups was from real wages to profits. Real wages show a very high

Table 2.5 The German real economy during inflation and stabilization

	Unemployment rate[1] (percent)	Index of physical volume of industrial production, per capita (1913=100)[2]	Index of physical volume of production of agricultural product, per capita (1913=100)[3]
1919	3.7	–	–
1920	3.8	61	62
1921	2.8	77	63
1922	1.5	86	69
1923	9.6	54	69
1924	13.5	77	71
1925	6.7	90	81
1926	18.0	86	67
1927	8.8	111	77

Sources:
1 Mitchell (1975)
2 Graham (1930)
3 Graham (1930).

variability in the period 1919–23. However, they never recover the pre-war level and they fall dramatically in 1923 to about 50–60 percent of their pre-war value (Bresciani-Turroni 1937).

Due to the collapse of the middle class, wealth distribution was made more unequal by the inflation. Most of the rich became richer and most of the middle class and lower class became poorer.[12] It is beyond doubt that this phenomenal redistribution of wealth deeply affected the political and social atmosphere of interwar Germany. The social and political consequences of such a massive and rapid redistribution of wealth played an important crucial role in the collapse of democratic institutions. Bresciani-Turroni (1937) for

Table 2.6 Interwar growth rates

	Average annual rates of growth of real GDP				
	France	Great Britain	Italy	Germany	"World"
1921–26	10.2	2.3	2.8	15.1	5.8
1927–30	5.0	1.3	1.4	2.4	0.3
1930–31	– 4.3	−5.1	−2.2	−10.9	−7.0
1931–38	– 1.6	3.1	2.8	8.0	2.8
1921–38	2.8	2.3	2.0	7.9	2.8

Source: Eichengreen and Wyplosz (1988), Table 1.

Table 2.7 Selected measures of French public debt
(billions of francs)

Year	Total internal debt	Nominal NNP	Total debt/NNP
1918	103.8	N.A.	N.A.
1919	154.1	N.A.	N.A.
1920	217.7	133	1.64
1921	244.4	140	1.74
1922	271.1	146	1.85
1923	274.4	163	1.68
1924	284.9	188	1.52
1925	289.2	208	1.39
1926	293.1	255	1.15
1927	286.5	259	1.10
1928	295.7	280	1.05
1929	298.5	300	1.00

Source: INSEE (1966), Annuaire Statistique.

Table 2.8 Ratio of short-term over total debt: France, Italy and Great Britain
(in percentages)

	France	Italy	Great Britain
1914	17.9	5.9	1.8
1918	45.2	34.0	23.7
1919	44.5	42.8	22.8
1920	38.8	29.8	19.7
1921	36.0	36.4	19.6
1922	35.7	39.0	15.4
1923	32.1	37.1	12.2
1924	30.7	35.1	11.8
1925	31.9	30.4	11.3
1926	32.2	30.5	10.8
1927	26.7	25.1	10.9
1928	15.5	1.9	10.5
1929	12.3	2.9	11.3

Source: Confalonieri and Gatti (1986).

example, suggests that "The paper inflation, by reinforcing the economic position of the classes which formed the backbone of the 'Right' parties, i.e. the great industrialists and the great financiers, encouraged the political reaction against the democracy."

Table 2.9 The French public budget
(Millions of current francs)

	Revenues			Expenses			
Year	Income taxes	Indirect taxes	Total revenues	Ordinary budget (a)	Extraordinary budget (b)	Total (a)+(b)	Surplus(+) Deficit(−)
1919	–	–	13,282	11,029	28,987	39,970	−26,688
1920	–	–	22,505	22,128	17,512	39,640	−17,135
1921	–	–	23,121	23,290	9,560	32,850	−9,729
1922	3,130	15,087	23,888	45,590	–	45,590	−16,702
1923	4,143	17,148	26,224	38,290	–	25,651	−12,066
1924	5,807	21,186	30,568	42,510	–	27,488	−11,942
1925	6,293	23,414	33,460	36,275	–	36,275	−2,815
1926	8,755	31,522	41,900	41,976	–	41,976	+76
1927	10,596	31,885	45,750	45,361	–	45,361	+389
1928	9,745	35,462	48,177	44,248	–	44,248	+3,929
1929	10,690	38,939	64,268	58,850	–	58,850	+5,419

Source: Bulletin Statistique (1966), and Mitchell (1975).

5 France

Both the dimension of the French public debt (around 1.5 of national product, Table 2.7) and its composition (Table 2.8) made the fiscal problem at the end of the First World War particularly dramatic. In addition, France suffered the highest physical costs of the war among the belligerent countries. During the decade after the war, the fiscal problem monopolized the political debate: the crucial question faced by France was who had to pay for the war debt.

5.1 Debt, deficits, inflation and politics

The years 1919–26 were marked by political instability and radical swings in the composition of the Chamber of Deputies. In November 1919 the most conservative Chamber of Deputies since 1871 was elected and a conservative government appointed. In May 1924 the Cartel des Gauches took office, and in August 1926 after several months of political chaos, the conservatives finally won the political struggle with the left and appointed a strong and very conservative government headed by Raymond Poincaré (1926–29). These political swings reflect the volatility of the French political situation of this period.

In the early 1920s the conservative government was unwilling to tax its own constituency (the wealthy and the business communities) and was constrained in its ability to tax the working class for fear of social unrest (Maier 1975). In this period (1919–22) a politically easy solution to the fiscal problem seemed achievable: war reparations from Germany. In 1919–21 the government showed complete confidence in receiving war reparations from Germany. For example, the French government presented two budgets: a "regular budget" with an optimistic small surplus and a large "extraordinary expenses" budget financed by borrowing and expected to be "covered" by German reparations (see Table 2.9). This show of confidence may have been a strategic move in the game between France and Germany over war reparations.

In the early twenties, France experienced three bursts of inflation: in 1919–20, in the winter 1923–24 and from the summer of 1925 to the stabilization in August 1926 (see Table 2.10). The index of wholesale prices increased about 80 percent between April 1919 and April 1920: this can be explained by the monetary expansion due to large government deficits. The following two bursts of inflation (winter 1923–24 and September 1925–August 1926) can hardly be attributed to current deficits; government deficits were in fact declining in both nominal and real terms (Table 2.9).[13] The fiscal problem in this period was the

Table 2.11 France: Index of exchange rate: francs per dollar (Base 100 Jan. 1919)

	Jan.	Feb.	Mar.	Apr.	May	June	July	Aug.	Sept.	Oct.	Nov.	Dec.
1919	100	100	106	110	117	117	126	142	154	158	171	200
1920	222	258	257	292	267	228	227	254	274	281	306	308
1921	284	255	259	250	222	228	235	237	248	255	257	241
1922	225	210	204	200	201	211	225	232	238	249	268	253
1923	275	299	292	275	276	291	311	324	314	308	334	349
1924	393	415	398	300	318	351	359	337	346	351	348	339
1925	340	347	353	353	356	385	390	391	389	413	465	491
1926	487	500	513	542	586	626	752	650	643	627	534	465
1927	463	468	469	468	468	469	469	468	468	467	467	466
1928	466	466	466	466	466	467	468	470	470	470	470	469

Source: Bulletin Statistique.

management of the public debt. The two inflationary episodes are a result of the effect of expectations on the behavior of investors and speculators.

By the end of 1922 it was hard to believe that the German taxpayers would have paid for the French debt; the French would have to pay. In his presentation of a new tax bill (November 1922) with a 20 percent across-the-board tax increase, the finance minister explained that "while reconstruction costs had been covered by non inflationary, long term bonds, the interest payments had piled up until they amounted to one quarter of total government expenditure. These had been charged against future German payments." (This quote is reported by Maier 1975.) Nevertheless, this tax increase proposed by the government was balked at by the Chamber, and thus postponed. Immediately, in December 1922, speculative attacks against the franc started. The failure of the invasion of the Ruhr as a means of collecting war reparations deflated even more the expectations of French holders of government debt.

The proposal of a 20 percent tax increase was opposed both by the left and the far right. The left called for an extraordinary (and progressive) tax on capital rather than a proportional and across-the-board levy. The Socialists also insisted, with some good cause, on the iniquity of the current tax structure which relied mostly upon indirect taxes as shown by Table 2.9. The system of personal income taxes was indeed fairly progressive, especially at the very high income brackets. However only 20 percent of the total revenues were collected with income taxes. Thus, the French tax structure bore heavily on the poor because of the high incidence of indirect taxes and on the very rich because of the progressivity, while the middle class mainly escaped from direct income taxes (Haig 1929). On the opposite side from the Socialists, the right wing of the conservative party argued against any progressivity in the tax system and proposed to rely even more heavily on indirect taxes. This debate continued throughout 1923. .

Only in February 1924 did the Chamber finally approve the tax bill, about 16 months after the original proposal was first presented. In the meantime the whole price index had increased about 60 percent (see Table 2.10). With the approval of the tax bill (March 1924) inflation stopped immediately (Table 2.10) but the election of the Cartel des Gauches made French investors nervous again.

This left-wing coalition was fairly divided: the Socialists and the Radicals disagreed on several issues, including fiscal policies. The Socialists favored a capital levy which was opposed by the Radicals (in agreement with the conservatives). They were afraid to compromise

Table 2.10 France: wholesale price index
(Base 100 Jan. 1919)

	Jan.	Feb.	Mar.	Apr.	May	June	July	Aug.	Sept.	Oct.	Nov.	Dec.
1919	100	98	97	95	94	95	100	100	103	110	117	122
1920	140	150	159	169	158	142	143	144	151	144	132	125
1921	117	108	103	98	95	94	95	95	99	95	95	94
1922	90	88	88	90	91	94	94	95	95	97	101	104
1923	111	121	122	119	117	117	117	118	122	121	127	131
1924	142	156	143	129	132	134	138	137	140	143	145	146
1925	148	148	148	147	150	156	160	160	158	165	174	182
1926	182	182	182	187	197	212	240	221	226	216	197	180
1927	179	181	184	183	181	179	178	178	178	173	169	171
1929	174	175	179	179	182	180	180	177	178	177	180	179

Source: Bulletin Statistique.

investors' expectations. "In practice this meant abandoning any effective taxing of dividends and interest . . . The split within the majority thus precluded any consistent financial policy" (Maier 1975). Also, the Radicals in the Cartel chained the government to ceilings on advances of the Bank of France to the government. However, the lack of new taxes (such as a capital levy) forced the government secretly to circumvent these ceilings. When this maneuver became known (April 1925), the political situation became more volatile. The following fifteen months were characterized by political chaos and by speculative movements against the franc. The wholesale price index increased almost 60 percent between April 1925 and September 1926; the franc depreciated about 85 percent against the dollar (Tables 2.10 and 2.11). In the summer of 1926 France was probably on the edge of a hyperinflation; prices were growing at an annual rate of almost 200 percent.[14]

5.2   Poincaré's stabilization 1926–28

Raymond Poincaré assumed the direction of a new solid conservative government on 22 July 1926 and kept the Ministry of Finance for himself. He announced a stabilization program which stopped inflation over-night. In July 1926 wholesale prices were rising at almost 15 percent (monthly) and the exchange rate depreciated 20 percent. In August, wholesale prices fell 8 percent and the Franc appreciated almost 16 percent against the dollar (Tables 2.10 and 2.11).

The Poincaré stabilization program was quite simple and its pre-condition was the defeat of the political left and increased political stability. The crucial elements of the plan were the following:

(a)   An increase in indirect taxes and income taxes on the lower middle class. Reduction from 60 percent to 30 percent of personal income taxes on the wealthiest fraction of the population. No capital levies were introduced with the exception of a mild "once for all" 7 percent tax on sales of real estate. This was the only concession to the Socialists. It is quite clear that "when the crisis came the remedy was sought in lightening the burden on rich taxpayers . . . and by increasing the levy on those of moderate means" (Haig 1929). The budget turned into a surplus in 1926 and remained in surplus for several years (Table 2.9).

(b)   The creation of a "Caisse d'Amortissement" to manage the outstanding public debt. The Caisse redeemed short term bonds (such as the "bons de la defense nationale") with the proceeds of some indirect taxes and by issuing long term bonds. The creation of the Caisse and the abolition of the practice of issuing short term debt freed the Central Bank from its role of pegging short-term interest rates (Makinen and Woodward 1986). The remarkable success of the Caisse in lengthening the composition of the debt (Table 2.8) is due to the confidence of investors in the program.

(c)   The appointment of a strong and independent personality such as Emile Moreau as Chairman of the Central Bank. The role of Moreau in the stabilization of the franc has not been emphasized enough in recent accounts of the French stabilization. His independence and resistance to the pressure of the Treasury to monetize the debt added credibility to the program.[15]

The stabilization program was completed on 23 June 1928 with the return of France to the gold standard. The gold value of the French franc was about 20 percent of its prewar value. From the appointment of Poincaré in 1926 and the return to gold, the economic and political debate focused on the alternative between revaluation of the franc to its pre-war value and stabilization at a much lower gold value. Unlike the political struggle of 1919–26 which was between "left" and "right" and was about who should be taxed, in 1926–28 two groups of the upper classes were confronting one another: "rentiers" who favored the appreciation of the franc, and "businessmen" who favored the "stabilization." Moreau (1954) provides a fascinating diary of this politico-economic debate: interestingly enough, although Poincaré was in favor of revaluation, the industrialists (in agreement with the Bank) succeeded in imposing the stabilization of the franc.

5.3   France in the 1920s: a miracle?

The rate of output growth of France in the 1920s was much higher than the world average and in Europe it was second only to Germany (see Table 2.6). Eichengreen and Wyplosz (1988) provide an excellent analysis of the French economy of this period and emphasize the role of the various components of aggregate demand in explaining output growth.

Despite the enormous public debt inherited from the war, France managed to avoid economic and political catastrophes. By the end of the decade the debt/output ratio had fallen to around one and its maturity structure had improved greatly (Tables 2.7 and 2.8). The "moderate inflation" of France in the first half of the 1920s contributed to the success of its debt-management problem. The French inflation sharply reduced the value of the long-term outstanding public debt at the end of the war.

Table 2.12 French nominal and real interest rates, inflation and growth

	Index nominal interest rates[1]	Inflation rate[2]	Real interest rate[3]	Growth in real national income[4]
1919	5.2	5.1	0.1	
1920	5.8	43.0	−37.2	
1921	6.1	−32.2	38.3	−7.4
1922	5.7	−5.3	11.0	21.6
1923	6.0	28.0	−22.0	8.2
1924	7.0	16.7	−9.7	15.8
1925	9.1	12.6	−3.5	0.8
1926	8.8	27.7	−18.9	4.4
1927	6.6	−12.1	18.7	−3.5
1928	5.3	0.0	5.3	5.9
1929	4.9	−1.4	6.3	10.4
Average 1921/29	6.6	3.8	− 2.8	6.25
Average 1919/29	6.4	7.5	−1.1	N.A.

Notes:
1. Index of interest rates on government bonds (Table VIII, p. 545).
2. Computed as the rate of growth of the index of retail prices given in Table II, p. 373.
3. Computed as nominal interest rate inflation.
4. Computed on the index estimated by Sauvy (Table XIV, p. 556).
Source: INSEE (1966), Annuaire Statistique.

For example the value of a 3 percent Rente Perpetuelle (which constituted about 40 percent of French Public Debt in 1925) had fallen to about 50 percent of its value from 1919 to 1926.[16] Blanchard, Dornbusch and Buiter (1986) emphasize (perhaps with some exaggeration) that "although the experience [of France] is less drastic than during the German Second World War hyperinflation, the reduction in the real value of public debt comes practically to the same thing." Table 2.12 displays the effects of inflation on real returns and compares the latter to the real growth of the economy. Clearly, inflation kept ex-post real interest rates on average well below the real growth of GNP.

The inflationary process may have also stimulated the French economy via a Phillips-curve effect on real wages. Alesina (1983) shows that real wages were indeed inversely related to inflation in this period.

On the costs side, one finds the effects of the stabilization of the franc in 1926–28. Dornbusch (1982), Spaventa (1982), Alesina (1983), and

DeLong (1986b) have emphasized that Sargent's (1982) claim that the stabilization had no real costs is overly optimistic. For example, industrial production fell about 20 percent between November 1926 and June 1927, reaching a level almost identical to that of 1913. Only two years later the index returned to the pre stabilization level. The index of real national product fell about 3.5 percent in 1927 (Table 2.12) and the (imperfect) available data on unemployment show a sharp increase of this variable in 1927–28 (see Alesina 1983).

In addition, in the summer of 1926, France was on the edge of a hyperinflation. The success of Poincaré's stabilization is due greatly to psychological effects: inflation stopped before Poincaré had time to actually do something. The program was credible because the political adversaries of the conservatives were defeated. This is the difference between the success of the stabilization program of 1926 and the "lack of success" of the program of 1923–24. Thus, it is hard to view French financial policies in the 1920s as a coherent plan. The observed outcome appears to be the result of a complex non-cooperative game between "players" with conflicting interests. In addition, as it will be argued later in this paper, it is not impossible that the debt policies of the 1920s had something to do with the poor performance of the French economy in the 1930s.

6   Italy

The "debt problem" of Italy at the end of the First World War was not only given by the dimension of government debt (about 75 percent of GNP) but also, and perhaps most importantly, by its composition. Almost half of the debt was short-term (Table 2.8): the maturity structure of the Italian debt was at least as "short" as that of the French debt. Interestingly enough, the maturity structure of the Italian debt shortened significantly after the disastrous military defeat of Caporetto in November 1917. (See Confalonieri and Gatti 1986.)

6.1   Debt, deficits and social conflicts 1919–22

The 1919–22 period was characterized by a revolutionary situation and social unrest. The weak centrist government of Giolitti was completely incapable of controlling the civil war exploding between the left (Socialists and from 1921 the newborn Communist Party) and the growing Fascist movement. Unlike in Germany, the Socialists refused to compromise with "bourgeois parties"; yet, on the other hand, the new-born

Table 2.13 The Italian public budget
(millions of current liras)

	Expenses	Revenues	Deficit or surplus	Revenues/expenses
1913	2843	2287	− 556	0.80
1914	2501	2287	− 214	0.91
1915	5224	2317	− 2907	0.44
1916	10550	3014	− 7536	0.29
1917	16920	4090	−12830	0.24
1918	25334	5812	−13552	0.23
1919	30857	7512	−23345	0.24
1920	21704	10210	−11494	0.47
1921	35139	13184	−20955	0.38
1922	33612	15444	−18168	0.46
1923	20172	15912	− 4260	0.79
1924	19264	17275	− 1989	0.90
1925	20202	18641	− 1561	0.92
1926	20107	20201	+ 94	1.00
1927	22967	20564	− 2400	0.90
1928	21481	19284	− 2107	0.90
1929	21711	20186	− 1525	0.93

Source: Ercolani in Fuà (1969).

Catholic Party refused to form a coalition with the anticlerical left. As a result, the political situation reached a stand still with the general elections of 1921: no majority was politically feasible in the new Parliament.[17] The Fascist Party took over on its own when Mussolini was appointed Prime Minister in October 1922.

In this period (1919–22) very little was done about the budget and the debt. Even though fiscal problems did not monopolize the political debate as in France and Germany, several tax proposals were discussed in Parliament. As in France and Germany, the Socialists asked for extraordinary taxes on wealth which were opposed by the right wing parties. In 1919 a broad based levy on wealth was introduced. However, the allowance for delayed payments (up to 20 years!) and the lack of enforcement of the new tax which allowed a very large fiscal evasion severely undermined the actual implementation of the new tax. This levy was almost completely ineffective.[18] As a result, deficits remained high and taxes covered much less than 50 percent of expenditures in this period (Table 2.13). In 1919–21 the Consumer Price Index (CPI) increased by about 60 percent and a similar pattern was followed by money supply (Table 2.14).

Table 2.14 The Italian money supply and CPI

	Checking accounts (in millions of liras)	Consumer Price Index
1914	8,252	100
1915	8,720	107
1916	11,088	134
1917	12,204	189
1918	18,620	264
1919	27,663	268
1920	34,854	352
1921	33,687	417
1922	36,016	414
1923	45,429	412
1924	52,709	426
1925	57,760	479
1926	66,859	516
1927	69,521	472
1928	73,703	437
1929	76,862	445
1930	77,508	430

Source: Confalonieri and Gatti (1986).

6.2   *Mussolini and the debt problem*

The improvement of the fiscal situation is perfectly correlated with the political consolidation of the Fascist regime and the increased political stability. In the period 1923–27 the Fascist government attacked the debt problem on two fronts: its dimension and its composition. The growth of the debt was reduced by a sharp decrease in government expenditure and an increase in taxes (especially taxes on consumption) in 1923–26 (Table 2.13). The achievement of budget balance in 1926 coincided with the complete annihilation of any political opposition to the Fascist regime. Due to the rapid economic growth of the period, the debt/GNP ratio fell from 75 percent in 1922 to about 50 percent in 1926–27 (Table 2.15).

It is fairly clear who had to "pay" for this fiscal adjustment: real wages fell by about 20 percent between 1921 and 1929 (Table 2.16). Industrial profits were increasing and no new extraordinary taxes on wealth or profits were introduced; consumption taxes (even on necessary goods) were increased and several social programs eliminated (Fuà 1969).[19] Zamagni (1975) illustrates the role of the Fascist unions in achieving nominal and real wage cuts when the government needed them.

Table 2.15 The Italian government debt

	Total government debt (millions of current liras)[1]	Debt/GNP
1914	15,766	65.6
1915	18,695	66.4
1916	23,857	58.9
1917	33,694	59.7
1918	48,402	70.3
1919	60,213	74.1
1920	74,496	60.1
1921	86,482	74.5
1922	92,836	74.8
1923	95,544	70.5
1924	93,163	65.1
1925	90,847	50.6
1926	93,789	49.7
1927	85,596	52.8
1928	88,287	53.8

Note: Computed at June 30.
Source: Confalonieri and Gatti (1986) for the debt; for CPI and GNP, ISTAT (1976).

Table 2.16 Italian wages, employment and output

	Index of nominal wages (1929=100)	Index of real wages (1929=100)	Index of employment (1929=100)	Index of GNP (1929=100)
1913	18	91		76
1919	22	135		80
1920	93	118	93	76
1921	115	123	81	75
1922	108	116	83	79
1923	120	121	84	84
1824	115	120	92	86
1925	124	115	100	90
1926	130	112	102	91
1927	121	114	94	91
1928	100	102	98	98
1929	100	100	100	100

Source: Ercolani in Fuà (1969).

The second line of attack on the debt concerned its cost and composition. The short maturity structure of the debt made the debt management very difficult: various unsuccessful attempts were made to achieve a "voluntary conversion" of short term bonds into long term bonds. The most dramatic failure was in 1924: five billion liras of long term (25 years) government debt were issued at 4.75 percent interest while only 1.5 billion were subscribed.

On 6 November 1926 the government adopted a legislative approach to the problem with a mandatory conversion ("conversione forzosa") of the debt. All the outstanding government bonds with a maturity shorter than seven years (for a total of 20.4 billion liras) were converted to a consolidated bond ("titoli del Littorio") at 5 percent interest. The conversion was at nominal face value with a small conversion premium (see Confalonieri and Gatti 1986 for details). The "Littorio" bond immediately lost more than 20 percent of its face value.

Less than eight years later (February 1934), the Littorio loan was converted into a 25 year loan at 3.5 percent interest. This new bond was clearly dominated by alternative assets available to the investors. In fact, there were massive attempts to cash in the bond. More or less legally, the Treasury refused to satisfy most of the requests; thus this second conversion was in practice "mandatory" even though formally "voluntary." The market value of the old "Littorio" bonds fell by about 30 percent in 1934.

6.3   Costs and benefits of the "conversione forzosa"

The two mandatory conversions of 1926 and 1934 represent in many respects a partially explicit default.

The benefits of this policy are self-evident: the government "adjusted" the maturity structure of the debt "once for all" in 1926 (Table 2.8) and reduced the costs of this adjustment in 1934. The cost of this policy was a loss of reputation. In the 10–15 year period after the first "conversione forzosa," the government found it very difficult and increasingly costly to borrow on a short term basis. The government was liquidity-constrained. In 1927 Mussolini was forced to announce that the traditional short-term bonds ("Buoni Ordinari del Tesoro") would no longer be issued. As a result, the Treasury in this period had to use various costly lines of short-term credit. The Treasury borrowed from banks at fairly steep rates and even illegal means of borrowing were used: for example the central government secretly borrowed from the cities of Milan and Rome (Confalonieri and Gatti 1986). The cost of short-term borrowing was probably about 2–3 percent higher after the first mandatory conversion.

The confidence of the investors was shaken even more dramatically in 1934 after the second conversion. This conversion (which followed the successful British conversion of 1932) was expected by the market. However, its timing was uncertain. The Treasury attempted to "sur‑ prise" speculators by announcing the conversion earlier than generally expected. As a result, many speculators attempted to cash in their bonds immediately after the announcement. The Treasury satisfied only a small fraction of these requests.

The conversions were rendered more costly by the financial difficulties incurred by several banks (particularly the Casse di Risparmio) which had invested heavily in government bonds. The government had to intervene to prevent financial panic.

7   Great Britain

By the end of the First World War Great Britain had accumulated public debt equal to about 1.3 times the GNP (Table 2.18). Even though its maturity structure was not as short as those of the Italian and French debt, repayments and renewals "followed each other so closely in the 1920s that the whole tended to coagulate into one single mass of war debt" (Pollard 1983).

7.1   A Conservative approach to the debt problem

As in France, Germany and Italy, the 2–3 year period after the war was characterized by social unrest and widespread strikes in Great Britain. Although this is one of the most turbulent periods in recent British history, it is clear that Great Britain had more stable democratic institutions and was a much more homogeneous society than Germany or Italy. Democratic institutions were never threatened by a revolutionary movement in Great Britain. The three British parties (Liberals, Con- servatives and the growing Labour Party) were also less polarized than the French parties.

With the exception of the brief interlude of the first Labour government in 1924, the Conservatives held office for the entire 1920s with a solid majority. Also, the Labour government headed by MacDonald in 1924 was very moderate. "The MacDonald government did more to adapt politicians of genuine working-class background . . . to the mainstream of British politics than vice-versa. . . . The MacDonald government was more a reaffirmation of economic liberalism . . . than a turn to the left" (Paxton 1975). In fact, this government was dependent upon Liberal votes for achieving a majority in Parliament; there were more moderate

Table 2.17 The British public budget (millions of current pounds)

	Expenditure	Revenue	Deficit (−) Surplus (+)
1913	192	198	+ 6
1914	559	227	− 332
1915	1559	337	−1222
1916	2198	573	−1625
1917	2696	707	−1989
1918	2579	889	−1690
1919	1666	1340	− 326
1920	1188	1426	+ 238
1921	1070	1125	+ 55
1922	812	914	+ 102
1923	749	837	+ 88
1924	751	799	+ 48
1925	776	812	+ 36
1926	782	806	+ 24
1927	774	843	+ 69
1928	761	836	+ 75
1929	782	815	+ 33
1930	814	858	+ 44
1931	819	851	+ 32
1932	833	827	− 6
1933	770	809	+ 39
1934	785	805	+ 20
1935	829	845	+ 16
1936	889	897	+ 8
1937	909	949	+ 40
1938	1006	1006	0

Source: Mitchell (1975).

Liberals than left-wing representatives in the Cabinet. After a brief second Labour government (1929–31), the Conservatives continued to dominate British politics in the 1930s.

Throughout this period the main preoccupation of the Conservatives and of the Central Bank was the stability of the pound. As soon as it was realized that the mounting unemployment was not a social threat, the Conservatives showed a "callous disregard for it" (Pollard 1983). Even in the 1930s, Great Britain was the only major European country which did not follow Keynesian fiscal policies to promote recovery.

The "economic orthodoxy" of the Conservatives, as prescribed in 1919 by the Cunliffe Committee, was very clear and simple: return to the gold standard at pre-war parities as soon as possible by revaluing the pound, create budget surpluses to reduce public floating debt, and promote a tight monetary policy to control inflation and capital flows.

Table 2.18 The British public debt

	Government debt (millions of current pounds)[1]	Government debt/GNP
1913	711.3	0.26
1919	7,481.1	1.30
1920	7,875.6	1.26
1921	7,623.1	1.44
1922	7,720.5	1.62
1923	7,812.6	1.71
1924	7,707.5	1.67
1925	7,665.9	1.57
1926	7,663.7	1.65
1927	7,652.7	1.58
1928	7,631.0	1.56
1929	7,620.9	1.53
1930	7,596.2	1.55
1931	7,582.9	1.68
1932	7,648.0	1.74
1933	7,859.7	1.78
1934	8,030.4	1.71
1935	7,992.4	1.63
1936	7,901.6	1.55
1937	7,909.9	1.44
1938	8,149.0	1.41

Note: Government debt is the "Aggregate Gross Liabilities of the State" from Mitchell and Deane, page 401. This variable includes government debt held by the Bank of Great Britain.

Source: Mitchell and Deane (1962) for debt; Mitchell (1975) for GNP.

7.2   Costs and benefits of Conservative policies

Tables 2.17, 2.18 and 2.19 need very few comments: they provide a self-evident description of the effect of the deflationary policies in interwar Great Britain.

The government pursued tight fiscal policies to create budget surpluses (Table 2.17): with the exception of a negligible deficit in 1932, the budget was in surplus every year from 1920 to 1939. The war debt had been contracted at very generous interest rates. These high nominal rates combined with a deflationary monetary policy (with declining prices) created very high ex-post real interest rates (Table 2.19): in the 1920s the average real interest rate on government debt was more than 6 percent, in the 1930s this average was 4 percent. These rates were much higher than the rate of growth of GNP, which was close to zero in the 1920s and

Table 2.19 Real interest rate, inflation, growth and unemployment in Great Britain

	Yield on consols (a)	Rate of inflation[1] (b)	Rate of growth of GNP	Real interest rate (a)–(b)	Rate of unemployment (percent)
1919	4.6	5.6	−9.1	− 1.0	2.4
1920	5.2	16.0	−6.6	−10.8	2.4
1921	5.2	− 9.2	−5.0	14.4	14.8
1922	4.4	−18.8	3.6	23.2	15.2
1923	4.3	− 5.4	3.5	9.7	11.3
1924	4.4	0.9	3.0	5.3	10.9
1925	4.4	0.0	5.4	4.4	11.2
1926	4.6	− 1.9	−4.1	6.5	12.7
1927	4.6	− 2.9	6.9	7.5	10.6
1928	4.5	− 1.0	1.6	5.5	11.2
1929	4.6	− 1.0	2.4	5.6	11.0
1930	4.5	− 4.0	0.0	9.5	14.6
1931	4.4	− 6.2	−5.1	10.6	21.5
1932	3.7	− 2.2	0.0	5.9	22.5
1933	3.4	− 3.4	2.0	6.8	21.3
1934	3.1	1.2	6.7	1.9	17.7
1935	2.9	1.2	3.9	1.7	16.4
1936	2.9	3.5	3.1	− 0.6	14.3
1937	3.3	4.4	3.8	− 1.1	11.3
1938	3.3	1.1	2.9	2.2	13.3
			Averages		
1919–29	4.61	− 1.8	0.1	6.4	11.1
1930–38	3.51	− 0.5	1.9	4.0	13.9

Note: Computed as rate of change of cost of living index.

Source: Mitchell and Deane (1962) for yield on consols; Mitchell (1975) for inflation, GNP and unemployment.

about 2 percent per year in the 1930s (Table 2.19). The debt service was about 7 percent of GNP in the 1920s and peaked to almost 9 percent of GNP in 1932 (Pollard 1983). Despite tight budget policies, the debt/GNP ratio did not fall in the 1920s; on the contrary, it reached a peak of about 1.7 in 1923 and remained well above 1.5 for the rest of the 1920s. This ratio had another peak during the recession years in the early 1930s reaching almost 1.8 in 1933. It is only in the mid-1930s, with the suspension of the gold standard (September 1931), the devaluation of the pound, and the reduction of real rates with the voluntary conversion of 1932 that the debt/GNP ratio started to fall (Table 2.18). Finally, note that in the entire interwar period, the British unemployment rate never fell below 10 percent (Table 2.19).

Table 2.20 Great Britain: taxation as a percentage of income

	Income of: (in pounds)				
	100	200	500	1,000	10,000
1918–19	9.9	7.9	10.2	16.9	42.5
1923–24	14.1	11.8	8.0	14.1	37.1
1925–26	11.9	10.2	6.2	11.0	31.2
1930–31	11.0	9.6	4.5	9.7	35.8
1937–38	10.4	8.4	5.6	11.8	39.1

Source: Pollard (1983).

It is quite clear that the British tax payers and recipients of government transfers suffered the burden of the war debt while the debt holders enjoyed very high returns on their assets.

It is interesting to examine briefly which taxpayers suffered most for the debt burden. Table 2.20 shows that the income tax structure was quite progressive, but this was reduced in the 1920s. In the 1930s this pattern was reversed, but overall it appears that the middle class was relatively more favored than the lower and the upper income classes. In addition, heavy duties on specific products (such as tea, sugar, tobacco, milk and others) had a regressive impact (Pollard 1983). The allocation of transfers and public expenditure also did very little in terms of income redistribution: the largest cut in government expenditure in the 1920s occurred in social services, including education. Barna (1945) estimated that in 1925 the working class contributed via taxes about 85 percent of the services received and in 1935 about 80 percent. He also computed that the income redistributed by the fiscal system was only 3 to 5 percent of national income.[20] The transfer from taxpayers to holders of government debt which was concentrated in the upper middle class introduced an additional regressive element to the system.

It is quite tempting to compare the French and the British approaches to the debt in the 1920s. John Maynard Keynes (1963) had clear views on this:

> In Great Britain our authorities have never talked such rubbish as their French colleagues or offended so grossly against all principles of sound finance. But Great Britain has come out of the transitional period with her debt aggravated, her obligations to the United States unabated, and with deflationary finance still appropriate to the former and a million unemployed as the outcome of the latter. France, on the other hand, has written down her internal war debt by four-fifths, and has persuaded her Allies to let her off more than half of her external debt; and now she is avoiding the sacrifices of Deflation. Yet she had contrived to do this without the slightest loss of reputation for conservative finance and

Table 2.21 The United States government debt

	Gross federal debt (billions of dollars)	Gross federal debt/ GNP
1946	271.0	1.34
1947	257.1	1.17
1948	252.0	1.03
1949	252.6	0.96
1950	256.9	0.97
1951	255.3	0.82
1952	259.1	0.76
1953	266.0	0.74
1954	270.8	0.74
1955	274.4	0.72
1956	272.8	0.66
1957	272.4	0.63
1958	279.7	0.63
1959	287.8	0.61
1960	290.9	0.58
1961	292.9	0.58
1962	303.3	0.55
1963	310.8	0.54
1964	316.8	0.51
1965	323.2	0.49
1966	329.5	0.46
1967	341.3	0.44
1980	914.3	0.35

Source: Economic Report of the President (1986).

capitalist principles. The Bank of France emerges much stronger than the Bank of Great Britain; and everyone still feels that France is the last stronghold of tenacious saving and the rentier mentality. Assuredly it does not pay to be good.

However, it is fair to add that the British economy suffered less than the French one in the depression of the 1930s. (DeLong 1968a provides a detailed comparison of these two economies.) Eichengreen and Sachs (1985) suggest that one of the reasons for the poor performance of France in the 1920s is the late devaluation of the franc. The French inflation in the 1920s could have generated an excessive anti-inflationary reaction in the 1930s, which aggravated the economic effects of the depression.[21]

8   The United States after the Second World War

At the end of the Second World War the United States had accumulated a public debt equal to about 1.3 times GNP, a figure very close to the

Table 2.22 The United States public budget

	Revenues (billions of dollars)	Outlays (billions of dollars)	Defense (percent of total)	Surplus(+) Deficit(−)
1940	6.5	9.5		−2.9
1941	8.7	13.7		−4.9
1942	14.6	35.1		−20.5
1943	24.0	78.6		−54.6
1944	43.7	91.3	88.6	−47.6
1945	45.2	92.7	75.9	−47.6
1946	39.3	55.2	18.8	−15.9
1947	38.5	34.5	11.4	4.0
1948	41.6	29.8	11.6	11.8
1949	39.4	38.8	13.6	0.6
1950	39.4	42.6	14.3	−3.1
1951	51.6	45.5	33.9	6.1
1952	66.2	67.7	46.4	−1.5
1953	69.6	76.1	49.3	−6.5
1954	69.7	70.9	41.2	−1.2
1955	65.5	68.4	39.1	−3.0
1956	74.6	70.6	40.3	3.9
1957	80.0	76.6	44.4	3.4
1958	79.6	82.4	44.8	−2.8
1959	79.2	92.1	46.0	−12.8
1960	92.5	92.2	45.1	0.3
1961	94.4	97.2	47.0	−3.3
1962	99.7	106.8	46.8	−7.1
1963	106.6	111.3	14.7	−4.8
1964	112.6	118.5	42.8	−5.9
1965	116.8	118.2	40.5	−1.4

Source: Economic Report of the President (1986).

debt/GNP ratio of Great Britain at the end of the First World War.

It is instructive to contrast the case of the interwar period in Great Britain and the post-Second World War case in the United States. In both cases the political situation is quite stable, particularly in the United States. American political parties after the Second World War were obviously much less polarized than European parties in the interwar period. Even though the two American parties may not have had identical redistributive goals (Hibbs 1987 and Hibbs and Dennis 1987), a political consensus was much more easily achievable in the United States in the 1950s than in Europe in the 1920s.

In many respects, British debt policies in the 1920s and American policies in the 1950s offer a remarkable comparison. Both are cases of

Table 2.23 United States real interest rate, rate of growth and debt/GNP ratio

	Nominal yields on US securities (average percent per annum)[1]	Rate of inflation of GNP deflator	Real rate of interest	Rate of growth of GNP (constant prices)	Debt/GNP ratio
1946	0.4	15.7	−15.3	−14.7	1.34
1947	0.6	12.9	−12.3	−1.7	1.17
1948	1.0	6.9	−5.9	−4.1	1.03
1949	1.1	−0.9	2.0	0.5	0.96
1950	1.2	2.1	−0.9	8.7	0.97
1951	1.6	6.6	−5.0	8.7	0.82
1952	1.8	1.4	0.4	3.7	0.76
1953	2.4	1.6	0.8	3.8	0.74
1954	1.7	1.2	0.5	− 1.2	0.74
1955	2.4	2.2	0.1	6.7	0.72
1956	3.0	3.2	−0.2	2.1	0.66
1957	3.6	3.4	0.2	1.8	0.63
1958	2.7	1.7	1.0	−0.4	0.63
1959	4.0	2.4	1.6	6.0	0.61
1960	3.6	1.6	2.0	2.2	0.58
1961	3.1	0.9	2.2	2.6	0.58
1962	3.3	1.8	1.5	5.8	0.55
1963	3.5	1.5	2.0	4.0	0.54
1964	3.9	1.5	2.4	5.3	0.51
1965	4.1	2.2	1.9	6.0	0.49
1966	5.0	3.2	1.8	6.0	0.46
1967	4.8	3.0	1.8	2.7	0.44
1968	5.5	4.4	1.1	4.6	0.43
Averages					
1948–58	2.0	2.7	−0.7	3.5	
1948–68	3.0	2.5	0.5	4.0	

Note: Average of interest rates on US Treasury Securities.
Source: Economic Report of the President (1986).

non-inflationary, non-defaulting approaches to the debt problem. In both cases no extraordinary capital levies of any significance were introduced. However, the United States since the Second World War has been much more successful than Great Britain in the inter-war years. 15 years after the end of the Second World War, the debt/GNP ratio of the United States was about one-half (see Table 2.21), and this ratio followed a downward trend until the early 1980s. This trend has been reversed only by the large budget deficits of the Reagan administration (see Barro 1987 on this point).

In the immediate aftermath of the war the debt/GNP ratio fell due to two factors: the budget surpluses (with debt retirement) of 1947–49 and the moderate inflation of 1946–49 (the average inflation was 12 percent per year). The budget surpluses were obtained with drastic cuts in government expenditures rather than with tax increases. The reduction in expenditure occurred almost exclusively in the military fraction which dropped in the period 1946–50 to only 10 percent of the total, before increasing again for the Korean war (Table 2.22).

The removal of price controls is partly responsible for the price increases in 1946–49 which inflated away a fraction of the outstanding, nominally denominated public debt. From 1949 onward, the reduction of the debt/GNP ratio was due to a sustained real growth in the economy, which was well above the real interest rate. The average growth of GNP in the period 1948–68 is about 4 percent and the average real rate is about 0.5 (Table 2.23).

This behavior of United States government debt has led Barro (1979, 1987) to conclude that the pattern of this variable is broadly consistent with the "optimal policy" of a social planner: the cyclically adjusted debt/GNP ratio peaked after wars and declined steadily in peaceful times. However, the recent experience of the current administration might have deviated from this pattern. Barro (1987) has documented this fact, and Alesina and Tabellini (1987a) and Persson and Svensson (1987) have provided a politico-economic explanation of this reversal.

In summary, the United States showed how "easy" it is to reduce the debt burden and the debt/GNP ratio in a rapidly growing economy with low real interest rates. Great Britain showed how difficult it is in the opposite case.

9   Conclusions: what have we learned that is relevant to the current Italian experience?

The current Italian public debt (about 80 percent of GNP) has been accumulated in "peaceful times": this debt is not the result of exceptional circumstances, such as a war or a natural disaster. In addition there has been no change of regime; the current political regime is the same as the one which issued the debt.

Based upon the discussion provided in this paper, let us examine how a reduction of the debt/GNP ratio could be achieved.

9.1   Inflation

Unlike in France or Germany in the interwar period, a depreciation of the nominally denominated debt with a burst of inflation would not work. Blanchard, Dornbusch and Buiter (1986) and Spaventa (1987) emphasize that the current public debt of industrialized economies, and in particular of Italy, are of such short maturity that it would not be easily depreciated by inflation. Spaventa (1987) notes that "the average maturity of the [Italian] interest bearing debt is [currently] of less than four years." In addition, "Treasury Bills (with a maximum duration of less than one year) [in 1985] accounted for almost 40 percent of total public debt, while more than 45 percent was in form of Treasury certificates, with a yield indexed to that of the six-month or ... of the one-year Treasury bills."

Thus, a burst of inflation would not work as a means of reducing the debt burden.

9.2   Default

The advantages of a debt repudiation are quite evident. The government can "start clean" by eliminating the need for taxation to service the debt. The advantage of such a solution to the debt problem in a situation where "interest payments have reached about the level of revenues from the personal income tax" (Spaventa 1987) should not be overlooked. However, it is important to emphasize (following Spaventa 1987) that such a remedy is permanently beneficial if and only if primary deficits are eliminated and "fiscal responsibility" established.

The costs of a repudiation are the loss of reputation incurred by the government. Unless the government can credibly commit not to default again, it would be "liquidity constrained" because no one would lend to a defaulting creditor, at least for a while. The ten year period after the "conversione forzosa" of 1926 is an example of this.[22]

With respect to the loss of reputation, there is an important difference between a post-war default and the default on public debt accumulated in peaceful times. A defeat in a war, especially if accompanied by the collapse of the old regime which had issued the debt (as in Germany), makes the default "excusable" (as in Grossman and Van Huyck 1986). A default is "excusable" if it was implicitly understood in the borrowing contract that a negative shock, such as war defeat, would have compromised the ability to pay off the borrower (i.e. the taxpayers). By way of contrast a repudiation of a debt issued in peaceful times may not be "excusable" and thus can potentially generate greater losses of reputation. In addition, a "new regime" may not lose credibility if it defaults on the debt issued by the collapsed old regime. On the contrary, if the same policymakers repudiate the debt issued by themselves in the past, and in "peaceful times," it is much more difficult to convince the public that "it will not happen again." The loss of reputation and the lack of confidence would be much bigger in the latter than the former case. Dornbusch (1986), however, expresses serious doubts about the dimension of these reputational costs in practice. Stein (1984) also suggests that the US should "throw away the National Debt" by not paying interest or principal on the outstanding debt.

A second cost of repudiation is redistributive. The default shifts the burden of the debt completely on to the debt holders. In Germany this implied the annihilation of the middle class which resulted in disastrous political and social consequences.

A third cost of a repudiation occurs if it generates financial instability. This is more likely to be the case if private financial institutions have heavily invested in government debt.

9.3   Capital levy

A "capital levy" is intended here as a broad based once and for all levy on all types of wealth, including government bonds. This is the remedy to the debt problem suggested by Keynes (1923). He thought that this was the best policy, even though he acknowledged that the political costs of such a policy would make it unfeasible.

An extraordinary broad-based tax on wealth to service and redeem the debt has some of the same costs and benefits of a default. However the advantage of a broad-based capital levy over a simple repudiation is that the former distributes the burden of taxation over a larger fraction of the public. For this reason, a capital levy is superior to a simple default.

A capital levy may be counterproductive if the government cannot commit itself to a fiscal plan which assures the public that in the foreseeable future no other "surprise" taxes on wealth would be introduced. Otherwise, such a policy might compromise the confidence of investors, propensity to save and possibly generate capital flights and financial turbulence.[23]

9.4   Increase regular taxes and reduce expenditures for several years

The fourth possibility is simply to run budget surpluses for several years without introducing extraordinary levies. The costs and benefits of this policy are the opposite to those of a default or capital levies. This policy implies no loss of reputation or confidence crisis but a long period of tight fiscal policies. The degree of success of such a policy depends very much on the growth of the economy, as shown by the British and the United States cases. Presumably, in terms of GNP growth and of real interest rates the Italian case of the next decade lies somewhere in between the case of Great Britain in the 1920s and the United States in the 1950s. Thus, even assuming fairly "optimistic" and responsible budget policies, this implies a long period of very high debt/GNP ratios for the Italian economy and thus a high debt/service ratio. The evaluation of the costs of such a large debt for the economy go beyond the scope of this paper (see Buiter 1985 for a survey of this issue): here we simply emphasize the difficulty of reducing this ratio without "extraordinary" measures.

Given the above discussion, consider the following fiscal plan:

(a)   Reduction of government expenditures to eliminate current and future primary deficits.

(b)   A credible commitment not to run primary deficits in the future; this commitment could be enforced by "fiscal rules" which limit the fiscal policies of future governments; the rule should be "flexible," namely it should prescribe escape clauses to account for exceptional circumstances, and should account for cyclical fluctuations of tax revenues.

(c)   A broad-based extraordinary tax on wealth to service and reduce "once and for all" the outstanding public debt.

This plan has many advantages over alternative policies, as emphasized above. It avoids a painful long period of tight budgetary policies and, unlike a default, it spreads the burden of the debt more evenly. If "fiscal responsibility" is established (point b) this plan may not imply a "loss of reputation."

However, the real question is the following: is the current political and institutional situation likely to adopt and enforce such a fiscal plan? As emphasized throughout the paper, lack of political stability makes a fiscal adjustment particularly difficult. The credibility of a weak and unstable political coalition is highly doubtful. Thus, the crucial ingredient of the plan could be missing. This is why the public debt is essentially a political problem.

NOTES

*   I am greatly indebted to my discussants, Marcello De Cecco and Barry Eichengreen for many useful suggestions. For comments on a previous draft and useful conversations I would like to thank Alessandra Barzaghi, Rudiger Dornbusch, Zvi Eckstein, Herschel Grossman, Anna Lusardi, Robert Miller, Angelo Porta, Richard Portes, Luigi Spaventa, Guido Tabellini, Susan Vitka and several participants of the conference. Saranna Robinson, Carol Goldburg and Anna Lusardi were valuable research assistants, and Alberta Ragan did a wonderful job in typing a messy manuscript. The usual disclaimer applies.

1 Henceforth the term "war" will be used to indicate any exceptional and temporary government expenditure.

2 How much the stock of outstanding debt should be reduced after the war is a function of the expectations of future "wars," i.e. of the expectations about future issuing of additional debt (See Lucas-Stokey 1983).

3 Graham (1930) and Bresciani-Turroni (1937) provide slightly different estimates of the deficits and of the war reparations; using either source the cumulated payments under the Treaty of Versailles amount to about 25 to 40 percent of the cumulated deficits in 1920–23.

4 The assassination of Ezreberg in August 1921 aggravated the fiscal deadlock by shifting political attention away from fiscal issues.

5 DeCecco (1983) documents the close relationship between the economic debate about the German inflation in the twenties and the current economic debate.

6 Graham (1930) writes that Havenstein's death was an "event which cannot be thought of as other than opportune." This quote is taken from Dornbusch (1987).

7 Holtfrerich (1985) provides a detailed history of the relationship between the Reich and the Reichsbank.

8 After the stabilization, some small compensation was paid to the holders of the worthless war debt. These compensations were, however, hardly significant (Bresciani-Turroni 1937).

9 Dornbusch and Fischer (1986) and Dornbusch (1987) emphasize that the stabilization of the mark automatically helped the fiscal stabilization by increasing real tax revenues.

10 However, several other factors affected the German real economy in this period (see Eichengreen and Wyplosz 1988). Thus it is not an easy task to isolate the effects of inflation on growth. Nevertheless, if one allows for the occupation of the Ruhr, Sargent's (1982) claim that there is no evidence of a Phillips curve in Germany in the twenties is debatable.

11 Grossman and Van Huick (1986) show how a sovereign who does not value its "reputation" enough can be "trapped" into an equilibrium with a sub optimally high rate of inflation, in an (unsuccessful) attempt to increase seignorage. Their argument does not rely upon distributional struggle but it is not incompatible with the approach taken in the present paper.

12 Needless to say, there were exceptions to this pattern. Bresciani-Turroni (1937) documents how several rich rentiers were ruined by the real government debt depreciation.

13 Barry Eichengreen cautioned me about the reliability of these official data on government budget, since they were probably manipulated for political reasons. However, the pattern of this data (namely a tendency to a reduction of the deficits) should be robust.

14 The idea that the French inflation was the result of a redistributive struggle is supported by Keynes (1963) who writes that "the level of the Franc is going to be settled in the long run . . . by the proportion of his earned income which the French taxpayer will permit to be taken from him to pay the claims of the French rentier."

15 In Moreau (1954) his role in cooperating and opposing (when necessary) Poincaré emerges very clearly.

16 These data are reported by Blanchard, Dornbusch and Buiter (1986).

17 For an overview of the Italian politico-economic history of this period see Toniolo (1978).

18 The lack of success of this levy resembles similar failures of other attempts to introduce capital levies in periods of economic and political instability. Rostas (1940) documents the failure of capital levies in Austria, Czechoslovakia, and Hungary in the aftermath of the First World War.
19 See Giovannini (1987) for a more detailed analysis of the fiscal policy of the Fascist regime.
20 Pollard (1983) compares various estimates of this figure and concludes that 5 percent is an upper bound.
21 In addition, the "good" reputation of being a non-defaulting government may have helped the British government in mobilizing resources for the Second World War. The non-defaulting approach followed by Great Britain may in fact imply that the British governments paid more attention to the reputation of the sovereign than, say, France or Germany, because they discounted less heavily the future given the higher degree of political stability. On this point see Grossman (1987).
22 Note, however, that one of the effects of this liquidity constraint on the government is actually to "enforce" fiscal responsibility. The problem is the government could be constrained even where additional borrowing was socially desirable and "responsible," such as in the case of a new "war."
23 On the effects of capital taxation on capital flights see Giovannini (1987) Alesina and Tabellini (1987b) and the references quoted therein.

REFERENCES

Alesina, Alberto (1983), "Inflation and Stabilization in France after the First World War," unpublished (May).
Alesina, Alberto and Guido Tabellini (1987a), "A Positive Theory of Fiscal Deficits and Government Debt in a Democracy," *National Bureau of Economic Research*, Working Paper.
   (1987b), "External Debt, Capital Flights and Political Risk," unpublished.
Barna, Thomas (1945), *The Redistribution of Incomes through Public Finance in 1937*. Oxford: Oxford University Press.
Barro, Robert (1979), "On the Determination of the Public Debt," *Journal of Political Economy*, Vol. 87, November.
   (1985a), "Government Spending, Interest Rates, Prices and Budget Deficits in the United Kingdom, 1730–1918," Working Paper, University of Rochester.
   (1985b), "US Deficits since World War I," *Scandinavian Journal of Economics*, Vol. 88.
   (1987), *Macroeconomics*. New York: John Wiley and Sons.
Bental, Benjamin, Devorah Kantorowitz and Dan Peled (1986), "Should Government Debt be Safe?" unpublished, November.
Blanchard, Olivier, Rudiger Dornbusch and Willem Buiter (1986), "Public Debt and Fiscal Responsibility" in *Restoring Europe's Prosperity*. Centre for European Policy Studies, Cambridge MA: MIT Press.
Bresciani-Turroni, Constantino (1937), *The Economics of Inflation*. London: Allen and Unwin.
Buiter, Willem (1985), "A Guide to Public Sector Debt and Deficits," *Economic Policy* Vol. 1, November.
Bulletin Statistique de la Republique Francaise (various issues).
Cagan, Philip (1959), "The Monetary Dynamics of Hyperinflation," in *Studies in*

the Quantity Theory of Money, edited by M. Friedman. University of Chicago Press.

Calvo, Gulliermo (1978), "On the Time Consistency of Optimal Policy in a Monetary Economy," *Econometrica*, Vol. 46, November.

Ciocca, Pierluigi and Giovanni Toniolo (eds.) (1976), *L'economia italiane nel periodo fascista*. Bologna: Il Mulino.

Clark, Colin (1945), "Public Finance and Changes in the Value of Money" *Economic Journal*, Vol. 60, December.

Confalonieri, Antonio and Emilio Gatti (1986), *La politica del debito pubblico in Italia 1919–1943*. Bari: Cariplo-Laterza.

Cukierman, Alex and Allan Meltzer (1986), "A Political Theory of Government Debt and Deficits in a Neo Ricardian Framework," unpublished.

DeCecco, Marcello (1983), "The Vicious/Virtuous Circle Debate in the Twenties and in the Seventies," Working Paper, Department of Economics, European University Institute, Florence.

DeLong, Bradford (1986a), "The Comparative Costs of Returning to Gold: Britain and France in the 1920's," unpublished.

(1986b), "The Severity of the 1927 Recession in France," unpublished.

Dornbusch, Rudiger (1982), "Some Comments on Thomas Sargent's 'Stopping Moderate Inflations'," unpublished.

(1986), *Dollars, Debts and Deficits*. Leuven: Leuven University Press and Cambridge, MA: MIT Press.

(1987), "Lessons from the German Inflation Experience of the 1920s," in *Macroeconomics and Finance: Essays in Honor of Franco Modigliani*, edited by Dornbusch, Fischer and Bossons. Cambridge, MA: MIT Press.

Dornbusch, Rudiger and Stanley Fischer (1986), "Stopping Hyperinflations Past and Present," *National Bureau of Economic Research* Working Paper.

Dulles, Eleanor (1929), *The French Franc 1914–1928*. New York: MacMillan.

Economic Report of the President 1986.

Eichengreen, Barry and Jeffrey Sachs (1985), "Exchange Rates and Economic Recovery in the 1930s," *Journal of Economic History*, Vol. 45, December.

Eichengreen, Barry and Charles Wyplosz (1988), "The Economic Consequences of Franc Poincaré," forthcoming in *Stabilization Policies*, edited by Helpman etal., London: MacMillan.

Fischer, Stanley (1980), "Dynamic Inconsistency, Cooperation and the Benevolent Dissembling Government," *Journal of Economics, Dynamics and Control*. Vol. 2, February.

Fuà, Giorgio, (ed.) (1969), *Lo sviluppo economico in Italia*, Milano: Franco Angeli Editore.

Giovannini, Alberto (1987), "Capital Controls and Public Finance: the Experience in Italy," this volume.

Graham, Frank (1930), *Exchange, Prices and Production in Hyperinflation: Germany, 1920–1923*. New York: Russel and Russel.

Grossman, Herschel and John Van Huick (1986a), "Sovereign Debt as a Contingent Claim: Excusable Default, Repudiation and Reputation," Working Paper, Brown University.

(1986b). "Seignorage, Inflation and Reputation," *Journal of Monetary Economics*, Vol. 18, July.

Grossman, Herschel (1987), "Lending to an Unsecure Sovereign," unpublished.

Haig, Robert (1929), *The Public Finance of Post War France*. New York: Columbia University Press.

Hibbs, Douglas (1987), *The American Political Economy: Electoral Policy and Macroeconomics in Contemporary America*. Cambridge MA: Harvard University Press, forthcoming.

Hibbs, Douglas and Christopher Dennis (1987), "The Politics and Economics of Income Distribution Outcomes in the Postwar United States," unpublished.

Holtfrerich, Carl Ludwig (1985), "Relations between Monetary Authorities and Governmental Institution. The Case of Germany from the 19th Century to the Present," unpublished.

INSEE (1966), "Annuare Statistique de la France," Paris.

ISTAT (1976), *Sommario di statistiche storiche dell'Italia 1861–1975*. Rome.

Keynes, John Maynard (1923), *A Tract on Monetary Reform*. London: Macmillan.

Keynes, John Maynard (1963), *Essays in Persuasion*. New York: Norton New York.

Lucas, Robert (1986), "Principles of Fiscal and Monetary Policy," *Journal of Monetary Economics*, Vol. 18, January.

Lucas, Robert and Nancy Stokey (1983), "Optimal Fiscal and Monetary Policy in an Economy without Capital," *Journal of Monetary Economics*, Vol. 12.

Maier, Charles (1975), *Restoring Burgeois Europe: Stabilization in France Germany and Italy in the Decade after World War I*. Princeton NJ: Princeton University Press.

Makinen, Gail and Thomas Woodward (1986), "Some Neglected Monetary Aspects of the Poincaré Stabilization of 1926," unpublished.

Mitchell, Brian (1975), *European Historical Statistics 1750–1970*, New York: Columbia University Press.

Mitchell, Brian and Phyllis Deane (1962), *Abstract of British Historical Statistics*. Cambridge: Cambridge University Press.

Moreau, Emile (1954), *Souvenirs d'un Gouverneur de la Banque de France*. Paris: Editions M-Th. Genn.

Paxton, Robert (1975), *Europe in the Twentieth Century*. New York: Harcourt Brace Jovanavich.

Persson, Torsten and Lars Svensson (1987), "Checks and Balances on Government Budget," University of Rochester, Working Paper.

Pollard, Sidney (1983), *The Development of the British Economy 1914–1980* Baltimore: Edward Arnold.

Poterba, James and Lawrence Summers (1986), "Finite Lifetimes and the Crowding Out Effects of Budget Deficits," *National Bureau of Economic Research*, Working Paper.

Rogers, Carol (1986), "Time Consistency and the Maturity Structure of Government Debt," unpublished.

Rostas, L. (1940), "The Capital Levy in Central Europe 1919–1924," *Review of Economic Studies*.

Sargent, Thomas (1982), "The Ends of Four Big Inflations," in *Inflation* edited by R. Hall. University of Chicago Press and *National Bureau of Economic Research*.

(1984), "Stopping Moderate Inflations: The Methods of Poincaré and Thatcher," in *Inflation, Debt and Indexation*, edited by R. Dornbusch and H. Simonsen. MIT Press.

Schacht, Hjalmar (1931), *La stabilizzazione del marco*, translated by Stanislao Scalfati. Milano: Fratelli Treves.

Spaventa, Luigi (1982), Comment on "Stopping Moderate Inflation: the Methods of Poincaré and Thatcher," unpublished.

——— (1987), "The Growth of Public Debt: Sustainability, Fiscal Rules and Monetary Rules," IMF Staff Papers, June, Vol. 34.

Spinelli, Franco and Silvio Formentini (1986), "Dimensione, composizione e costo del debito pubblico interno dal 1861 al 1985," Associazione per lo sviluppo degli studi di banca e borsa, Quaderno n. 78, Universita Cattolicà del Sacro Cuore, Milano.

Stein, Herbert (1984), "Throw Away the U.S. National Debt," *Wall Street Journal*, March 30.

Toniolo, Giovanni (editor) (1978), *L'economia Italiana 1861–1940*. Bari: Laterza.

Youal, Ran (1986), *The Effects of the Horizon of the Policymakers on the Path of Inflation: Germany 1919–1924*. M.A. Dissertation, Tel-Aviv University (in Hebrew).

Zamagni, Vera (1975), "La dinamica dei salari nel settore industriale 1921–1939," *Quaderni Storici*, No. 29/30.

Discussion

BARRY EICHENGREEN

Economic historians generally dislike the way economists analyze the political economy of debt and deficits. The typical neoclassical model of fiscal policy is highly aggregated and based on the assumptions of a representative agent and a social welfare maximizing government. Historians assume in contrast that fiscal policy is fundamentally redistributive, that policy formulation is fundamentally political, that its outcome is fundamentally uncertain, and that the distribution of tax burdens turns fundamentally on the origins and sources of the public expenditures in question.

As an economic historian, I therefore had a ready-made set of comments on Alberto Alesina's paper. I don't know whether to be delighted or disappointed by not being able to make them. For Alesina has written an exemplary paper which is at the same time good economics and good history.

At the heart of Alesina's paper is a disaggregated model of the political economy of debt management. Alesina distinguishes three classes of agents and three strategies for dealing with an existing public debt. The mapping from interest groups to policy preferences can be represented as follows, in Table 2.24.

Rentiers are the holders of the public debt. The alternative they prefer is for the government to manage the debt by raising taxes and cutting public expenditures sufficiently to balance the budget (inclusive of interest payments). If inflation has been suffered since the time of debt issue, they argue that distributive justice requires an offsetting deflation to restore the real value of assets. The alternative they prefer least is a special capital tax levied on outstanding government obligations. The extent to which they prefer inflation to a capital levy depends on the maturity structure of the debt (the extent to which they are protected from the inflation tax by the adjustment of short-term interest rates).

Wage laborers have opposing priorities. They prefer the capital levy

Table 2.24 Interest groups and policy preferences

Policy preference	Rentiers	Entrepreneurs	Workers
1st preference	deflation	inflation	capital levy
2nd preference	inflation	(? capital levy ?)	inflation
3rd preference	capital levy	deflation	deflation

because it falls most heavily on others, and prefer inflation and budget deficits over deflation and budget surpluses because inflation may be conducive to employment growth and because the working class is a principal beneficiary of public expenditures. Entrepreneurs, following Keynes's argument in the *Tract* (Keynes, 1923), prefer inflation to deflation because it increases the profitability of enterprise. But whether entrepreneurs prefer the capital levy to deflation depends on whether the former is defined narrowly (so as to fall only on claims on government) or broadly (so as to include also industrial and commercial assets). This ambiguity is indicated in Table 2.24 by the question marks in the second column.

Like any good model, this one is highly stylized, incorporating only what is essential to the author's argument. In particular, the model neglects overlap among groups – the extent to which workers also held government bonds and shared the interests of rentiers, for example. Yet it has the merit of highlighting political and distributive aspects of debt management and of shifting the focus away from representative agent models of at best questionable relevance to the policy debate – in other words, of reintroducing into debate among economists the blood, sweat and tears of politics.

Using this model, Alesina characterizes the question of debt management as whether to bleed the rentier, sweat the worker, or tax the entrepreneur to tears. He explains the outcome of the debate in terms of which interest group dominated party politics. France in the 1920s, he concludes, converged on inflation because of the political dominance of labor, while Britain settled on deflation because of the political dominance of the rentier. While agreeing that the political struggle over distribution was central to the debate, I am struck by the suppression of other vital aspects of the political process. First, Alesina makes little mention of the endogeneity of political outcomes. Models of the political business cycle, to which he has made important contributions elsewhere, emphasize feedbacks from fiscal policies through macroeconomic outcomes to the balance of political power. Second, there is the issue of interest group alliances. In virtually all the European experiences Alesina considers, Parliamentary politics were coalition politics. Which view triumphed depended critically on the success with which interest groups formed coalitions. While rentiers and workers are natural antagonists in Alesina's model (in the sense that the policy preferences of each are inversely related to those of the other) it is unclear with whom the entrepreneurs logically ally. Much depends on the precise form of the capital levy and of deflationary policies.

Another underemphasized aspect of the political process is its international dimension. Although Alesina mentions German reparations by way of indicating how such considerations might be appended to his model, in several of the instances he considers the international struggle over who should pay for the war did not merely supplement but dominated purely domestic considerations. In the case of France, running a budget deficit (resisting both the capital levy and deflation) was a way of pressuring Germany to finance reconstruction costs. It is no coincidence that the French labeled reconstruction expenditures extraordinary and segregated them in special budgetary accounts to which few tax revenues were assigned. Raising taxes or cutting public spending was seen as an admission that German reparations might not be forthcoming. In the case of Germany, running a deficit was a strategy for signaling the difficulty of raising the resources needed for reparations transfers. The breakdown of German public finances following the Ruhr invasion was only the most dramatic instance of the phenomenon. Just as France ran deficits and inflated to increase the pressure for reparations, Germany ran deficits and inflated to increase its ability to resist. Ultimately, reparations were not paid and inflation was the legacy for both countries. This points to the fact that inflation was no one's first choice. Even entrepreneurs preferred cuts in social programs. Inflation was an outcome of a different sort, one which resulted from the international deadlock over distribution.

One might object to this emphasis on reparations on the grounds that they were owed to Britain and France alike, rendering it difficult to explain on this basis both Britain's choice of the deflationary solution and France's choice of inflation. But the French felt more strongly than the British about reparations, both because their country had served as the battlefield for much of the war, and because they had been forced to pay reparations to Germany following their defeat at the hands of the Prussians in 1871.

Britain also differed from France by virtue of its role in the international gold standard. Both the Labour and Conservative Parties embraced the argument that a return to the gold standard, implying the deflationary solution, was essential to British economic prosperity. Returning to gold would strengthen the balance of payments, so the argument ran, and by relaxing the external constraint would permit full employment to be restored. Since Britain was a net external creditor and her foreign investments were denominated in sterling, appreciation might serve to raise the real value of her external assets. In other words, the British solution differed not so much or not merely because of different preferences (equivalently, because of differences in the political balance of power) but because of different constraints.

The most controversial passages of Alesina's paper concern the capital levy. Many analyses stress the parallels between capital levies and unilateral debt repudiation. Alesina transcends this literature by emphasizing the distinction between excusable and inexcusable default. Default (taken to mean in this context either inflation or an extraordinary tax on government bonds) is regarded as excusable in the sense of not undermining the government's subsequent ability to borrow when the source of the debt is extraordinary. The appropriate analogy is with corporate bankruptcy law, as invoked by advocates of sovereign debt forgiveness. In the absence of bankruptcy statutes, an extraordinary event which leads to corporate insolvency will ignite a destructive scramble of creditors each seeking to attach the firm's remaining assets. Corporate reorganization under judicial protection prevents the firm from being dismantled and its productive capacity from being destroyed, increasing the size of the pie to be distributed among the creditors. Analogously, governmental insolvency can set off a destructive scramble of creditors which leads to hyperinflation and attendant inefficiencies. Not only may a modest capital levy be Pareto superior to runaway inflation, but it may erode the real value of the debt by less than inflation, leaving even rentiers better off. If the source of the insolvency was extraordinary (war or a failure to receive reparations, for example) and if default is succeeded by a convincing change in regime, it need not follow that the defaulting government will find itself unable to borrow subsequently.

While the distinction between excusable and inexcusable default is sound in theory, it may be problematic in practice. If default through inflation is ever excusable, this should have been true of France in the 1920s, where the reparations tangle was to blame. If default was ever succeeded by a convincing change in regime, this should have been true of France after Poincaré's return to power in 1926. Yet France was so traumatized by her experience with inflation that she stayed on the gold standard through the depths of the Great Depression, long after her major competitors had devalued, at considerable cost to employment and national income. She did so precisely in order to avoid a recurrence of inflation. Similarly, current German attitudes belie the notion that the German hyperinflation was excusable, despite the very extraordinary circumstances under which it occurred and the very convincing change in regime coinciding with its termination. These experiences suggest that the concept of excusable default, like the fashionable concept of credibility, is more elusive in practice than simple theoretical models would suggest.

Another way to think about the concept of excusable default is in terms of taxpayer compliance. A necessary condition for the benefits of default through a capital levy to exceed the costs is that the levy raise revenues – that it not elicit widespread taxpayer resistance. For this to be the case there must be a social consensus that circumstances are sufficiently unusual to justify extraordinary taxes. Keynes's shifting views of the advisability of a capital levy can be understood in terms of his concern over whether the public would regard the circumstances as extraordinary and hence comply with the tax. As time passed and memories of the First World War faded, Keynes regarded the case as harder to sustain, although he noted exceptions to the rule. But the point is general: it is extremely hard for policymakers to know when extraordinary measures will meet with public acceptance. One section of Alesina's paper concludes with a delightful quote from Keynes who wrote, in comparing British and French debt management, that "Assuredly it does not pay to be good." But Keynes was aware of difficulties of putting even assured principles into practice. As he wrote on another occasion, "Bright ideas in the realm of taxation are seldom worth while" (quoted in Gottlieb, 1952).

REFERENCES

Gottlieb, M. (1952), "The Capital Levy After World War I," *Public Finance.*
Keynes, John Maynard (1923), *A Tract on Monetary Reform*, London: Macmillan.

Discussion

MARCELLO DE CECCO

Let me say first of all that I have read Alesina's paper with great pleasure. The approach he takes to the subject brings us back to the world of traditional political economy, away from the never-never land of representative agents, benevolent despots, "the unloading of burdens on future generations" and the like. It is also an interdisciplinary approach, which goes well along the path traced by historical research. Furthermore, it is consonant with the spirit of the debate on public debt which took place in the interwar years, among the people who actually benefitted or suffered from the alternative solutions available to the problem of large public debts.

To provide further comfort to Alesina, I have retrieved from my files the photocopy of the work of an illustrious Italian economist, Piero Sraffa. It is his "opera prima," his B.A. dissertation, which carries the suggestive title "L'inflazione monetaria in Italia durante e dopo la guerra." Published in 1920, by the 22-year old Sraffa, it was written under the supervision of Luigi Einaudi. Sraffa must have been a very independent pupil, because the main argument of the book is very far from what Einaudi used, in the same years, to preach and write on the same subject. Sraffa debated the point whether a rise in the real value of money in Italy, through a slump of domestic prices brought about by a return to convertibility at the prewar parity, would, to quote him verbatim "re-establish justice in the relations between creditors and debtors, because the creditors hurt by inflation are not the same creditors who would benefit from a price level contraction and it would be impossible to look for each of the original creditors, to indemnify them for the damage they had suffered."

To reinforce his point Sraffa reproduced, for Italy, the calculations Irving Fisher had made for the United States (Fisher 1920). Sraffa's table showed that, if the lira had been deflated by the full price inflation, the subscribers to Italian loans would receive, in real terms, five times what

Table 2.25 Italian government loans

		(1) Date of issue	(2) Price index number (Bachi)	(3) Nominal amount of issues (in milliards of lire)	(4) =(2)×(3)
Redeemable loan	4½%	Jan. 1915	133	1.0 milliar.	1.33
Redeemable loan	4½%	July 1915	164	1.1 milliar.	1.80
Redeemable loan	5 %	Jan. 1916	232	3.0 milliar.	6.96
Consolidated loan	5 %	Feb. 1917	303	3.8 milliar.	11.51
Consolidated loan	5 %	Jan. 1918	458	6.1 milliar.	27.93
Consolidated loan	5 %	Jan. 1920	631	20.0 milliar.	126.80
				35.0 milliar.	176.33

Source: P. Sraffa (1920).

they had lent the State. And the Italian State, following the same reasoning, would shoulder a public debt revalued from 100 to 700 billion lire.

Sraffa concluded that a policy of price deflation would give an unjustifiable capital gain to creditors, and an unjustifiable penalty to private debtors, including firms, and to the State.

As can be gleaned from Table 2.25, his calculations yielded the extravagant benefits for creditors that they did because both public debt and price inflation were concentrated in the last two years of the period considered. Bringing the lira back to its full prewar real value would have given people who had lent bad money in the last two years the good money of 1914.

As a matter of curiosity, I will add that Sraffa, having clearly enunciated that the Italian government would have to choose between stabilizing the exchange rate and stabilizing prices, suggested that the best course would be to let the exchange rate float. Domestic price level stability was, in his opinion, much superior to exchange rate stability, since the latter could only be purchased at the cost of ruining entrepreneurs and workers.

One of the problems with the approach chosen by Sraffa and Alesina is indeed to disentangle exactly which groups of people benefitted or suffered from each of the debt inflation policies adopted in the countries under scrutiny. Economists are used to categorizing income distribution as taking place between Rent, Profits and Wages. The categorization serves us well in the case of Britain. In the three episodes of re-entry from large public debts which that country experienced in the last two hundred

Table 2.26 Sectoral gross debt/GNP ratios 1975 and 1985
(in percentages)

		Public sector	Personal sector	Corporate sector
United States	1975	42	49	37
	1985	54	61	42
	(1986)	(56)	(65)	(45)
United Kingdom	1975	64	33	46
	1985	59	51	44
Germany	1975	25	42	63
	1985	43	57	73
Japan	1975	39	33	93
	1985	90	46	102
Canada	1975	77	52	65
	1985	107	51	64

Source: E. P. Davis, "Rising sectoral debt/income ratios: a cause for concern?" BIS Economic Papers, n. 20, June 1987.

years, the rentiers clearly won in each case, at the expense of profit and wage earners. Real interest rates soared and remained very high after the Napoleonic Wars, after the First World War, and after 1979. This did not happen anywhere else with anything like the same starkness. It is instructive to look at the other table I have provided (Table 2.26). From it, it appears clearly that, in the decade 1975–85, only the British have managed to actually reduce their debt/GNP ratio, while other major governments have increased it, sometimes very much, as in the case of Japan and of Italy, which is not on the table, but whose figures are well known to members of this Conference.

How did the British do it, not only in the episode analyzed by Alesina, but also in the other two I have quoted? I do not think it is possible to understand the case without making reference to the truly remarkable power wielded by the City over the government and public opinion in Britain. Geoffrey Ingham has written an excellent book, *Capitalism Divided*, which describes the very close links the financial community has always had in Britain with governments and the top level bureaucrats. This clear hegemony of one interest group over all others only exists in Britain. Everywhere else debt deflation, when it occurred, could never be carried to British extremes. The rentier class was always mixed with the profit makers, the entrepreneurs, to an extent which made it impossible to achieve and maintain for any length of time the two targets of debt deflation and a strong currency.

Moreover what I called the financial community was never as homogeneous elsewhere as it was in Britain. In the American episode quoted by Alesina, for instance, stable and low real interest rates could be maintained not only because GNP kept growing at a brisk rate, but also because the financial community was utterly divided. The large money center banks were interested in a return to high real rates, because they relied on interbank deposits and on foreign deposits, i.e. they worked with "purchased money," short-term funds which could only be obtained if remunerative real rates were offered. Local banks were, for a long time, very happy to live off the modest but secure income generated by intermediating between local savers and the governments, whose bonds the banks accumulated.

Had Alesina brought his data forward to more recent years, he would have noticed that the American financial community brought this policy to a gradual end, with the eventual victory of the money center banks, who managed to "liberate" monetary policy and real interest rates and to bring them up to higher levels, in order to increase the volume of funds they borrowed abroad and thus the volume of loans they made, especially to foreign governments. Their lending policies have recently come unstuck, but it is undeniable that, for about 20 years, the money center banks have ruled the roost. Recent events have, however, demonstrated once again how different the American socio-political set-up is from the British one, and how volatile and ephemeral is the power of the money center banks.

At a more general level, we may advance the conjecture that bringing a large public debt to an end by a policy of budget surpluses, entailing price and income deflation, is a policy option only really open to societies where the financial system does not have a stake in inflation. It must be a financial system not locked into illiquid loans to industry, which severe deflation might transform into insolvent ones. As indebted industrial firms went bankrupt, because of the deflation, banks would unfailingly follow them. This type of policy, with its full complement of dire consequences, was tried by both the Weimar Republic and Fascist Italy, between 1926 and 1931. It was heavily influenced by the pressure brought to bear on the two countries by the international financial community, i.e., by the international committee of creditors informally formed and headed by the British, and in particular by Montagu Norman, the Governor of the Bank of England. But the same policy could be successful in Britain in the same years, because British banks had traditionally stayed clear of industrial loans. British industry was not heavily in debt, hence the deflationary policy could be backed by industrialists as a means of bashing the workers, by the banks as a way of giving back to London its role as center of the world financial system, and by the rentier class, who saw their Consols' yield in real terms handsomely increased.

If we apply the same analysis to contemporary Italy, we find that the modest decline in the Public Deficit/GNP ratio which appears to have occurred in the last couple of years has been made possible by the "Act of God" of the oil price slump which has raised profits, and by the strategy pursued by Italy's industrial sector of transforming their debt to the banking sector into equity sold to the general public. How long can these two factors continue to operate? The Bank of Italy has already pointed to a recent recrudescence of large indebtedness on the part of the company sector. Were this to continue, it would swing the companies again to the side of debtors, and the coalition which made the modest decline in the Public Deficit/GNP ratio possible would collapse. The only option realistically open would be again de facto cancellation through monetization and inflation.

It will be seen that my comments are obviously inspired by what amounts to the exact opposite of the "Treasury View." When Public Debt is accompanied by private enterprise indebtedness, the only realistic policy will be cancellation through monetization and inflation. When Public Debt coincides with private asset accumulation, a coalition is likely to be formed, which includes rentiers and bankers, which will not be opposed by industry, and which will enforce a policy of budget surpluses, high real interest rates, severe deflation and unemployment. To these two extreme cases, a whole array of intermediate ones can be added, with weaker solutions or even open stalemates.

REFERENCES

Davis, E. P. (1987), "Rising sectoral debt/income ratios: a cause for concern?" *Bank for International Settlements Economic Papers*, no. 20, June.
Fisher, Irving (1920), *Stabilizing the Dollar*, New York: Macmillan.
Ingham, Geoffrey (1984), *Capitalism Divided*, London: Macmillan.
Sraffa, Piero (1920), *L'Inflazione monetaria in Italia durante e dopo la guerra*, Milan.

3 Monetary and fiscal policy coordination with a high public debt*

GUIDO TABELLINI

1 Introduction

Monetary policy in Italy has large repercussions on the size of the government budget. For instance, it can be calculated that at the end of 1985, because of the short duration of public debt, a 1 percent rise in the market real interest rate would have added to the fiscal deficit a flow of interest payments equal to 0.64 percent of GDP within one year. Moreover, the revenue collected through money seignorage in 1986 amounted to approximately 1.2 percent of GDP.[1]

Despite these repercussions, for the last several years the Italian monetary regime has evolved towards an increased decentralization between the monetary and the fiscal authorities. As a result of a series of institutional reforms that started in the early 1980s, the Bank of Italy has increased its autonomy from the Treasury and has pursued its monetary objectives with more determination than ever before.

At the same time that this process of decentralization was taking place, the Italian public debt was soaring at extremely high rates. Public debt is now over 100 percent of GDP (according to the unrevised national income accounts), and it is forecast to remain above this level for several years to come (see Cividini, Galli and Masera 1987). According to several authoritative Italian economists, the growth of public debt in Italy cannot be arrested without a concerted effort on the part of both monetary and fiscal policies. (This point of view is argued most forcefully in Spaventa 1984 and 1985.)

These facts pose a natural question: is there any contradiction between the institutional reforms that increased the decentralization of the monetary and fiscal authorities, and the goal of stabilizing public debt?

This question is examined in the paper from two points of view. From a purely theoretical point of view, it is argued that there is no contradiction between the monetary reforms and the goal of stabilizing public debt. On the contrary, the change in the monetary regime and the resulting monetary restraint may facilitate the task of correcting the fiscal imbalances. The central point here is that the incentives of the fiscal authority, and hence its behavior, are not invariant to the features of the monetary regime. In a monetary regime in which the course of monetary policy is predetermined independently of the outstanding public debt, the fiscal authority internalizes the costs of deficit financing to a greater degree than in a regime where the debt is eventually monetized. Hence, a less accommodative monetary regime reinforces the incentives of the fiscal authority to pursue a more balanced fiscal policy.

Looking at the empirical evidence, however, suggests a more cautious conclusion. There is some indication in the data of a more balanced fiscal policy under the new monetary regime. However this evidence is not very robust. Moreover, the private sector did not seem to perceive a regime change. The overall picture that emerges here is that the new monetary regime has been shaped more by concrete monetary policy actions of the Bank of Italy than by binding external institutional reforms. In this new regime the link between fiscal deficits and future monetization has not been cut – even though it now seems less automatic than before.

Combining these two points of view suggests the following tentative conclusion: the ambiguities of the new monetary regime force the Bank of Italy to pursue a restrictive monetary policy in order to maintain its credibility. At the same time, they weaken the incentives of the fiscal authority to bear the whole burden of stabilizing public debt. As a result, these ambiguities could generate a non-coordinated monetary and fiscal policy mix that would compromise the stabilization of public debt. If this conclusion is correct, it suggests that the remaining ambiguities of the new Italian monetary regime should be removed, and the process of monetary reform be completed as soon as possible.

The outline of the paper is as follows. Section 2 briefly summarizes the evolution of the Italian monetary regime from 1970 up to now. Section 3 describes a simple theoretical model in which the behavior of the fiscal authority is not invariant to the regime change. It is a game theoretic model with three players: the private sector, the fiscal authority and the central bank. The model predicts an inverse relationship between the size of fiscal deficits net of interest payments and the extent of debt monetization by the central bank. Section 4 looks at the empirical evidence, in order to determine whether the monetary regime change of the 1980s was indeed accompanied by a more disciplined fiscal policy. Section 5 contains some concluding remarks.

2   Monetary policy and monetary institutions in Italy: 1970–86

This section summarizes the transformation of the Italian monetary regime in the period under consideration. The introductory chapter of this volume, by Luigi Spaventa, describes the evolution of public debt and of fiscal policy in this period. Here I focus on monetary policy and particularly on the interaction between the monetary and the fiscal authorities.

Institutional changes generally occur gradually over time, and any attempt of periodization involves some inescapable arbitrary judgment. In this case, three distinct subperiods can be identified. Even though it is not always possible to identify precisely the beginning and end of each period, important aspects of monetary policy and/or of monetary institutions differ sharply across these three subperiods. For clarity of exposition, this section proceeds as if the three subperiods are sharply identifiable. The empirical analysis of section 4, however, performs some sensitivity analysis with respect to this periodization.

In the first subperiod, 1970–76, the Bank of Italy pursues the goals of stabilizing the interest rate and facilitating the monetary financing of fiscal deficits. The second subperiod, 1977–80, is a transition phase: the Bank of Italy begins to pay attention to monetary aggregates and gradually tries to gain independence from the fiscal authority. Monetary policy is less accommodative than in the previous subperiod. However the institutional position of the central bank is still relatively weak, and the instruments of monetary control remain inadequate to implement an independent monetary policy. Finally, in the third subperiod, 1981–86, the new monetary regime takes a precise shape and important institutional reforms are implemented. As a result, the course of monetary policy becomes largely independent of the fiscal constraint.

This periodization is clearly reflected in the statistics reported in Table 3.1. The coefficient of monetary financing of the deficit is much higher in the first subperiod than in the other two. The same applies to the creation of monetary base against Treasury liabilities, as a fraction of GDP. The rate of growth of the total monetary base drops sharply in the third subperiod. The marginal real interest rate on public debt, which is negative on average in the first two subperiods, becomes positive and high in the third period.[2] Finally, as reported in Table 3.2, the share of public debt held by the Bank of Italy rises in the first subperiod, to reach 40 percent in 1976; and it steadily declines thereafter, to reach 16.5 percent at the end of 1986.

The remainder of this section describes the events of the three subperiods in more detail.[3]

Table 3.1 Monetary policy in Italy

	Coefficient of deficit mone- tization[1]	Real interest rate[2]	Monetary base creation against liabilities of the Treasury[3]		Rate of growth of monetary base
			Total	Overdraft a/c	
1970–76	47.73	− 1.27	4.72	2.73	17.7
1977–81	14.10	− 1.47	1.32	4.25	16.9
1982–86	12.83	3.84	1.97	6.38	13.6

All data are yearly averages.
Notes:
1 Creation of monetary base against Treasury liabilities, as a fraction of the public sector borrowing requirement.
2 1974–86: Nominal interest rate on 6 months Treasury bills (weighted average of returns based on biweekly auctions) less CPI inflation rate.
   1970–73: Average nominal rate of return on total public debt less CPI inflation.
3 Scaled to nominal GDP.
Source: Bank of Italy.

Table 3.2 Share of public debt held by the Bank of Italy

1970	25.62
1971	24.40
1972	23.36
1973	28.01
1974	31.67
1975	37.07
1976	40.32
1977	30.74
1978	27.40
1979	23.58
1980	23.36
1981	23.67
1982	21.90
1983	17.56
1984	16.57
1985	17.64
1986	16.56

Note: The debt aggregate refers to the public sector.
Source: Bank of Italy.

2.1   Accommodative monetary policy: 1970–76

The attitude of the monetary authorities during this subperiod is adequately summarized in a well known official statement of Guido Carli, Governor of the Bank of Italy until the summer of 1975:

> We asked and we keep asking ourselves whether the Bank of Italy could have refused, or could refuse, to finance the budget deficit by refraining from the faculty, attributed by the law, of buying government debt. Such a refusal would leave the government in the impossibility of paying wages to public employees ... and pensions to all citizens. It would look like an action of monetary policy: essentially it would be an act of rebellion. We cannot avoid the downfall by means of the tools of monetary policy only: we can try and make it less deep

(Report of the Bank of Italy, 1973).[4] Faced by a budget deficit of unprecedented dimensions, with a market for Treasury bills still largely undeveloped, in the years 1970–73 the Bank of Italy completely subordinates its monetary policy to the goals of facilitating deficit financing and stabilizing interest rates. The behavior of monetary aggregates is completely disregarded. The yearly report of the Bank of Italy does not even publish any ex-post statistics concerning the quantity of money.[5] The quantity of money is mentioned for the first time in the 1975 report. But even then, a precise definition of the relevant aggregates is not provided, and the quantity of money is mentioned exclusively for its presumed correlation with the stock market – see *Tendenze Monetarie*, December 1975.

In the summer of 1973 the inflationary consequences and the adverse external effects of this policy become evident. But the Bank of Italy cannot (or does not want to) reduce debt monetization.[6] Hence, it cannot rely on monetary base control and interest rates to implement a more restrictive monetary policy. Instead, it introduces administrative controls on financial markets: first a portfolio constraint obliging commercial banks to invest a fraction of their deposits in long-term bonds (and in Treasury bonds); and then a ceiling on the quantity of bank loans. This method of credit control is continued in subsequent years, and finds official recognition in the "letter of intent" signed with the IMF in 1974: the monetary policy target identified in this document is the quantity of total domestic credit, an aggregate that can be controlled by the central bank mainly through administrative methods. This intermediate target will continue to guide monetary policy for several years and it is deemphasized by the Bank of Italy only in the 1980s.

The years of 1975 and 1976 are important and yet contradictory in the evolution of the Italian monetary system. Some institutional reforms are initiated, specifically designed to enhance the effectiveness of indirect methods of credit control. More importantly, the public debt auctions in the primary market are modified: they are made more competitive, but at the same time the Bank of Italy is required to act as the residual buyer of all the unsold public debt. The central bank is then free to resell the debt in the secondary market if it so wishes (possibly incurring a capital loss, however).

In 1975 Guido Carli is replaced by Paolo Baffi as Governor of the Bank of Italy. The new Governor publicly expresses some disagreement with the accommodating policy of his predecessor. However, the Bank of Italy continues to disregard the behavior of monetary aggregates. The monetary base and the quantity of money grow at extremely high rates throughout 1975. As a result, in January 1976 the Italian lira falls under speculative attack. The weakness of the lira continues throughout 1976. In the summer of 1976 the Communist party scores a major victory in the political elections. This shakes the confidence of some Italian savers and possibly of foreign investors. In June and in September the lira falls again under speculative attacks and the Bank of Italy is forced to return to the old policy of debt monetization accompanied by strict administrative controls. Finally, in 1976 short-term Treasury bills are offered for the first time to the non-banking public.

2.2 The transition phase: 1977–80

These can be called the years of "compensatory," or "ex-post," monetary policy.[7] The administrative credit controls begin to lose some effectiveness and impose increasing efficiency costs on the economy. The target for total domestic credit is systematically missed whenever the fiscal deficit turns out to be larger than forecast, which happens most of the time. As a result, the Bank of Italy gradually turns towards indirect methods of monetary control, that rely on controlling the quantity of monetary base. A secondary market for public debt is now in existence and operates quite smoothly. This enables the Bank of Italy to drain liquidity from the banking system through open market operations. The typical pattern of monetary policy during this period is as follows: the Treasury creates large amounts of monetary base through the overdraft account and in the primary market for public debt. (Recall that since 1975 the Bank of Italy is obliged to act as the residual buyer of public debt at the Treasury auctions.) The central bank then destroys the monetary base created by the Treasury, through open market operations. To a large extent, the private sector holders of public debt are now the households rather than the banking system. Thus, the growth of a well

Table 3.3 Real interest rate differentials
between Italy and West Germany

1974	− 6.4
1975	− 4.9
1976	− 0.7
1977	− 3.4
1978	− 1.3
1979	− 4.7
1980	− 7.7
1981	− 3.2
1982	0.3
1983	1.7
1984	3.4
1985	3.0

Note: The real interest rate is computed as the difference between the nominal interest rate and the actual CPI rate of inflation. The nominal interest rate is the monthly average of all money rates.
Source: Tables 43 and 31 in Ungerer et al. (1986).

organized market for public debt is accompanied by a large disintermediation of the financial system.

Throughout this period, the compensatory monetary policy of the Bank of Italy manages to limit the size of the overall creation of monetary base against Treasury liabilities (see Table 3.1). However, the Treasury is still responsible for large variations of liquidity during the course of each year. Moreover, the Treasury sometimes receives an implicit subsidy from the Bank of Italy, since it forces the central bank to buy the debt in the primary market at a price which can occasionally exceed the price subsequently formed in the secondary market.

In 1979 Italy enters the European Monetary System (EMS) and Paolo Baffi is replaced by Carlo Azeglio Ciampi as Governor of the Bank of Italy. However, none of these events substantially alter the course of monetary policy. During the first two years of its existence, the EMS does not place a binding constraint on Italian monetary policy, as indicated by the low level of real interest rates in Italy relative to other European countries (see Table 3.3), and by the frequent realignments of the Italian lira in the system.[8] And the new Governor continues the "compensatory" monetary policy of his predecessor.

2.3   The new monetary regime: 1981–86

The transformation of the monetary regime begins in the summer of 1981, when the Bank of Italy is freed from the obligation of buying the unsold public debt at the Treasury auctions. The "divorce" between the Bank of Italy and the Treasury, as the reform is called in the Italian press, has one main motivation (see Salvemini 1983): to block the mechanism described in the previous subsection, whereby the Treasury creates monetary base and the Bank of Italy destroys it in the secondary market. This mechanism has several drawbacks. From a technical point of view, it adds variability to the monetary base and it forces the Bank of Italy to operate in the secondary market exclusively as a net seller of public debt. More importantly, from a political point of view, it places the responsibility for the level of interest rates on the monetary rather than on the fiscal authorities. The "divorce" has the effect of increasing the visibility and hence the unpopularity of deficit financing.[9] In this regard, it is worth noting that one of the most active and influential supporters of the "divorce" was the Secretary of the Treasury himself, Beniamino Andreatta. The Secretary of the Treasury and his advisers, perhaps even more than the Bank of Italy, were convinced that the "divorce" would have positive repercussions on the incentives of the government and the political authorities.

However, the reform is incomplete in two important respects. Firstly, it still leaves the Treasury with the opportunity of creating liquidity through the overdraft account. Since the ceiling on this account is 14 percent of public expenditure in the current period, this is by no means a trivial channel of base creation. Indeed, as indicated in Table 3.1, the Treasury makes heavy use of this account throughout this period of time. Secondly, the "divorce" gives the Treasury the ability to choose the minimum base price at the public debt auctions. Any offer below such a minimum price is not accepted. Hence, the Treasury can fix the maximum interest rate in the primary market. Since the debt traded in the primary market is a very good substitute of the debt traded in the secondary market, the Treasury can set a ceiling to a key interest rate in the Italian money market. In practice, this ceiling on the level of interest rates has very seldom been binding. The Treasury has regularly asked the Bank of Italy for "technical advice" about the appropriate base price. Generally this advice has been followed. It is not clear, however, whether this would continue to happen under all possible Secretaries of the Treasury. Nor is it clear whether the "technical advice" offered by the Bank of Italy has been conditioned by the perceived reaction of the Treasury to this advice.

Even in the presence of these constraints, however, the "divorce" has had relevant effects on the visibility of fiscal imbalances. This is well exemplified by events that took place in 1982. The Treasury had to raise a large amount of cash. It was unwilling to raise the interest rate in the primary market, and the size of the overdraft account was insufficient to cover its liquidity needs. The Bank of Italy chose not to monetize the debt in the primary market. And the Treasury was forced to ask Parliament to ratify by law the temporary overshooting of the legal limit on the overdraft account. We are clearly very far away from the logic of Guido Carli, that a refusal to monetize would amount to an "act of rebellion" (see subsection 2.1).

A second important institutional change that occurs in this period concerns the methods of monetary control. In 1983 administrative credit controls are abandoned, in favor of more indirect methods that rely on interest rates and monetary aggregates. There are several reasons for this change. Financial innovation is making administrative controls less and less effective (see Cottarelli *et al.* 1986). To the extent that the controls are not evaded, they impose increasing efficiency costs on the economy (see Bruni, Monti and Porta 1980). Finally, the expansion of the public sector borrowing requirement is forcing the monetary authorities to deemphasize total domestic credit as a target of policy and to replace it with monetary targets. In 1974, when a target for total domestic credit was first announced, the public sector borrowing requirement amounted to less than 50 percent of total domestic credit. In 1983 it is over 70 percent. In such a situation, total domestic credit is largely determined by fiscal policy, not by monetary policy. Suppose for instance that the fiscal deficit turns out to be larger than expected. The scope for offsetting the resulting increase in total domestic credit through a curtailment of credit to the private sector is severely diminished. Hence the shift towards monetary targets and indirect methods of control (see Ciampi 1986 and Caranza and Fazio 1983). As in the case of the "divorce," much of the impetus in favor of the deregulation comes initially from the Treasury, and in particular from the influential report of the Treasury Commission chaired by Mario Monti (see *Report* 1984). One of the points stressed in the report is that the regulatory constraints on financial markets confer a hidden subsidy to the Treasury. The removal of this subsidy, it is argued, restores new incentives towards a more disciplined fiscal policy.

Two interest rates now play a key role in the strategy of the Bank of Italy: the real interest rate on Treasury bills, that is perceived as being systematically related to the demand for financial assets in general, and the differential between the rate on short term Treasury bills and the rate on bank deposits, that determines the demand for public debt on the part of households, and hence money demand (see Masera 1983 and Caranza and Fazio 1983). As documented in Tables 3.1 and 3.3, the real interest rate sharply increases during the 1980s both in absolute value and relative to other European countries.

The third and final milestone of the Italian monetary regime change is the increased willingness to accept the external constraint imposed by the EMS. This constraint was disregarded in the first couple of years of the EMS's existence; but in more recent times it plays a major role in publicly justifying a severe monetary policy. As documented in Table 3.3, the real interest rate differential between Italy and West Germany rises sharply after 1981. The elimination of the controls on international capital flows, that is about to take place, will obviously consolidate the bite of this external constraint on Italian monetary policy.

2.4 What next?

As stated in the previous pages, the monetary reform is yet to be completed. Among the industrial countries, Italy is still one of the few in which the Treasury has such large monetary powers through the over-draft account, and in which the central bank has access to the primary market for public debt. In most other countries the central bank operates exclusively in the secondary market; and the size of the Treasury overdraft account with the central bank is limited to a maximum of 2 or 3 percent of current expenditures. (In the case of Denmark, the UK and the US, the Treasury cannot receive any direct financing from the central bank – see Bank of Italy 1983.) The reduction of the degree of monetary financing of the deficit that occurred in the 1980s is the result of discretionary choices of the Bank of Italy, not of binding external constraints. As such, the new course of monetary policy in Italy is easily reversible. Moreover, even the reforms described in the previous pages can be easily reversed, since they occurred through administrative decisions of the monetary and fiscal authorities and have not been ratified by a legislative act of Parliament.

In order to consolidate the process of monetary reforms, other important steps have to be taken. They are: (i) to curtail the monetary powers of the Treasury, through a reduction in the size of the overdraft account; (ii) to tolerate more upwards flexibility of interest rates, by further reducing the participation of the Bank of Italy in the primary market for public debt. This can be done partly by making the public debt auctions more competitive and more generally by increasing the separa-tion of responsibilities between the conduct of monetary policy (the concern of the Bank of Italy) and the management of public debt (the concern of the Treasury); (iii) to ratify these reforms by law, so as to transform them into external constraints on the policymakers, since now, the reforms rely for their survival exclusively on the goodwill and reputation of the policymakers themselves.

Should these additional steps be carried out in the near future? Or should they instead wait until the debt to GDP ratio has been stabilized by means of a coordinated monetary and fiscal policy strategy?

In the remainder of the paper I argue that the completion of the monetary reforms should not be delayed. Not only is there no contradiction between the completion of the reforms and the goal of arresting the growth of public debt. On the contrary, the monetary reform can be regarded almost as a prerequisite for achieving that goal. As stated in the introductory section, the argument is that reforming the monetary regime changes the incentives of the fiscal authority, in the direction of making fiscal stabilization more desirable. This argument will be presented in two steps. The next section analyzes some theoretical results supporting this point of view. Section 4 then considers the empirical evidence in the light of these theoretical results.

3   A theoretical interpretation of the monetary reforms

The monetary reforms described in the previous section grew out of an intellectual climate that stressed the positive incentive effects of adding visibility and transparency to forms of taxation that had hitherto been hidden and implicit (see for instance Monti 1983a, 1983b, Masera 1986, Bruni and Giavazzi 1987, and Salvemini 1983). This line of thought can be traced back to the research of Buchanan and his associates (see Brennan and Buchanan 1980 and Mueller 1979), and before them to the work of Italian economists such as Puviani (1903). Fiscal policy decisions are viewed as reflecting political considerations about the redistributive effects of the policy. The political gains associated with the redistributions (in cash or in kind) in favor of certain groups of the population are weighted against the political costs of effecting these transfers. This weighting process, however, is highly imperfect. Because of irrationality on the part of political agents, or because of the existence of information gathering costs, some forms of taxation have smaller political (but not necessarily economic) costs than others. Typically, deficit financing, money seignorage and regulatory constraints are implicit taxes bearing smaller political costs than more explicit forms of taxation. According to this point of view, therefore, the desirable incentive effects of the reforms on the behavior of the fiscal authority operate by increasing the visibility and the transparency of the taxes implicit in the process of deficit financing.

In this section I analyze a second incentive effect of the monetary reforms that can facilitate the correction of fiscal imbalance. This effect operates by improving the strategic position of the central bank, in the context of a dynamic game between the monetary and fiscal authorities.

The key idea is as follows. Suppose that, for the same reasons considered by the school of Public Choice (information gathering costs, logrolling and vote trading, budget maximizing bureaucrats, and so on), the fiscal authority desires a large amount of public expenditure or transfers. Suppose further that the central bank is shielded from the political pressures that direct the incentives of the fiscal authority towards large public expenditure. Hence, assume that the central bank assigns a smaller weight to public expenditure. We then have two decentralized taxing authorities with different objectives.

In this situation, the Treasury finds it optimal to run a deficit. For by doing so, it forces the central bank to increase the future rate of money seignorage. Moreover, the incentive to run a deficit for the fiscal authority is stronger the larger is the extent of debt monetization. Hence, a monetary reform that reduces the extent of future debt monetization has the effect of reducing the equilibrium size of the budget deficit. Naturally, the desirability of the reforms depends on a judgment concerning the optimal size of the inflation tax. If the inflation tax that would be chosen by the Treasury exceeds the optimum, then the monetary reforms can be welfare improving, since they lead to less inflation and smaller deficits.

Note that this effect of the reforms is purely strategic. It does not depend on the fact that the reforms increase the visibility (and hence the political costs) of the deficit. However, these two effects reinforce each other. The reason for focusing on this particular aspect of the monetary reforms is because it has been neglected so far in the Italian public policy debate.[10]

3.1 The model

The model is the simplest one possible in order to analyze the idea summarized in the previous pages. The nature of the results should extent to much more general settings even though the analysis would be more complex.

The economy is open to the rest of the world and is a price taker in international capital markets. The only tool of monetary policy is the domestic component of the monetary base. Thus, exchange rates are perfectly flexible. Moreover, purchasing power parity is assumed, so that there is no need to distinguish between the price level and the nominal exchange rate. The time horizon lasts two periods. At the end of the second period all debt (private or public) has to be repaid.

The private sector consists of a representative consumer that lives two periods and maximizes:

$$V = \text{Max}\{ln\,C_1 + \beta ln\,C_2 + ln\,m_1 + \beta ln\,m_2\}$$
$$1 > \beta > 0 \tag{1}$$

where: $C_i \equiv$ consumption in period i; $m_i \equiv M_i/P_i \equiv$ real money balances held at the end of period i, M_i and P_i being respectively nominal money balances and the price level in period i. Real money balances enter the utility function because of the liquidity services that they provide.

The consumer is endowed with a positive quantity E of real output in each period; this endowment is taxed at the rate τ_i in period i. Moreover, at the beginning of the first period of his life, the consumer also owns a positive quantity of nominal money balances, M_0, and of real government debt, B_0.[11] Finally, he faces a given real interest rate in international capital markets, r, that coincides with his subjective rate of intertemporal preference: $1/(1 + r) = \beta$. Under all these assumptions, and denoting the inverse of the expected inflation rate in period 2 by $\pi_2^e \equiv P_1/P_2^e$, the consumer's intertemporal budget constraint can be written as:

$$W \equiv E(1 - \tau_1) + \beta E(1 - \tau_2) + B_0 + M_0/P_1$$
$$= C_1 + m_1(1 - \beta\tau_2^e) + \beta C_2 + \beta m_2 \tag{2}$$

where W denotes his lifetime real wealth.

The first order conditions of this simple optimization problem yield the consumer's demand for private consumption and for real money balances in the two periods of his life:

$$C_1 = C_2 = m_2 = \frac{W}{2(1 + \beta)}$$
$$m_1 = \frac{W}{2(1 + \beta)(1 - \beta\tau_2^e)} \tag{3}$$

The conflict of interest between the two policy makers is modelled in the simplest possible way. The fiscal authority behaves like Buchanan's Leviathan: it only cares about public expenditures, G, and maximizes:

$$U = \text{Max}\{ln\,G_1 + \beta ln\,G_2\} \tag{4}$$

The central bank, by contrast, only cares about the private sector and totally disregards public consumption. Making a less extreme hypothesis about the divergence of preferences between the two policymakers would complicate the notation and the algebra, but would not alter the nature of the results in any respect. The only essential feature of the model is that the inflation tax desired by the fiscal authority is larger than that desired by the central bank. Even though this feature does not have universal validity, it seems to capture an important aspect of the interaction between the monetary and fiscal authorities in Italy from 1970 up to now.

The action of the two policymakers is constrained by the intertemporal government budget constraint:

$$
\begin{aligned}
G_1 + B_0 &\leqq \tau_1 E + \beta B + M_1/P_1 - M_0/P_1 \\
G_2 + B &\leqq \tau_2 E + M_2/P_2 - M_1/P_2
\end{aligned}
\tag{5}
$$

where B is the (real) public debt issued by the government in period 1 that has to be repaid in full at the end of period 2.

It is clear that the fiscal authority always sets taxes at 100 percent. Hence, to simplify the notation, I will denote the excess of public expenditure over tax revenue by $g_i = G_i = E$. Thus, g_i is the fiscal deficit net of interest payments in period i. The fiscal authority chooses g_i, and the central bank chooses M_i, $i = 1, 2$.

The imposition of the government budget constraint implies the loss of one degree of freedom in setting monetary and fiscal policies. Who is going to bear the residual burden of satisfying this constraint? Obviously, there is no general answer: it depends on the institutional set-up.[12] Here this feature of the institutional setting is parameterized as follows. It is assumed that a fraction $(1 - \theta)$ of the burden of satisfying the budget constraint falls on the fiscal authority, and that the remaining fraction θ falls on the central bank. Thus, in the second period of the game, g_2 and M_2 are constrained by:

$$
\begin{aligned}
g_2 &\leqq -(1 - \theta)B \\
M_2/P_2 - M_1/P_2 &\leqq \theta B
\end{aligned}
\tag{6}
$$

If $\theta = 1$, we have a regime where fiscal policy is dominant and the burden of repaying the debt falls entirely on monetary policy. This regime resembles the one analyzed by Bryant and Wallace (1979); it corresponds to a situation in which the fiscal authority acts as the Stackelberg leader and has the first move in each period of the game. If $\theta = 0$ we have the opposite extreme: a regime where monetary policy is dominant and the burden of repaying the debt falls exclusively on fiscal policy. This regime would arise if the central bank could act as the Stackelberg leader and could precommit to a course of action for the current period before fiscal policy has been chosen. Intermediate regimes correspond to values of θ between 0 and 1. Throughout the paper I will refer to θ as the "degree of fiscal dominance."

The monetary regime prevailing in Italy in the first half of the 1970s clearly resembles the case of a dominant fiscal policy, with a θ very close to 1: a non-accommodating monetary policy would have been an "act of rebellion" – see section 2.1 above. The reforms of the 1980s can be interpreted as having had the effect of reducing the value of θ: the divorce between the Bank of Italy and the Treasury officially recognizes that monetary policy should not automatically bear the burden of financing the fiscal deficit; the increased importance of the Italian participation in the EMS limits the autonomy of domestic monetary policy; and more generally, the reforms denote the emergence of a political and intellectual climate in which monetary policy is partially shielded from fiscal pressures. Even though Italy is still far away from the extreme regime of a dominant monetary policy, nonetheless it seems plausible that the reforms of the 1980s have reduced the value of θ.

The remainder of this section analyzes the impact that a change in θ has on the equilibrium of the game, and in particular on the rate of inflation and on the size of the fiscal deficit in the first period.

3.2   The macroeconomic equilibrium

The demand for real money balances in period 1, and hence the price level in that same period, depend on expected future inflation. Under rational expectations, expected future inflation is determined by the equilibrium condition of the money market in period 2. From equations (6) and (3) we obtain

$$m_2 = \theta B + m_1 \pi_2 = \theta B + m_2 \pi_2/(1 - \beta \pi_2^e) \tag{7}$$

Equating π_2 and π_2^e, and using (3) again, equation (7) can be solved for the actual and expected inverse of the inflation rate:

$$\pi_2 = \pi_2^e = \frac{W - 2\theta(1 + \beta)B}{[W - 2\theta\beta B](1 + \beta)} \tag{8}$$

By taking partial derivatives of (8), it can be shown that π_2 is increasing in W and decreasing in θ and (if $\theta > 0$) in B. Thus a higher debt to be repaid, B, or a higher proportion of debt to be monetized in the second period, θ, tends to raise the inflation rate. Whereas a higher private real wealth, W, by increasing the demand for real balances in period 2, has the opposite effect of reducing the inflation rate.

The price level in period 1, P_1, is also determined by the equilibrium condition in the money market:

$$1/P_1 = \frac{m_1}{M_1} = \frac{W}{2(1 + \beta)(1 - \beta\pi_2^e)M_1} \qquad (9)$$

Defining $\mu = M_1/M_0$ as the gross rate of growth of money supply in period 1, recalling from (2) that $W = B_0 + M_0/P_1$, and using (8) to form π_2^e, we can solve (9) for the inverse of the price level:

$$\frac{1}{P_1} = \frac{2B_0 - \theta\beta B}{2(2\mu - 1)M_0} \qquad (10)$$

Equation (10) implies:

Proposition 1
P_1 is increasing in μ and B. The effect of B on P_1 is proportional to θ.

That is, an expansionary monetary policy (a larger μ) increases prices in the current period. And issuing more public debt, B, is also inflationary in the current period, since the private sector realizes that issuing debt leads to future inflation and hence reduces its real money demand today. Moreover, the larger the degree of fiscal dominance (the larger is θ), the more inflationary are the consequences of issuing public debt. In the limit, if monetary policy is dominant (that is, if $\theta = 0$), issuing debt has no effect on prices, since the debt will not be monetized at all in the future.

This result suggests an empirical conjecture. Namely, the Italian monetary regime change should be reflected in a diminished response of the rate of inflation to the time path of public debt in the 1980s relative to the earlier period. This conjecture is tested in subsection 4.3 below.

3.3   Fiscal deficit and monetary reforms

It is now possible to evaluate the effect of changing θ on the behavior of the fiscal authority and on the players' welfare in the feedback–Nash equilibrium. In such an equilibrium, the two policymakers move simultaneously in each period and take into account the effect of the state variable on the outcome of the game in the second period, i.e., they take into account equations (6) and (8). This is the appropriate solution concept, given that neither player can precommit to a course of action forever.[13]

The government budget constraint in period 1 is:

$$B = \frac{1}{\beta}\left[g_1 + \frac{M_0}{P_1}(1 - \mu) + B_0\right]$$

or, using equation (10):

$$B = g_1 \Phi(\mu, \theta) + \Omega(\mu, \theta) \tag{11}$$

Where

$$\Phi(\mu, \theta) = \frac{4\mu - 2}{\beta[(4 - \theta)\mu + \theta - 2]}$$

$$\Omega(\mu, \theta) = \frac{2B_0}{\beta[(4 - \theta)\mu + \theta - 2]} \tag{12}$$

The fiscal authority maximizes (4) with respect to g_1 and B, subject to (6), (11) and (12), and taking current monetary policy, μ, as given. Its first order conditions imply:

$$1/G_1 \gtreqqless \beta(1 - \theta) \Phi(\mu, \theta)/G_2 \tag{13}$$

with an equality sign in an interior optimum. The left hand side of (13) is the marginal utility of public expenditure in the current period. The right hand side is the marginal cost of financing it by issuing public debt. This cost is given by the marginal disutility of the future reduction in expenditure that is necessary to repay the debt, under the existing monetary regime, as parameterized by θ.

Monetary policy is chosen by the central bank so as to maximize the welfare of the private sector, subject to the private sector first order conditions (equation 3), the equilibrium condition in the money market (equations 8 and 10), the government budget constraints (equations 5 and 6), and for a given value of the fiscal policy variable, g_1. Appendix 1 characterizes more precisely the central bank optimization problem and applies the envelope theorem to prove that under plausible conditions the welfare of the central bank (and hence the welfare of the private sector under the hypothesis of this model) is a monotonically decreasing function of θ. That is, the more dominant is monetary policy, the better off is the central bank. Not surprisingly, given the assumptions of the model, the optimal monetary arrangement for the private sector's welfare has the central bank completely shielded from fiscal pressures (that is, the optimal value of θ is 0). This result would survive several generalizations of the underlying model, as long as one retains the assumption that the rate of inflation desired by the central bank is closer to the social optimum than the inflation rate that would be chosen by the Treasury.

Finally, applying the implicit function theorem to (13) and to the central bank first order conditions, it is possible to prove that, for large values of B_0 and for θ not too close to 1:

Proposition 2
The fiscal deficit net of interest payments in period 1, g_1, is an increasing function of θ.

That is, a monetary reform that decreases the degree of fiscal dominance, θ, forces the fiscal authority to reduce the size of the budget deficit in period 1. The intuition is straightforward. The cost of issuing public debt here is mitigated by its future partial monetization. A monetary reform that cuts the link between public debt and subsequent money creation thereby tends to raise the marginal cost of running a fiscal deficit. In the limit, if monetary policy is dominant and money creation is absolutely independent of the stock of public debt in circulation (that is, if $\theta=0$), equation (13) reduces to $G_1=G_2$, in which case the fiscal authority finds it optimal to balance the budget in both periods.

3.4   Further remarks

The results presented in the previous pages seem in strident contrast to two related common sense considerations that recur in public policy discussions of the Italian financial problems: namely, that fiscal deficits are *de facto* determined independently of the stance of monetary policy; and that their size is purely the macroscopic consequence of several myopic political decisions, rather than being the deliberate and strategic choice of a rational agency.

The first consideration, however, reflects a confusion between monetary policy actions and monetary institutions. In the model of the previous pages too, it is true that fiscal policy is not affected by current monetary policy. The crucial determinant of fiscal policy is the monetary regime: that is, the link between current deficits and future monetization. This link does not depend on the goodwill (or bad will) of the Bank of Italy. It is determined exclusively by factors that the monetary authority controls only indirectly and in the very long run, such as institutions, political constraints, and the intellectual climate. The analytical results of this section therefore should not be interpreted as an argument in favor of more restrictive monetary policies within the current institutional set up. Such a policy choice would merely substitute less monetization today for even more monetization in the future, as in the model of Sargent and Wallace (1981). The results do, however, argue in favor of a continuation of the monetary regime change initiated in the 1980s. To the extent that such a change in monetary regime would credibly reduce future debt monetization, it would also decrease the incentives of the fiscal authority to run a deficit.

The second objection to the approach taken in this section is more damaging and more difficult to handle. But even if fiscal policy decisions are not taken by a rational player, the fact that changing the monetary regime may increase the cost of running a fiscal deficit remains valid. All that is necessary for the argument to go through, then, is that, at some stage of the political decision process, these costs be taken into account.[14]

4   Monetary reforms and fiscal policy: the evidence

This section tests the conjecture formulated in the previous pages, namely that the Italian monetary reforms brought about a fiscal policy more disciplined by the intertemporal budget constraint. Two kinds of evidence are considered: direct indicators of fiscal policy, and indirect evidence reflecting private sector expectations of future debt monetization. The evidence is mixed. The fiscal policy indicators give ambiguous results, depending on the particular indicator that is chosen and on the specification of the econometric regressions. And the indirect evidence suggests that the private sector expects the currently outstanding debt to be repaid by future monetization rather than by future fiscal surpluses.

4.1   Simple fiscal policy indicators

A commonly used indicator of intertemporal fiscal policy decisions in Italy is the public sector borrowing requirement (PSBR) scaled to nominal GDP. This variable has steadily grown throughout the period under consideration. However, its growth exclusively reflects the increasing flow of interest payments on government debt.

Table 3.4 reports the PSBR net of (net) interest payments, scaled to GDP:[15] it is roughly constant throughout the period. Its yearly average is 7.5 percent for the period 1970–76, 6.68 percent for 1977–81, and 7.32 percent for 1982–86. Hence, this indicator suggests that no change in fiscal policy occurred as a result of the monetary reforms.[16]

The PSBR net of interest payments however is not a good indicator of fiscal policy, since it reflects both discretionary decisions and the automatic impact of the business cycle on tax revenue and on some components of public expenditure. In order to isolate those discretionary decisions, Table 3.4 also reports the PSBR net of interest payments and

Table 3.4 PSBR without interest payments, with and without cyclical adjustments

Year	Fy	Fay
1970	4.57	3.18
1971	6.93	4.16
1972	8.02	5.71
1973	8.85	5.99
1974	7.05	5.21
1975	10.82	4.30
1976	6.91	3.14
1977	5.47	1.52
1978	9.78	2.56
1979	6.51	3.50
1980	5.24	2.21
1981	6.39	3.93
1982	8.02	1.92
1983	8.14	0.79
1984	7.24	0.29
1985	8.22	1.62
1986	5.00	0.12

Note: Fy is the PSBR net of (net) interest payments – see note 15. Fay is the PSBR net of (net) interest payments and cyclically adjusted – see note 17. All variables are scaled to nominal GDP – see note 16.
Source: Bank of Italy and OECD.

cyclically adjusted.[17] This variable suggests a fiscal policy change: its yearly average is 4.53 percent for the period 1970–76, 2.74 percent for the period 1977–81 and 0.63 percent for the period 1982–86.[18]

The computation of the cyclical adjustment, however, is subject to serious errors of measurement.[19] Moreover, a simple comparison of cyclically adjusted PSBR conceals the effects of political and economic factors besides the monetary regime change that may have influenced the course of fiscal policy throughout the period under consideration. The next subsection therefore estimates a reaction function of the fiscal authority, using two different methods.

4.2 The Treasury reaction function

This subsection exploits the following simple idea: if fiscal policy is conditioned by the goal of stabilizing public debt, then the size of the cyclically adjusted PSBR net of interest payments should be inversely related to the stock of debt outstanding at the beginning of each period

(and possibly in previous periods).[20] Moreover, this inverse relation
should be stronger in the periods in which this goal is pursued more
actively. This result follows, for instance, from a model in which the
Treasury loss function includes a quadratic term in public debt, or
equivalently in the deviations of public debt from its desired time path.
Tabellini (1986) analyzes a dynamic game theoretic model exhibiting this
feature. Tabellini and La Via (1986) estimate the reduced form of such a
model on US data.

This simple insight suggests the following research strategy: to estimate a Treasury reaction function, including lagged values of public debt
as explanatory variables, and then to test whether the coefficients on the
lagged debt variables have become more negative under the new
monetary regime.

This strategy faces a number of difficulties: there are only 17 annual
observations (before 1970 there was no serious fiscal imbalance). Despite
the fact that there are relatively few observations, the period is sufficiently long that the assumption of stability of the coefficients may fail.
Finally, there is no theory to guide us on the specification of the reaction
function.

Of these, the final difficulty is really the fundamental one: even with a
large data set, in any non-experimental setting and in the absence of
sharp theoretical priors, there is always a "degrees-of-freedom-deficit"
(see Leamer 1983). For this reason, in the following pages particular
attention is paid to the robustness of the results with respect to alternative specifications.

To save on the degrees of freedom, I follow two alternative
approaches. I estimate first a reaction function with sharp prior constraints on the lag structure and loose priors on the set of explanatory
variables to be included. Then I do the opposite: I impose no prior
constraints on the lag structure but I restrict more severely the set of
included explanatory variables.

4.2.1 Sharp priors on the lag structure
The general form of the reaction function estimated in this subsection is:

$$f_t = \beta_0 + \beta_1 f_{t-1} + \beta_2 d_{t-1} + \beta_3 D d_{t-1}$$

$$+ \sum_{i=1}^{2} \delta_i x_{it} + u_t \tag{14}$$

where:
f_t = PSBR, cyclically adjusted and net of interest payments, scaled to
    nominal GDP.

d_t = stock of public debt held by the private sector at the end of year t, scaled to nominal GDP.

D = dummy variable taking a value of 0 up through 1981 and a value of 1 thereafter.

x_{it} = some exogenous economic variable that can influence the size of f_t, either because the Treasury responds to it, or because it has some automatic effect on either tax revenues or public expenditure.

u_t = unobservable error term.

The β coefficients correspond to variables for which I assume no specification uncertainty. Thus, the corresponding variables are included in all the regressions. The δ coefficients instead correspond to variables to which I assign loose prior beliefs, in the sense that I ignore whether or not they should be included as explanatory variables, and how. This second set of variables will be the object of some formal specification search. The focus coefficient is β_3: I want to find out whether fiscal policy has responded more vigorously to the goal of stabilizing public debt after 1981 than before. The conjecture is that β_3 is negative.

The variables x_{it} are the CPI inflation rate, x_{1t} (that may affect f_t automatically through the fiscal drag or it may induce a discretionary response), and the real interest rate on Treasury bills, x_{2t} (that alters the Treasury intertemporal tradeoffs). The expected sign on the coefficient of both variables is negative. In order to avoid simultaneous equation bias, the predicted rather than the actual values of these variables are used in estimating equation (14). These predicted values were generated by means of an OLS regression of the variable in question on itself lagged twice and on lagged values of: f, d, a measure of cyclical output fluctuations, and the creation of the Treasury component of the monetary base scaled to nominal GDP. The hypothesis of no first order autocorrelation in the residuals of these OLS regressions could not be rejected. If the Treasury responds with a lag and tries to forecast the future, then these predicted values of x_1 and x_2 can be regarded as instruments for unobservable Treasury expectations (see McCallum 1976).[21] The results are not sensitive to the way in which these predicted values of x are generated. In particular, the result of a negative estimated β_3 coefficient referred to in the following paragraph is reinforced if the variable Dd_{t-1} is added to the OLS regressions generating the values of x.

Table 3.5 reports the estimates of the coefficients in (14), when no constraint is imposed and all the variables are included.[22] None of the coefficients on public debt is significantly different from zero. However, whereas β_2 is positive, β_3 is negative as expected. Moreover, when either δ_1 or δ_2 or both are constrained to be equal to zero, β_2 remains positive

Table 3.5 Unconstrained estimates of equation (14)

β_0	β_1	β_2	β_3	δ_1	δ_2
4.963	0.260	0.007	− 0.028	− 0.193	− 3.09
(5.326)	(0.526)	(0.069)	(0.035)	(0.137)	(0.487)

$\bar{R}^2 = 0.617$
$F = 6.159$

SE = 1.210
MLM = 1.211
LM = 1.715

Note: Standard errors are in parentheses. LM is the Lagrange Multiplier test for the hypothesis of no first order serial correlation of the residuals. MLM is the LM test modified for small samples (Kiviet 1981). The regression SE is corrected for degrees of freedom.

Table 3.6 Estimates of equation (14) when the constraint $\delta_2 = 0$ is imposed

β_0	β_1	β_2	β_3	δ_1
1.889	0.562	0.036	− 0.046	− 0.120
(2.156)	(0.218)	(0.050)	(0.021)	(0.071)

$\bar{R}^2 = 0.636$
$F = 7.997$

SE = 1.179
MLM = 0.9132
LM = 1.29

Note: Standard errors are in parentheses. LM is the Lagrange Multiplier test for the hypothesis of no first order serial correlation of the residuals. MLM is the LM test modified for small samples (Kiviet 1981). The regression SE is corrected for degrees of freedom.

and insignificant, whereas β_3 remains negative, but rises in absolute value and becomes significant. Table 3.6 reports the estimates when δ_2, the coefficient on the real interest rate, is constrained to be zero. Not only does β_3 become significant, but the overall regression improves.

In order to verify further that the negative sign of β_3 is robust to alternative specifications of (14), Appendix 2 reports the results of some sensitivity analysis done with the help of "SEARCH," a Bayesian statistical package designed by Leamer and Leonard (1983). This analysis confirms that uncertainty about the prior constraints on the

δ coefficients does not invalidate the inference that β_3 is negative. Finally, the same inference remains valid if a different, more gradual, periodization of the monetary regime change is chosen,[23] and if the relevant variables are scaled to a log linear trend of nominal GDP (rather than to its actual value).[24]

The results however are sensitive to the specification of the lag structure. If the variables d_{t-2}, Dd_{t-2} and f_{t-2} are added to the right hand side of (14), an F test cannot always reject the hypothesis that the coefficients of Dd_{t-1} and Dd_{t-2} are both equal to zero. These two coefficients turn out to be of opposite sign, and their algebraic sum is negative, but for some specifications it is very small. Only when δ_2 is constrained to be equal to 0 one can reject the hypothesis that the sum of the coefficients on Dd_{t-1} and Dd_{t-2} is zero.

Summarizing, the evidence reported in this subsection suggests that the monetary regime change forced the fiscal authority to pay more attention to the goal of stabilizing public debt. This evidence is robust to alternative specifications of the Treasury reaction function, as long as one is willing to maintain the prior hypothesis about the lag structure explicit in equation (14): namely, that the PSBR is influenced by f_{t-1} and d_{t-1}, but not by the same variables in earlier periods. When this prior hypothesis is relaxed, some of the results change.

The next subsection asks the same question, but with no prior constraints on the lag structure.

4.2.2 Unrestricted lag structure

The equation estimated in this subsection is:

$$f_t = \alpha_0 + \beta_1(L)f_{t-1} + \beta_2(L)d_{t-1} \\ + \beta_3(L)Dd_{t-1} + \delta_2(L)x_{2t-1} + u_t \qquad (15)$$

where the variables are defined as in equation (14) above. Unlike the previous subsection, lagged actual values rather than predicted values of the real interest rate, x_2, are used, since now there is no simultaneous equation bias problem.[25] $\beta(L)$ and $\delta(L)$ are second degree polynomials in the lag operator. The focus coefficients are again those of $\beta(L)$. The conjecture is that the sum of these two coefficients is negative.

Table 3.7 reports the estimates for $\beta_3(L)$ unconstrained. The two β_3 coefficients are of opposite sign and of similar magnitude. An F test cannot reject the hypothesis that they are both insignificantly different from zero.

Thus, the evidence here points in the opposite direction from that considered in the previous subsection: with a relatively unrestricted lag

Table 3.7 Estimates of equation (15)

α_0	β_{11}	β_{12}	β_{21}	β_{22}	β_{31}	β_{32}	δ_{21}	δ_{22}
4.854	0.826	− 0.589	0.009	− 0.063	0.200	− 0.235	− 0.198	0.153
(4.032)	(0.420)	(0.492)	(0.102)	(0.117)	(0.440)	(0.473)	(0.257)	(0.147)

$\bar{R}^2 = 0.611$ SE $= 1.220$
$F\ \ = 4.136$ MLM $= 2.702$
      LM $= 5.74$

Note: Standard errors are in parentheses. LM is the Lagrange Multiplier test for the hypothesis of no first order serial correlation of the residuals. MLM is the LM test modified for small samples (Kiviet 1981). The regression SE is corrected for degrees of freedom.

structure, there is no indication that the monetary regime change had an impact on the attitude of the Treasury towards the goal of stabilizing public debt. Since there is no theoretical ground on which to choose between the specification of this and of the previous subsection, it seems impossible to draw any reliable inference. The evidence concerning the Treasury reaction function is not sufficiently robust to assess whether the regime change had an impact on fiscal policy.

4.3   Indirect evidence: the inflationary consequences of budget deficits

According to Proposition 1 in section 3.2, the inflationary consequences of budget deficits depend, through the expectations of the private sector, on a feature of the institutional setting: namely, the degree of fiscal dominance (the parameter θ of subsection 3.3). This result is more general than the model from which it was derived. Sargent and Wallace (1981), for instance, analyzing an overlapping generations model, note that the growth of public debt is not inflationary if it occurs in a regime where monetary policy is dominant (in the sense that its future time path is independent of the stock of public debt outstanding). But it is inflationary if, instead, fiscal policy is dominant, since the debt will then be repaid through future money seignorage (see also Aiyagari and Gertler 1985). Moreover, in a regime where fiscal policy is dominant, the inflationary consequences of the deficit are larger with a more restrictive monetary policy, since such a policy further increases future money creation.

   This suggests an indirect test of whether the monetary reforms of the 1980s reduced the degree of fiscal dominance in Italy. If they did, then we

Table 3.8 Summary statistics

Variables	Mean	Std. Dev.	r_1	r_2	r_3	r_4	r_5	r_6
					Autocorrelation			
Period 1970: 1 – 1986: 4								
P	3.09	1.56	0.66	0.57	0.52	0.41	0.37	0.35
y	0.6	5.83	− 0.53	0.15	− 0.57	0.95	− 0.53	0.12
m	3.62	3.85	− 0.33	− 0.19	− 0.22	0.61	− 0.15	− 0.20
d	5.04	1.66	0.17	0.08	0.25	0.44	0.09	0.23
Period 1970: 1 – 1981: 2								
P	3.35	1.66	0.65	0.57	0.51	0.38	0.33	0.41
y	0.69	6.22	− 0.50	0.09	− 0.54	0.94	− 0.50	0.03
m	3.76	4.05	− 0.38	− 0.14	− 0.20	0.54	− 0.11	− 0.16
d	4.87	1.81	0.14	0.12	0.23	0.40	0.11	0.30
Period 1981: 3 – 1986: 4								
P	2.55	1.17	0.63	0.52	0.65	0.70	0.73	0.48
y	0.52	5.05	− 0.62	0.35	− 0.68	0.98	− 0.64	0.37
m	3.34	3.44	− 0.21	− 0.39	− 0.31	0.82	− 0.28	− 0.35
d	5.38	1.27	0.21	− 0.27	0.15	0.48	− 0.22	− 0.19

should find that fiscal deficits had more capacity to predict inflation before the monetary reforms than afterwards. If instead the degree of fiscal dominance was unchanged, then the opposite should be true: monetary policy has been more restrictive in the 1980s than in the earlier period. If fiscal policy is dominant, then, this tends to increase the inflationary consequences of budget deficits, as noted by Sargent and Wallace (1981). Naturally, this is a joint test of the nature of the institutional setting, of the hypothesis of rational expectations, and of the hypothesis that the monetary reforms were unexpected.

In order to perform this test, I estimate an equation of the following general form (all variables are expressed in deviations from their mean):

$$P_t = \alpha(L)P_{t-1} + \beta(L)m_{t-1} + \sigma(L)y_{t-1} + \delta(L)d_{t-1} + u_t \qquad (16)$$

where: $P \equiv$ CPI inflation rate; $m \equiv$ first difference of the log of base money; $y \equiv$ first difference of the log of real output; $d \equiv$ first difference of the log of total public debt (expressed in liras and not as a percentage of GDP). The null hypothesis is that $\delta(L) = 0$ for the period 1981: 3 – 1986: 4.

The data are quarterly. Table 3.8 reports the summary statistics of the whole sample and of the two subperiods. The hypothesis of no pairwise

Table 3.9 Unconstrained estimates of equation (16)

Period 1970: 1 – 1986: 4

α_1	α_2	α_3	α_4	β_1	β_2	β_3	β_4
0.280	0.290	0.298	− 0.139	0.026	− 0.021	0.022	0.072
(0.137)	(0.135)	(0.141)	(0.138)	(0.056)	(0.058)	(0.059)	(0.054)

σ_1	σ_2	σ_3	σ_4	δ_1	δ_2	δ_3	δ_4
0.190	0.216	0.166	0.152	0.304	0.089	0.040	− 0.120
(0.059)	(0.052)	(0.061)	(0.067)	(0.102)	(0.100)	(0.095)	(0.093)

$\bar{R}^2 = 0.59$ SE $= 0.999$ LM $= 0.204$
$F = 7.032$ MLM $= 0.153$

Period 1981: 3 – 1986: 4

α_1	α_2	α_3	β_1	β_2	β_3
− 0.220	0.424	0.460	0.051	− 0.282	− 0.165
(0.383)	(0.256)	(0.297)	(0.107)	(0.116)	(0.178)

σ	σ_2	σ_3	δ_1	δ_2	δ_3
− 0.186	− 0.059	0.048	0.407	0.159	0.008
(0.106)	(0.137)	(0.085)	(0.218)	(0.207)	(0.187)

$\bar{R}^2 = 0.71$ SE $= 0.631$ LM $= 1.54$
$F = 5.277$ MLM $= 0.63$

Period 1970: 1 – 1981: 2

α_1	α_2	α_3	α_4	β_1	β_2	β_3	β_4
0.238	0.250	0.250	− 0.099	− 0.020	− 0.040	0.008	0.069
(0.184)	(0.179)	(0.198)	(0.192)	(0.083)	(0.086)	(0.082)	(0.073)

σ_1	σ_2	σ_3	σ_4	δ_1	δ_2	δ_3	δ_4
0.207	0.216	0.189	0.149	0.304	0.144	0.061	− 0.089
(0.080)	(0.080)	(0.082)	(0.090)	(0.152)	(0.145)	(0.142)	(0.149)

$\bar{R}^2 = 0.504$ SE $= 1.17$ LM $= 0.22$
$F = 3.866$ MLM $= 0.14$

Note: Standard errors are in parentheses. LM is the statistic for the Lagrange Multiplier test on first order serial correlation. MLM is the LM test modified for the degrees of freedom, as in Kiviet (1981). The regression SE is corrected for degrees of freedom.

cointegration for the whole sample between the CPI and the stock of base money, the CPI and the stock of public debt, and the stock of base money and the stock of public debt could not be rejected at the 5 percent confidence level. The unconstrained estimates are reported in Table 3.9, for the whole period and for the two subperiods. The log polynomial is chosen to be of order 3 for the period 1981: 3 – 1986: 4, in order to preserve degrees of freedom. The two longer subperiods have instead a distributed lag of order 4 for all the variables. The results are not

Table 3.10 F tests on the hypothesis that $\delta(L) = 0$

Period 1981: 3 – 1986: 4		
	F	t
When:		
$\delta(L)$ of order 3:	1.91	
$\delta(L)$ of order 2:	3.18*	
$\delta(L)$ of order 1:		2.43*
Period 1970: 1 – 1981: 2		
	F	t
When:		
$\delta(L)$ of order 4:	1.42	
$\delta(L)$ of order 3:	1.81	
$\delta(L)$ of order 2:	2.74*	
$\delta(L)$ of order 1:		2.14*

Note: The (*) indicates that the F or t value is significant at the 5 percent level.

sensitive at all to the choice of the lag length. The LM statistics cannot reject the hypothesis of no autocorrelation of the residuals for any of the equations.

Table 3.10 reports the F statistics for testing the null hypothesis that all the coefficients of $\delta(L)$ are zero, given that the maximum length of $\delta(L)$ is assumed to be n, for $n = 1, 2, 3, 4$. The hypothesis is strongly rejected for the period 1981: 3 – 1986: 4. It is also rejected, though a bit more weakly, for the period 1970: 1 – 1981: 2. Also note that the coefficients of $\delta(L)$ in Table 3.9 tend to be larger in the period 1981: 3 – 1986: 4 than in the preceding period.

If the total stock of public debt is replaced by the public debt held by the private sector (except base money), the hypothesis is still rejected for 1981: 3 – 1986: 4, but not for the period 1970: 1 – 1981: 2. Similarly, the same pattern (a strong rejection for 1981: 3 – 1986: 4 and a weaker and more sensitive rejection for 1970: 1 – 1981: 2) is maintained if $\delta(L)$ in (16) is constrained to be zero, if the lag length for some of the variables is altered, or if base money is replaced by M1. If lagged import prices of consumption goods are added to the regressions and the lag lengths of all variables are shortened so as to save degrees of freedom, the results remain unaffected and the coefficients on the import prices are generally insignificant.[26]

Finally, if the subperiods are redefined as 1970: 1 – 1976: 4 and 1977: 1 – 1986: 4, the null hypothesis is again strongly rejected in the second subperiod, whereas the first subperiod gives more ambiguous results.

This result is quite striking. Not only are deficits inflationary under the new monetary regime, but they seem to be more inflationary than under the old one! This finding strongly contradicts the conjecture that the monetary reforms were perceived to have reduced the degree of fiscal dominance.

Three interpretations are possible. The first one is simply that the regression is misspecified, either because of omitted variables or because of the choice of the lag length. This is of course always possible, in any atheoretical test of this kind. However it does not seem very likely, given the robustness of the results to the different specifications reported above.

The second interpretation is that a reduction in the degree of fiscal dominance did take place. But it did not show up in the data for two reasons. Firstly the institutional reforms were implemented gradually throughout the 1980s and secondly, the private sector expectations may have reacted slowly to the reforms, maybe through some kind of learning process.

The third possible interpretation is that the process of monetary reform is still largely incomplete, and as such it lacks credibility. It is incomplete in two respects. First of all because, as discussed in section 2, a few important reforms are still to be implemented (reducing the size of the Treasury overdraft account, further limiting the participation of the Bank of Italy in the primary market for public debt, and increasing the upwards flexibility of interest rates in the primary market). Secondly, and perhaps more importantly, because it is not clear yet that the reforms already implemented will not be reversed in the future. Many of these reforms were the result of purely technical and administrative decisions. These decisions are very easily reversible if the Minister of the Treasury or if the leadership of the Bank of Italy find it expedient to do so. More generally, the new monetary regime contains several ambiguities; its general features have been shaped more by the actual behavior of the policymakers themselves than by the imposition of external constraints. As a result, a promise of no future debt monetization may lack credibility. And in this case, as shown by Sargent and Wallace (1981), a restrictive monetary policy enhances the inflationary consequences of fiscal deficits. Further support in favor of this interpretation is provided by the difficulty that the Treasury has had in issuing fixed interest public debt throughout the 1980s (with the possible exception of 1985).

5   Conclusions

The paper started with a question: is there any contradiction between the institutional reforms of the 1980s that increased the decentralization of the Bank of Italy and the Treasury, and the goal of coordinating monetary and fiscal policies so as to stabilize public debt? The theoretical analysis of section 3 suggests a negative answer. This answer relies crucially on a distinction between a monetary regime and monetary policy actions. According to this distinction, the institutional reforms of the 1980s can be interpreted as creating a regime in which monetary policy is dominant, in the sense that there is no automatic link between fiscal deficits and money creation. Such a regime gives credibility to a refusal to increase future debt monetization, and consequently strengthens the Treasury incentives to pursue a more balanced fiscal policy. Within this regime, the Bank of Italy can choose to coordinate with the Treasury on an adjustment path of public debt. Moreover, such a coordinated action would not undermine the credibility of the monetary authority. Its credibility is guaranteed by the external rules of the game, that is, by the institutional features that define the regime.

The historical and empirical analysis of sections 2 and 4 convey the impression that the distinction between the Italian monetary regime and the policy actions of the Bank of Italy is in practice much more blurred. The reforms are still incomplete. Evidence of a more disciplined fiscal policy is mixed. There is no indication in the data that the private sector perceived a reduction in the degree of fiscal dominance. It seems plausible to infer from all this that the new monetary regime contains several ambiguities. It is not precisely defined independently of concrete monetary policy actions. In this situation a contradiction between the need to stabilize public debt and the goal of reducing the degree of fiscal dominance could emerge. A coordinated accommodative monetary policy could damage the credibility of the Bank of Italy, and this in turn could have deleterious effects on the incentives of the fiscal authority, thereby nullifying the purpose of the reforms. But on the other hand, a restrictive monetary policy could lack the credibility to induce the fiscal authority to bear the whole burden of stabilizing public debt.

If this formulation of the problem is correct, it seems possible to draw an important normative implication from the foregoing analysis: namely, that the current ambiguity of the Italian monetary regime should be removed. If the ambiguity persists, the combination of future monetary and fiscal policies in Italy might resemble the equilibrium outcome of a game of "chicken": a tight monetary policy motivated by the goal of establishing some credibility, accompanied by large fiscal deficits based on the expectation of future debt monetization.[27]

Some of the legislative and administrative steps that are necessary to give a more precise shape to the new Italian monetary regime have been outlined in section 2. These steps might also increase the independence of the central bank from the Treasury. As such, however, they would also increase the independence of the central bank from the political authorities. And this would create another, perhaps even more dangerous, confusion of responsibilities. Monetary policy, like explicit forms of taxation and any other major economic policy decision, involves a choice between conflicting goals and opposed political interests. Only democratically elected representatives have the political legitimacy to make such choices. As noted by Poincaré: "Money is too important to be left to central bankers";[28] "and to Treasury officials," one is tempted to add.

A corollary of the arguments developed in this paper, therefore, is that the additional reforms outlined in subsection 2.4, some of which have been advocated on several occasions by the Bank of Italy, should be accompanied by reforms that explicitly limit the independence of the central bank from the legislative authority. Not in the sense of creating direct parliamentary control over the appointment and terms of office of the leadership of the Bank of Italy.[29] But rather in the sense of limiting the range of actions that the Bank of Italy can take without explicit parliamentary approval. For instance, along the lines suggested in Monti (1985 p. 39),

> the ideal regime would be that in which the monetary authorities, on the basis of the inflationary targets expressed by the government and by Parliament, propose to Parliament a plan for the growth of monetary aggregates. Once the plan has received Parliamentary ratification, during its implementation, the central bank can discretionally deviate from its planned course of action, if it can prove that the behavioral parameters of the economy have unexpectedly changed. If instead the deviation implies the acceptance of a higher rate of inflation, the central bank should obtain the authorization–imposition of Parliament. Not technocracy, therefore, in which the monetary authorities choose the final goals, but a strengthening of the monetary authorities by depriving them of some discretionary powers that should belong to the legislative authority.

APPENDIX 1

Proposition 3
If in equilibrium $\mu \geq 1$, then the central bank welfare is a strictly decreasing function of θ.

Proof
Substituting (8) and (10) in (3) and then in (1), we obtain the central bank (and private sector) objective function as a function of μ, B and θ:

$$V = \text{Max}\left\{(1 + 2\beta)\ln W + \ln\left[\frac{W}{2} - \theta\beta B\right]\right\} \tag{A.1}$$

where W is the private sector real wealth defined by (2). The central bank maximizes [A.1] with respect to μ and B, subject to (11). Its Lagrangian is accordingly:

$$L = V + \lambda[B - g_1 \Phi(\mu, \theta) - \Omega(\mu, \theta)] \tag{A.2}$$

Αππλυινγ τηε ενωελοπε τηεορεμ το (A.2), θε ηαωε:

$$
\frac{\partial V}{\partial \theta} = \frac{\partial L}{\partial \theta} = \frac{1 + 2\beta}{W} \frac{\partial W}{\partial \theta} + \frac{1}{m_1} \frac{\partial m_1}{\partial \theta}
$$
$$
+ \lambda \left[-g_1 \frac{\partial \Phi}{\partial \theta} - \frac{\partial \Omega}{\partial \theta} - \frac{\partial g_1}{\partial \theta} \right] \tag{A.3}
$$

where all the partial derivatives are computed for given values of the control variables, μ and B. Specifically:

$$\frac{\partial W}{\partial \theta} = \frac{-\beta B}{4\mu - 2} < 0$$

$$\frac{\partial m_1}{\partial \theta} = \frac{1}{2} \frac{\partial W}{\partial \theta} - \beta B < 0$$

$$\frac{\partial \Phi(\mu, \theta)}{\partial \theta} = \frac{(4\mu - 2)(\mu - 1)}{\beta[(4 - \theta)\mu - 2 + \theta]^2} \geq 0 \quad \text{if} \quad \mu \geq 1$$

$$\frac{\partial \Omega(\mu, \theta)}{\partial \theta} = \frac{2B_0(\mu - 1)}{\beta[(4 - \theta)\mu - 2 + \theta]^2} \geq 0 \quad \text{if} \quad \mu \geq 1$$

$$\frac{\partial g_1}{\partial \theta} > 0, \text{ as remarked in the text.}$$

Hence, $\dfrac{\partial L}{\partial \theta} < 0$, if $\mu \geq 1$

QED

Remark
The condition that in equilibrium $\mu \geq 1$ (i.e. that in equilibrium the central bank does not decrease the stock of nominal money balances in period 1) is very plausible and should be satisfied for most parameter values.

APPENDIX 2. SENSITIVITY ANALYSIS FOR THE SPECIFICATION OF EQUATION (14)

This section reports on the results of some sensitivity analysis performed using "SEARCH," a program elaborated by Leamer and Leonard (1983).

The program combines prior and sample information in several ways. The goal is to characterize the mapping from priors into posteriors, for alternative specifications of prior beliefs. I want to find out how the estimate of β_3 in equation (14) is affected by the imposition of alternative linear constraints on δ_1 and δ_2, the coefficients of the "doubtful" variables, x_1 and x_2. "SEARCH" computes the answer for all possible combinations of linear constraints on δ_1 and δ_2, as long as one is willing to specify a prior location for the remaining β coefficients. For lack of better information, the chosen prior location for the β's corresponds to the OLS estimate of the constrained model (i.e., $\delta_1 = \delta_2 = 0$). Given this prior location for the βs, the posterior estimate of β_3 is bound to lie in the interval:

$$- 0.056 < \beta_3 < - 0.006$$

This interval also includes as special cases the constrained OLS estimates corresponding to $\delta_1 = 0$ and/or $\delta_2 = 0$.

The range of this interval (0.05) exceeds in absolute value the estimated standard error of β_3 reported in Table 3.5 (0.035). However, the interval lies on the negative axis and is bounded away from zero. Hence, we can conclude that the specification uncertainty about the variables x_1 and x_2, though numerically relevant for the absolute value of β_3, and large relative to the sampling uncertainty as summarized by the estimated standard error, does not affect the validity of the inference that β_3 is negative. This inference is robust to alternative specifications of constraints on δ_1 and δ_2.

NOTES

* I am grateful to Alberto Alesina, Stanley Fischer,Vincenzo La Via, Patrick Minford, Mario Monti, Richard Portes, Riccardo Rovelli, Luigi Spaventa and several conference participants for very helpful comments on a preliminary version, and to the UCLA Academic Senate for financial support. Luca Molteni and Alessandro Prati provided able research assistance. This paper was completed while I was visiting Bocconi University. The usual disclaimer applies.

1 This number is obtained by multiplying the rate of growth of the monetary base (about 7 percent) by the stock of monetary base as a fraction of GDP (about 18 percent).

2 The surge in the ex-post real interest rate begins in 1981. However the ex-ante real interest rate (computed according to survey data) begins to rise earlier, in mid-1980. The differential between the Italian ex-post real interest rate and other European rates also rises in 1981 (see Table 3.3).

3 Masciandaro (1986) contains a more detailed analysis of these years, focusing on the same question of monetary and fiscal policy coordination.

4 This well known statement by Carli is almost identical to a remark that Rudolf Havenstein, the head of the German central bank in the 1920s, presented in defense of the monetary policy that it pursued during the German hyper-inflation: "The Reichsbank has done all it could do with any chance of success. For years . . . it has continually called attention to these [fiscal] conditions and demanded a remedy in the most serious and urgent way, but it was not in a position to stop the discounting of Treasury bills as long as the Reich had no other available means to cover its deficit, and as long as all groups in the legislature were not fully convinced that such means absolutely have to be found. For the Reich must live, and real renunciation of discounting in the face of the tasks set by the budget . . . would have led to chaos. The threat of a general refusal to discount Treasury bills would have been nothing but a futile gesture" (Rudolf Havenstein, "Defending the Policy of the Reichsbank,"

address to the Executive Committee of the Reichsbank, 25 August 1923, in Fritz K. Ringer 1969). I am grateful to Marcello De Cecco for this reference.

5 The behavior of M_1 and M_2 is described for the first time in 1973 by *Tendenze Monetarie*, a private publication of Banca Commerciale Italiana directed by Mario Monti.

6 A large portion of the public debt outstanding becomes due in 1973.

7 See also Masciandaro (1986).

8 The Lira was realigned 4 times in the period March 1979–October 1981.

9 Tabellini (1987) argues that the "divorce" may have had a second important effect on the incentives of the policy makers: by raising some uncertainty about the future behavior of the monetary authorities, it created new reputational incentives that gave the Bank of Italy some credibility in pursuing a less accommodative monetary policy.

10 However, see Tabellini (1986, 1987) for a related analysis.

11 The assumption that public debt is indexed to the price level simplifies the analysis but does not affect the results in any respect.

12 Note that this issue is not an artifact of having a finite horizon. It would also arise in an infinite horizon model, as long as the time path of public debt is bounded from above. Specifically, the question that would arise in our infinite horizon version of this same model is: who will bear the burden of satisfying the budget constraint when the upper bound of public debt is reached? The answer to this question will determine the strategic interaction among the monetary and fiscal authorities throughout the rest of the game, just as in the two period model analyzed in the text.

13 Because of the feedback nature of the strategies chosen by both players, the equilibrium is subgame perfect and hence *a fortiori* time consistent.

14 Monti (1976) contains similar considerations.

15 Interest payments are net of interest received. They are computed as follows: it is assumed that the average interest rate is the same on passive and active interest rates. The flow of gross (passive) interest payments is then multiplied by the ratio of net to gross general government debt (source: OECD).

16 The GDP data on which all the ratios reported in this section have been computed do not incorporate the recent revision of April 1987. According to this revision, nominal GDP should be revised upwards during the 1980s by as much as 15 percent in some years. The reasons for using the old data are that these were the data available to the policymakers at the time at which policy decisions were taken and that the revisions do not go up to the early 1970s yet.

17 The cyclical adjustment reported in Table 3.4 is done by the OECD, according to the following method (see also European Economy, November 1984). The interpolation of output peaks gives a measure of "full employment" output. The cycle is computed as the difference between actual and "full employment" output. This measure of the cycle is then used to compute the cyclical component of tax revenues and of a small fraction of public expenditures. See OECD (1983) for more details.

18 Because of the method according to which it is computed (interpolation of output peaks), the level of the cyclically adjusted PSBR is not particularly meaningful, since it reflects an overly optimistic assumption about the natural rate of output. However, a fiscal policy change in the 1980s relative to the earlier period is apparent even if one considers the first difference of the cyclically adjusted PSBR, rather than its level.

19 Ceriani and Di Mauro (1986) report three different estimates of the Italian cyclically adjusted PSBR net of interest payment, for the period 1970–84. Two of these are based on log-linear trends of the natural level of real output. The third one is based on middle reference points of the business cycle, along the same lines of De Leeuw and Holloway (1983) for the US. The three estimates differ markedly. Only one of them suggests a smaller cyclically adjusted PSBR in the years 1982–84 relative to the previous period.

20 The cyclical adjustment and the subtraction of interest payments help to isolate the policy component from the automatic components of the PSBR.

21 As shown by Pagan (1984), this two-step procedure may tend to overestimate the standard errors of all the coefficients of the final regression.

22 The hypothesis of no first order serial correlation of the residuals cannot be rejected.

23 Specifically, a second dummy was added to the debt variable. This dummy took a value of 1 in the years of gradual monetary regime change (1977–81), and 0 elsewhere. Its estimated coefficient is negative and significant, but the same applies to β_3. Hence, the inclusion of this second dummy strengthens the inference that the first period, 1970–76, was different from the other two. The results are also invariant to redefining the dummy variable D as being 0 up through 1982 rather than 1981.

24 It can be argued that, because of the Treasury information lag, only d_{t-2} rather than d_{t-1} ought to be included in the regression as an explanatory variable. However, since d_{t-1} and d_{t-2} are highly collinear, the results of such a regression should be very similar to those reported in Tables 3.5 and 3.6 of the text, where only d_{t-1} is included.

25 When x_1 rather than x_2 is used in (15), the results are virtually unchanged, but the hypothesis of white noise residuals is strongly rejected.

26 Note that the import prices of consumption goods account for the direct inflationary effects of changes in the Lira exchange rate, but do not capture shocks to the price of imported inputs (such as oil price shocks).

27 Blinder (1982), Loewy (1976) and Sargent (1985) suggest a similar interpretation of the current US monetary-fiscal policy mix.

28 Quoted by Friedman (1962).

29 Kane (1980) contains some convincing criticisms of such a form of legislative control over monetary policy.

DATA SOURCES

Bank of Italy for the following variables: PSBR, Interest payments, Stock of public debt, CPI inflation rate, Monetary base, Overdraft account.

OECD for the cyclically adjusted PSBR and for the computation of net interest payments.

Masera (1986) for nominal GDP.

Ceriani and Di Mauro (1986) for a measure of cyclical output fluctuations.

Macchiati and Prati (1986) for the nominal interest rate (period 1974–86: average rate on return on 6 months Treasury Bills at the biweekly auctions; period 1968–73: rate on commercial bank loans).

ISTAT for real output.

All quarterly data are seasonally adjusted.

REFERENCES

Aiyagari, S.R. and M. Gertler (1985), "The Backing of Government Bonds and Monetarism," *Journal of Monetary Economics*, July.

Bank of Italy (1983), "I Finanziamenti del Tesoro da Parte della Banca Centrale in Italia e in Altri Paesi Industriali," *Bolletino Economico*.

Blinder, A. (1982), "Monetary and Fiscal Policy Coordination," NBER Working Paper.

Brennan, J. and J. Buchanan (1980), *The Power to Tax*. Cambridge: Cambridge University Press.

Bruni, F. and F. Giavazzi (1987), "Debito pubblico, debito estero e protezionismo valutario," in *Debito pubblico e politica monetaria in Italia*, edited by F. Bruni, forthcoming.

Bruni, F., M. Monti and A. Porta (1980), "Bank Lending to the Public Sector: Determinants, Implications and Outlook," *Giornale degli Economisti*, Nov.–Dec.

Bryant, J. and N. Wallace (1979), "The Inefficiency of Interest Bearing National Debt," *Journal of Political Economy*, April.

Caranza, C. and A. Fazio (1983), "L'Evoluzione dei metodi di controllo monetario in Italia: 1974–83," *Bancaria*, September.

Ceriani, V. and F. Di Mauro (1986), "Finanza pubblica e politica di bilancio: i risultati di alcuni indicatori," Banca d'Italia, Temi di Discussione, No. 72.

Ciampi, C.A. (1986), "Mercati finanziari in evoluzione: riflessi per il governo della moneta e del credito," *Bolletino Economico*, Bank of Italy.

Cividini, A., G. Galli and R.S. Masera (1987), "Vincolo di bilancio e sostenibilita del debito: analisi e prospettive," in *Debito pubblico e politica monetaria in Italia*, edited by F. Bruni, forthcoming.

Cottarelli, C., G. Galli, P. Marvello Reidtz and G. Pittaluga (1986), "Monetary Policy Through Ceilings on Bank Lending," *Economic Policy*, 3, October.

De Leeuw, F. and T.M. Holloway (1983), "Cyclical Adjustment of the Federal Budget and Federal Debt," *Survey of Current Business*, November.

Friedman, M. (1962), "Should There be an Independent Central Bank?", in *In Search of a Monetary Constitution*, by L. Yeager.

Kane, E. (1980), "Politics and Fed Policymaking," *Journal of Monetary Economics*, April.

Kiviet, J. (1981), "On the Rigour of Some Specification Tests for Modelling Dynamic Relationships," mimeo, University of Amsterdam.

Leamer, E. (1978), *Specification Searches*, John Wiley.

—— (1983), "Let's Take the Con Out of Econometrics," *American Economic Review*.

Leamer, E. and L. Leonard (1983), "Search," mimeo, UCLA.

Loewy, M. (1976), "Reagonomics and Reputation Revisited," George Washington University, mimeo.

Macchiati, A. and A. Prati (1986), "La domanda di attivita finanziare delle imprese: un indagine empirica su un gruppo di società Italiane," in *Sistema Finanziario e Industria*, edited by M. Onado, Bologna: Il Mulino.

Masciandaro, D. (1986), "Assetto istituzionale della banca centrale e condotta della politica monetaria," Tesi di Laurea, Universita Bocconi.

Masera, R.S. (1983), "Politica monetaria e politica di bilancio: intreccio o dicotomia?" *Rivista di Politica Economica*.

(1986), "Per un risanamento della finanza pubblica in Italia," Banca d'Italia, Temi di discussione, N. 61.

McCallum, B. (1976), "Rational Expectations and the Natural Rate Hypothesis: Some Consistent Estimates," *Econometrica*, January.

Meltzer, A. and S. Richard (1981), "A Rational Theory of the Size of Government," *Journal of Political Economy*, October.

Monti, M. (1976), "Riflessioni sulla politica monetaria in Italia," *Giornale degli Economisti*, January–February.

(1983a), Comment presented at the conference on "Lo stato e i soldi degli Italiani," *Rivista di Politica Economica*, January.

(1983b), "Più autonomia monetaria e meno poteri fiscali occulti," *Politica ed Economia*, April.

(1985), "Politica monetaria disinflazionistica e assetto instituzionale," in *Politiche di rientro dall'inflazione, Rivista Milanese di economia*, Serie quaderni n. 11.

Mueller, D. (1979), *Public Choice*, Cambridge University Press.

OECD (1983), "Public Sector Deficits: Problems and Policy Implications," *Occasional Studies*, June.

Pagan, A. (1984), "Econometric Issues in the Analysis of Regressions with Generated Regressors," *International Economic Review*,Vol. 25, No. 1, February.

Puviani, A. (1903), *Teoria della Illusione Finanziaria*, Palermo.

"Report of the Treasury Commission on the Italian Financial and Credit System," (1984), *Banca Nazionale del Lavoro Quarterly Review*.

Ringer, F. (1969), *The German Inflation of 1973*, New York: Oxford University Press.

Salvemini, M.T. (1983), "The Treasury and the Money Market: the New Responsibilities After the Divorce," *Review of the Econometric Conditions in Italy*, January–April.

Sargent, T. (1985), "Reagonomics and Credibility," in his *Rational Expectations and Inflation*, New York: Harper and Row.

Sargent, T. and N. Wallace (1981), "Some Unpleasant Monetarist Arithmetic," *Federal Reserve Bank of Minneapolis, Quarterly Review*.

Spaventa, L. (1984), "The Growth of Public Debt in Italy: Past Experience, Perspectives, and Policy Problems," *Banca Nazionale del Lavoro Quarterly Review*.

(1985), "Adjustment Plans, Fiscal Policy and Monetary Policy," *The Review of Economic Conditions in Italy*, January–April.

Tabellini, G. (1986), "Money, Debt and Deficits in a Dynamic Game," *Journal of Economic Dynamics and Control*, December.

(1987), "Central Bank Reputation and the Monetization of Deficits: The 1981 Italian Monetary Reform," *Economic Inquiry*, April.

Tabellini, G. and V. La Via (1986), "Money, Deficit and Public Debt in the US," UCLA, mimeo.

Tendenze Monetarie, various issues. Published by Banca Commerciale Italiana.

Ungerer, H., O. Evans, T. Mayer and P. Young (1986), "The European Monetary System: Recent Developments," *Occasional Paper*, No. 48. I.M.F.

Discussion

STANLEY FISCHER

This is a clear and admirably honest paper that deploys historical narrative, theory, and econometrics to examine the important topic of the benefits of central bank independence. The main point of the paper is stated in the introduction, that non-accommodating monetary policy forces the fiscal authority to confront its budget constraint. The tentative conclusion based on both the theoretical and empirical work is also stated in the introduction, that the remaining ambiguities in the obligations of the Banca d'Italia to accommodate Treasury deficits complicate the task of non-inflationary policy-making and should be removed.

I shall discuss in turn the three main sections of the paper – the narrative history of monetary policy since 1970, the analytical model, and the empirical work. I conclude with general comments on the approach adopted and on the subject of central bank independence.

1 Italian monetary history, 1970–86

There are three periods of monetary history, corresponding roughly to the Governorships of Carli, Baffi and Ciampi. The first is seen as a period of full accommodation of government deficits, the second as a transitional period, and the last as a period in which the Banca d'Italia began to run an independent monetary policy.

There is one mystery in the early narrative: how is it that a fiscal policy that had come close to balancing the budget in the 1950s and 1960s suddenly became extraordinarily lax thereafter? One possible explanation, provided by Antonio Pedone, is that fiscal drag produced unexpectedly high tax revenues in the early 1970s, that spending adjusted to the new level of revenue, but which then fell while spending stayed high.

The fiscal policy data presented in Table 3.4 are not fully informative. First, the data presented do not include interest payments. But if the

127

concern is over money financing of deficits, the most relevant deficit measure should include real interest on the debt. Similarly, the data on the cyclically adjusted PSBR may be slightly misleading; unless the economy will return very soon to what is taken to be full employment in calculating the series Fay, the actual deficit is more relevant to predicting future deficits than the full employment deficit. Indeed, one would welcome in this paper predictions of future deficits under a variety of assumptions about future taxes and spending.

The paper rightly emphasizes the shift in monetary regime two years after Italy joined the EMS. Looking at Table 3.2 one is even more struck by a major change in monetary policy between 1976 and 1977. The share of national debt held by the Banca d'Italia fell by 10 percent in that period, indicating a major change in policy. Similarly, looking at Table 3.1 at monetary base creation, one sees again a major change between the first two periods, with the Banca d'Italia selling over 3 percent of GNP worth of Treasury liabilities to offset money base creation through Treasury overdrafts.

Although Tabellini emphasizes the Treasury's ability to require central bank financing of 14 percent of its spending, and the reluctance of the Banca d'Italia to deviate from interest rates set by the Treasury, it is striking from Table 3.1 that the Banca has evidently engaged in massive open market sales since 1977. Despite the increases in the use of the Treasury's overdraft account after 1977, the Banca d'Italia was able to reduce sharply its net purchases of government bonds below the 1970–76 level. I am thus less certain than he that monetary policy has been much constrained by the remaining formal constraints on central bank behavior.

Tabellini rightly enjoys the Carli quotation about central bank rebellion. This was to be sure an exaggerated comment, but Carli has a point in that central bank independence is always a matter of political judgment. The constitutional position makes a difference, but any central bank that decides to take on an elected government has to make sure its rear is protected before it enters battle. Indeed, it appears from the paper that the Treasury was as much responsible for the greater independence as the Banca d'Italia.

2   The model

The model presents an extreme version of the central banker's view of the world. The fiscal authority wishes to spend, the more the better, and government spending has no social value. The central bank has the same welfare function as society. Tabellini is almost certainly right, though, in arguing that a less extreme formulation, in which the fiscal authority gave more weight to government spending than society does, would produce similar results.

The fiscal authority has at its command lump-sum taxation which enables it to take the entire endowment in each period. The fiscal authority uses all the taxes it can, but also may have access to monetary financing of whatever deficit it can run in period one. The extent of the deficit it can run depends on how much money financing the central bank is allowed to provide. Although Tabellini describes central bank independence as forcing the government to confront its budget constraint, the actual maximization appears to mean rather that the central bank chooses the size of the deficit. In any event, it is clear that the more monetary financing the fiscal authority can call on, the larger is the deficit it will run, and the higher is the first period inflation rate (relative to period zero).

Tabellini presents an interesting discussion of two common objections to this model: first, some argue that the deficit is determined independently of monetary policy; and second, some argue that no rational calculation underlies the deficit. Neither position seems especially defensible, but the distinction that Tabellini draws between monetary policy and a monetary policy regime in disposing of the first objection is too sharp. The appointment of a strong governor after a weak predecessor in a system in which the law is unchanged will likely produce more change in fiscal policy than a change in the law which permits the central bank not to finance budget deficits but leaves it the option of buying government debt in the open market.

3   The evidence

The regressions are less impressive than the remainder of the paper. Two questions are investigated. First, whether a larger debt leads to smaller primary deficits, indicating a desire by the Treasury to stabilize the debt; and second, whether a larger deficit creates inflationary pressure.

Both these implications emerge from the first period equilibrium in the model. There is mild evidence that a larger debt reduces the primary deficit, despite the ambiguities that emerge when the lag distributions are lengthened. There seems to be a general problem here with a lack of degrees of freedom. It is also unclear whether the dependent variable should be the primary or the actual deficit. It is the latter that creates the pressure for future monetization that is the focus of this paper, so perhaps that should be the dependent variable. If it were, the negative coefficient would be likely to become less negative, since the left hand side variable would be larger in later periods, in which the debt was also larger.

The inflation regressions are not consistent with the implications of the model. Remarkably, deficits seem to be more inflationary in the 1980s than before. This is in fact hard to believe, given Italian membership of the EMS, and must mean that some other regressor is picking up responsibility for lower inflation in the 1980s. Perhaps it is the growth rate of money. In this case, using the actual deficit rather than the primary deficit as the regressor might produce results that accord more with the theoretical implications. It is, furthermore, not clear that it is the deficit rather than the stock of debt that belongs in the regressions.

4   General comments

Perhaps the most striking omission from the paper is any discussion of dynamic consistency. To avoid the problem, Tabellini makes the debt real, thereby making it impossible to inflate it away. If the debt were nominal, the central bank could inflate away the first period debt and probably improve social welfare.

In the Italian context it is generally argued that unanticipated inflation would be ineffective in reducing the debt burden because the debt is effectively very short-term. Certainly the debt cannot be inflated away by a preannounced policy of raising inflation – though to be sure the increase in seignorage would make it possible to reduce the debt that way. However, it is possible that a sudden program of massive open market purchases could effectively reduce the debt first and pay the inflation consequences later. A policy of this type was followed in Argentina when Domingo Cavallo was governor of the central bank in 1982.

How large could such an inflation blow-out be? The money base is about 20 percent of GNP, and the debt about 100 percent. A policy that doubled the money base in a week would reduce the debt by 20 percent – unlikely to be enough to justify the consequent chaos, but nonetheless an interesting theoretical possibility.

Once dynamically inconsistent policies are considered, the possibility of a capital levy or debt default should also be weighed. To be worthwhile, a debt default would have to be on so large a scale that it would bring widespread inequity, particularly to widows and orphans who had trusted in government debt. It also creates the difficulty pointed out in Alesina's paper, that financial institutions which had invested in government bonds would find their capital severely depleted, possibly to the extent of bankruptcy. Regular taxation of capital income which reduced the budget deficit and thereby made it possible to reduce the debt gradually would probably be preferable.

One frequently expressed objection to the use of a capital levy or levy on government debt is that it would make it difficult for the government to borrow in future. The spirit of this paper suggests that such a change would be for the better, for it would force the Treasury to confront its true budget constraint.

At the end of the paper Tabellini draws back to re-examine the underlying implicit premise of the model: the proposition that central banks represent the will of the people while elected governments do not. Although this is now becoming a commonplace in discussions of macroeconomic policy, it is not self-evident. Going back to the 1920s, Montagu Norman, in his role as Governor of the Bank of England, was not obviously better for Britain than the Treasury which wanted to have lower interest rates at the time. The Bundesbank performs its task of keeping inflation low with devotion, but the rise in German unemployment since 1980 is not clearly the best thing that could have happened. There is a short-run trade-off (and if modern theories of hysteresis are right, a long-run trade-off) between inflation and unemployment, and central banks cannot be relied on to choose it correctly.

The Fed was wise enough to let up on slow money growth in August 1982, but the Fed is closely watched by the Congress. Economists who approve of the inflation fighting propensities of central banks should ask themselves when one of their number was last unemployed.

None of this is to detract from an interesting paper, merely caution against exaggerating the important component of truth that is contained in the Tabellini model.

Discussion

PATRICK MINFORD

I much enjoyed and admired much of this paper, which forms part of Tabellini's research programme – some of it joint with Alesina – on the political economy of public policy. This is an interesting and worthwhile area of research; for example in forecasting, the assessment of political pressures is both a key input into any forecast and a key source of error, according to my own experience.

The paper theorizes that the Italian Treasury and Central Bank are involved in a two-period game where the Treasury maximizes public spending, while the Bank maximizes consumers' welfare; the constraints are a single economic model and an institutional limit, θ, on the fraction of second-period public debt the Bank must monetize. The result of the game is that the higher θ ("fiscal dominance"), the more the Treasury will spend because it has access to a higher second-period inflation tax. Tabellini applies the model to Italy, arguing that monetary reform from 1979 (the "divorce") gave the Central Bank more independence; therefore a lower θ was set. Empirically, however, and with praiseworthy honesty, he finds disappointingly little support. The Treasury *may* have shown more of a tendency since the reforms to restrain the deficit in response to increased public debt; but this predicted effect is not robust. And inflation has, if anything, responded *more* to deficits since the reforms, whereas it should respond less with less systematic debt monetization. Tabellini concludes there may have been credibility problems with the reforms, because of questions about the permanence of such recent innovations.

Obviously, the set-up of the game is peculiar. Apart from the curious choice of preference functions for the Bank and Treasury, which are not clearly motivated by either public choice theory or casual empiricism, there is the assumption that taxes are costless to raise and have no incentive effects so that the Treasury automatically levies a 100 percent tax rate. Having done so, it then wants more! This "more" comes from

132

the inflation tax; the higher θ the more it can obtain. But since it has already taken 100 percent of GNP, the budget constraints dictate that it must come from *negative* private consumption!

It is hard to say whether removal of these peculiarities would destroy the principal theoretical prediction that a higher θ generates more public spending. It may well not. In any case my concern about this as a framework for understanding Italian deficit and money creation runs deeper. The key parameter in the model is θ; yet θ was itself set by politicians. Why? If we take the model at face value, the story must be that the "good guys" at the Bank managed to slip these reforms past the "bad guys" at the Treasury; they hijacked the monetary constitution somehow. If so, it would not indeed be surprising that they have little credibility. Yet, though Tabellini does find little credibility, it is not a story which from a public choice viewpoint is satisfying theoretically. Possibly a more plausible alternative would be: politicians deliberately set out to limit the discretion of the public spending process – reforms and EMS are an attempt to supply the punishments that would make monetary and fiscal pre-commitment credible.

Without the back-up of some such deeper theory, it is hard to rule out Sargent and Wallace's game of chicken. The Treasury could be playing to break the reforms and raise θ. It certainly looks like that to the outsider viewing the rise and rise of Italian public debt. Also bond markets – with rates in excess of 10 percent – appear to be discounting a return of higher inflation; they regard θ and the EMS as inadequate mechanisms to penalize such time-inconsistency by Italian politicians.

A couple of further points strengthen me in my agreement with the markets. First, Tabellini's treatment of the PSBR in this paper is quite cavalier. By excluding debt interest and applying a generous cyclical adjustment, he conveys the impression that the momentum driving up public debt in Italy is being reduced. This is clearly false. The real interest burden of debt is large and growing, with positive real interest rates. Cyclical adjustment must take into account a rising natural unemployment rate, as taxes, benefits, and the black economy interact to keep many fruitfully "unemployed" in their villages.

Second, optimal tax theory recommends equalizing the marginal distortions from different taxes. The inflation tax is the only one that can touch Italy's large black economy; attempting to raise revenues without the inflation tax is likely to raise marginal distortions on "conventional" tax of the white economy to severe proportions. The popular backlash must generate strong political incentives to return to the inflation tax, once public debt is eventually perceived to be out of hand.

To conclude, that *something* remarkable is happening in Italy, to have brought inflation down so far without reducing public deficits, cannot be denied. But this paper, interesting as it is, has not got to the bottom of it. Meanwhile, alternative ideas suggest pessimistically that nothing fundamental has changed.

4 The management of public debt and financial markets*

MARCO PAGANO

1 The Italian experience

Public debt management has come to be regarded as a serious policy issue in Italy only since the beginning of the 1970s. Before that time, the Italian economy experienced moderate deficits, mainly financed *via* seignorage and issues of fixed-rate long-term debt. Placing this type of debt instrument raised no problems at times of low and stable inflation, rapid growth of disposable income and Central Bank commitment to interest rate pegging. From 1970 onwards, however, public sector deficits have soared dramatically (as shown by the data in the introductory chapter by Spaventa), and at the same time, all the other factors that had previously eased the placement of public debt also disappeared. The rapid increase in the level and volatility of inflation (due to the oil shocks and to the accommodating policy of the Central Bank) and the abandonment of interest rate pegging inflicted very large capital losses on holders of outstanding public debt and made it increasingly difficult to finance the deficits via debt issues.

Actually, in the early 1970s even placing new issues of short-term Treasury Bills proved arduous. The most visible symptom of the crisis was the desertion of T-Bills auctions by the banks: in the 10 auctions open to the participation of banks that were held in 1973–74, only 46.2 percent of the total supply offered to the market was sold, and no relief came from raising base rates in line with the inflation rate in the spring of 1974. At that point, the only way open to the Treasury was extensive recourse to credit from the Central Bank: in those two years, the Treasury financed most of the deficit by drawing from the overdraft account it held with the Central Bank and by selling T-Bills to the Bank (with the result of fueling inflation even further).

Starting from 1975, reducing the maturity of newly issued debt and opening T-Bills auctions to non-bank intermediaries, the government

Table 4.1 Percentage composition and average maturity of public sector debt[1]

Years	T-Bills	Medium and long-term securities BTP[2]	CCT[3]	Other	Postal deposits	Overdraft loans from Central Bank	Foreign debt	Other debts	Average maturity (months)
1971–75									70
1976	27.0	6.2	—	25.5	15.7	5.1	1.4	19.1	43
1977	26.0	6.1	4.4	29.7	15.5	3.9	1.3	13.1	39
1978	24.0	10.9	9.6	23.9	15.2	4.3	1.2	10.9	36
1979	25.0	9.9	13.3	18.6	16.2	5.3	1.3	10.4	30
1980	31.9	7.5	12.3	14.3	14.5	8.4	1.5	9.6	22
1981	37.6	7.4	10.9	11.9	12.6	8.9	2.3	8.4	15
1982	38.6	5.4	16.3	8.7	10.8	8.8	2.7	8.7	15
1983	33.0	5.1	27.7	6.8	9.7	6.9	2.7	8.1	19
1984	28.4	5.7	32.6	5.3	9.0	7.5	2.9	8.6	30
1985	25.3	5.3	38.5	6.0	8.7	7.1	2.7	6.4	41
1986	23.8	8.4	39.2	5.4	8.1	7.2	2.5	5.4	45

Notes:
1 End-of-period data. Source: *Bollettino Economico*, Banca d'Italia.
2 "Buoni Poliennali del Tesoro": medium or long-term fixed rate nominal bonds.
3 Credit Certificates of the Treasury: medium-term floating rate bond indexed to the T-Bill issue rate.

successfully placed increasing amounts of T-Bills on the market and thus decreased direct borrowing from the Central Bank. Initially, T-Bills were bought mainly by banks, in part as a result of the constraint imposed by credit ceilings on the growth of their loans. Over time, however, a growing number of T-Bills found their way into the portfolio of households, mainly at the expense of the share of monetary assets in the wealth of Italian families: by the beginning of the 1980s, these directly held over half of the outstanding stock of T-Bills.[1]

The increased reliance on short-term debt, coupled with the fast growth of public debt, caused a rapid decline in the average maturity of outstanding debt (as shown in Table 4.1, last column); this in turn forced the government to step up the pace of new issues and diminished control by the Treasury over the timing of its recourse to the market. To recover some degree of flexibility in the management of the escalating mass of public debt, in 1977 the Treasury introduced a medium-term floating rate note known as CCT (Treasury Credit Certificate), with coupons indexed to the return on T-Bills (*plus* a spread). The indexation clause was due to the fear that, owing to persisting uncertainty about the future course of monetary policy, a fixed-rate medium-term instrument would not have been favorably received by the public. The role of CCTs in financing the Italian public debt rapidly increased in the following years: from 4.4 percent of total public debt in 1977, they have risen to 12.3 percent in 1980 and to 38.5 percent in 1985, thus becoming the most widely used public debt instrument – a position kept by T-Bills until 1983 (see Table 4.1).

The monetary authorities have been instrumental in fostering the development of the market for T-Bills, and later of that for CCTs. The birth of these markets has gradually restored independence to the conduct of monetary policy, which until 1975 was dominated by the need to satisfy the growing borrowing requirement of the public sector via the creation of monetary base. Also the lengthening of the maturities of public debt, made possible by the introduction of the CCTs, has been encouraged by the Central Bank as a tool for smoothing over a longer time horizon the large and erratic fluctuations of the gross borrowing requirement by the Treasury, and the implied jumps in the creation of monetary base. Another step towards the separation of monetary policy from debt management was taken in July 1981 when the Bank and the Treasury agreed that the Central Bank's policy of acting as a residual buyer for new issues of T-Bills should be discontinued. However, an important link between the Treasury and the Bank was retained: the statutory obligation of the Central Bank to extend credit to the Treasury via its overdraft facility up to 14 percent of public expenditure. As a matter of fact, the burden of this constraint on the conduct of monetary policy has increased since then, due both to the growing size of public spending relative to monetary aggregates and to increasing recourse by the Treasury to the overdraft facility. The line of credit with the Bank has in fact been exploited almost fully in the 1980s (an average 96 percent of the statutory limit in 1980–85, versus 70 percent in 1975–79), and has provided a larger share of deficit financing than in the 1970s (see Table 4.1).[2]

In the 1980s, aside from much increased reliance upon CCTs, there have been no remarkable changes in the mix of debt instruments issued by the government. The Treasury has started reintroducing fixed-rate debt (BTP) with somewhat longer maturities, and has otherwise widened somewhat the menu of its liabilities, issuing Treasury Certificates denominated in European Currency Unit (ECU) (named CTE) and, in 1987, discount Treasury Certificates with a coupon indexed to T-Bills (a hybrid called CTS). After a long debate on the opportunity of issuing indexed debt, a single issue of real bonds (CTR) was timidly tried in 1985, with little success – largely because of mispricing by the Treasury and insufficient dissemination of clear information about the indexation scheme. To date, these innovations have had a minor quantitative impact on the overall debt structure: Italian public debt is mostly composed of short-term debt (T-Bills) or of medium-term debt indexed to the short-term interest rate (CCTs), so that the interest rate bill of the government is very sensitive to movements in the short-term rate. Given the current magnitude of interest payments (an average 71 percent of the net increase in debt per year, in the period 1981–85), movements in the short-term rate translate directly into wide swings in the deficit itself.

Recently, refinements have been introduced in the placement system: T-Bill auction participants can now choose between submitting "competitive" bids (*i.e.* bids for given price-quantity combinations, each to be settled at its own price) and bids to buy a given amount at the average transaction price. The new system, which seeks to extract "rentiers' surplus" from the competitive bidders via price discrimination, was first adopted for the 3-month T-Bills in May 1983, and extended one year later to 6-month T-Bills (an attempt to extend it to the issue of CCTs was made in 1985, and then abandoned in favor of the old method of selling the whole issue at a preset price). Moreover, to ease the placement of new issues, an underwriting syndicate of banks has been engaged since March 1984 in buying a predetermined share of each issue. Unluckily, in this case, the potential of the innovations has not been fully exploited: the frequent practice of setting the auction base rate very close to the current market rate has often prevented the successful placement of new issues, irrespective of the auction method used (except for a brief period in 1983–84). The availability of the overdraft credit facility with the Central Bank has probably encouraged the Treasury in this behavior, as indicated by the fact that recourse to this source of finance has been most intense when auctions have turned out to be unsuccessful.

The overall picture of the current debt policy in Italy is thus characterized by the following elements: rather short average maturity and massive indexation of the interest bill of the government to short-term interest rates, use of monetary financing to the maximum extent allowed by the existing rules of the game, very limited adoption of innovations both in the menu of assets supplied to the public and in the methods of placement of new debt issues. In the meanwhile, with a stock of debt almost equal to GDP and interest payments around 9 percent of GDP, the numbers involved in the management of the Italian public debt are such that the adoption of alternative policies will have first-order effects on the welfare of current and future generations.

Let us then turn to economic analysis to deal in a consistent fashion with the main policy options, and to appraise them.

2   Debt management: options and objectives

Should the Italian government strive to reduce public debt to some target level or should it rather regard the current level of its debt as irrelevant in deciding on the future time-profile of public deficits? Should one advise the Treasury to issue bonds with returns indexed to the inflation rate (or, for that matter, indexed to other macroeconomic variables)? Is there a point in lengthening the average maturity of outstanding debt? These questions define the two most important choices currently facing the Italian government in the management of public debt: the choice of the future path of deficits and that of the menu of debt instruments to be issued. Economic analysis can assist in these choices in two ways: first, by requiring that the questions be posed in a meaningful way; second, by proposing normative models capable of answering them, and providing appropriate policy rules.

This section is devoted to the first task: setting up the questions so that economic models can meaningfully be applied to answering them. This involves specifying what are the *instruments* that the government can control, what is their *effectiveness* and what should be the *objective function* of the government. In the remaining sections of the paper I will turn to some simple normative models of debt management to try and get some answers.

2.1   Policy instruments

In deciding how to finance a given path of public expenditure, a government has in principle a rich set of instruments it can choose from: it can use *taxes* (including the inflation tax, if monetary policy is set cooperatively with the Central Bank), it can decide to issue *debt* or sell off government-owned *equities*. At a second level, the government can choose to issue *different debt instruments*: debt can be safe or risky, nominal or real, short- or long-term. These classes obviously intersect each other: nominal debt is risky if inflation is uncertain, real debt can also be risky if it is long-term and fixed-rate (since the debt-holder is still exposed to interest rate risk in case of liquidation before maturity), and so on. At a third level, the policy-maker can choose what kind of stochastic behavior the return on *risky debt* should have: debt whose return is indexed to that of UK gilt-edged securities will have different risk characteristics from Italian T-Bills.

This distinction between different "levels of choice" by the government is primarily an expository device, because in general the effects of the corresponding decisions are interdependent: there is no *a priori* reason to suppose that the overall choice set of the government should separate neatly into several mutually independent choices, allowing the policymaker to decide first upon the path of taxes and debt, and then upon the optimal debt menu. The amount of taxes that will be optimal to raise at each date may depend on the risk characteristics of outstanding debt and of debt to be issued in the future. Conversely, choosing a certain debt structure will in general impose a constraint on the future path of taxes – a constraint that is more binding the richer the maturity structure of debt (it is precisely using this constraint that Lucas and Stokey (1983) show that a government can bind successive governments to follow the optimal tax policy program that it has devised, thus overcoming time inconsistency problems in debt policy).

Nevertheless, there are practical reasons why a stage-wise approach to government financial policy may be warranted. First, decisions about the level and future path of taxation are much more difficult to change than decisions about the menu of assets to be issued. Second, the set of events on which the payment of taxes and transfers can be conditioned is quite restricted (primarily by law, but also by administrative costs), whereas the returns on government debt can in principle be indexed to any publicly known variable: the rate of inflation, the stock market index, GNP, foreign currencies' exchange rates, etc. Finally, choices about taxes and choices about the characteristics of public debt are taken by different authorities, and they can hardly be considered so coordinated as to be equivalent to the result of a joint decision process. Thus it may be reasonable to analyze decisions about the optimal debt menu *as if* the path of taxes were given, and this is in fact the assumption that will be made in Section 4 of this paper.

2.2   Policy effectiveness

The recent literature on public financial policy is replete with proofs about its irrelevance (see Barro 1974, Levhari-Liviatan 1976, Wallace 1981, Stiglitz 1983 and Peled 1985). In a number of cases, it turns out that the real allocations produced by market equilibria are invariant both to government choices about tax *versus* deficit financing and to those involving the precise menu of assets issued to pay for the deficits. What effectively happens in these cases is that private agents behave so as to offset the impact of government actions on their intertemporal allocation of consumption or on their contingent consumption plans (if there is uncertainty). Formally, this amounts to showing that their budget constraints are invariant to government policies. Thus, the general rule to identify the cases where public financial policy is *not* irrelevant is that the government should be able to redistribute real income across different periods or different states of the world at terms that differ from those that are available to the private sector. An important subset of these cases is that of missing markets: if the government can implement trades that private agents cannot perform *at all* – not even at very unfavorable terms – then we can be sure that financial policies that involve those trades will not leave the real equilibrium of the economy unaffected.

Typically, *intergenerational trade* provides an instance where markets are missing. Consider in fact a standard overlapping generations model with no uncertainty (and no dynastic altruism): whatever redistribution of the tax burden the government implements across any two non-overlapping generations via the issue or the retirement of debt will be non-neutral, because there are no markets through which those two generations can trade. Moreover, if the two generations overlap for only one time period, those that belong to the old generation have nothing to sell to younger agents in exchange for current consumption: thus also reallocations of income between those two generations cannot be "undone" by the private sector. If instead government policy tries only to reallocate consumption over the lifetime of people belonging to the same generation, it will have no real effect, provided that the generation affected by the policy can change its saving so as to keep its consumption profile invariant. For example, suppose a person receives a debt-financed transfer when young and knows that additional taxes will be levied on him when old, to pay for the corresponding debt (*plus* interest): his lifetime income is unchanged, and so will his optimal consumption path. To keep consumption invariant at each date, he will then save up the entire transfer, buy the corresponding extra debt issued by the government and use the return to pay the extra taxes due in his old age.

Exactly the same reasoning applies to *any* change in the structure of public debt, as shown by Stiglitz (1983) in the context of a model where each generation lives for three periods: temporary swaps of short- for long-term debt, or of indexed for non-indexed debt, are neutral if the implied reallocations only affect the lifetime income of a single generation, and the presence of uncertainty does nothing to alter this general result. The famous Ricardian neutrality proposition of Barro (1974) is nothing but a special case of this principle: in the dynastic model all consumers behave as if they were effectively going to live forever, so that any redistribution that public financial policy can bring about over time is irrelevant.

Obviously, there is no reason to assume that the only missing markets are those that allow intergenerational trade. If some markets for *intra-generational trade* are imperfect or missing, public debt management has an even larger opportunity to affect the outcomes. Take the case of *liquidity constraints*: some agents may be unable to borrow and lend at the same rate of interest at which the government can; in fact, they may be totally rationed if they try to borrow beyond a given amount (something that one would expect to observe if, for instance, some agents are dishonest, as in Hammond (1986), or if moral hazard is an issue). In general, in the presence of *uncertainty*, it is natural to suppose that markets for intragenerational trade are incomplete: real-world capital markets can hardly provide the opportunity to insure against any possible contingency. Thus, if the government financial policy relaxes some liquidity constraint or conditions upon events for which people cannot insure, it will generally have real effects. In fact, it is reasonable to conjecture that the set of effective financial policies available to the government will, *ceteris paribus*, be richer in an economy where the number of imperfect and missing markets is higher. For instance, if transaction costs or the structure of the tax system have discouraged the issue of private indexed debt, a swap between nominal and indexed debt by the government will in general not be neutral, even if it affects only a single generation. This would not be the case if capital markets already provided indexed bonds.

Finally, the effectiveness of public financial policies may arise from *imperfections in the "tax technology,"* i.e. in the method used to raise taxes or to transfer income across different agents or different generations, rather than in the technology that the market offers to private agents to carry wealth over time. Such is the case, for instance, if the government cannot levy taxes without incurring a real resource cost, or without imposing deadweight losses on its taxpayers: in this case transfers of income over time can be operated "less efficiently" by the government than by the private sector via capital markets. The resulting wedge between public and private intertemporal terms of trade will, once more, cause public debt management to be non-neutral. To see this by means of an example, recall the temporary tax-debt switch considered above, and assume that the tax can only be levied at a real resource cost: then, when an individual receives the transfer in his youth, he knows that the tax that will later be levied on him to balance the budget will exceed the value of the transfer plus interest – the excess being due to tax collection costs. This implies that the lifetime income of that agent has been decreased by the discounted value of the tax collection cost, and his consumption path will accordingly be altered.

2.3   The objective function of the government

Having seen that in general debt management can affect real outcomes, one has to ask what this potential should be used for. Selecting the government's objective function in the management of public debt is far from obvious. For instance, since choosing the path for debt and taxes (given government expenditure) generally redistributes income across generations, it raises basic issues of intergenerational equity. Any reasonable objective function will have to assign weights to the welfare of different generations in deciding how to distribute over time the tax burden implied by the initial level of debt and by the future flow of public expenditure. The optimal path of taxes, transfers and deficits will then be obtained by maximizing the value of this welfare function subject to the intertemporal budget constraint of the government and to a transversality condition on the path of public debt.

One problem with this approach is that it can end up imposing binding commitments onto agents that are not currently alive (and thus have no say in designing the objective function): for instance, a debt-financed tax cut in favor of the current generation imposes a burden on all future generations, even though they may not be happy about it. A standard of intergenerational equity may be found along the lines of contractarian political philosophy. One could require the social welfare function to be such that members of any generation would agree on it if they could evaluate it *before* knowing the particular age and circumstances in which they will live – "behind the veil of ignorance," to use the expression of Rawls (1971). In a sense, public action should raise the *ex ante* welfare of all future generations, transferring wealth, say, from those living in peaceful and rich times to those struck by wars and catastrophes. It should be noticed, anyway, that each generation is not without protection against unfair policies by preceding ones: it can always choose to repudiate the debt.

One may also wonder whether this approach to the issue of debt management is robust. If the resulting optimal debt path were highly dependent upon the specific objective function and the assumptions about private sector behavior, a policy-maker would be justified in treating this approach with some skepticism. We shall instead see below that quite different (simple) models generate qualitatively similar solutions – and that in addition the optimal path implied by these solutions can be summarized by simple fiscal policy rules.

When uncertainty is introduced into the picture, it has been suggested that the criterion for the welfare evaluation of public financial policy may be that of *unconditional Pareto optimality* (see Fischer, 1983). Policy actions should result in an *ex ante* Pareto-improvement, in the sense that the unconditional expected utility of all agents should be raised in equilibrium (although their *ex post* utility may actually be lower). Also this criterion can be defended by use of the contractarian method. If an unconditionally Pareto-improving policy were proposed, and agents could vote on the proposal "behind the veil of ignorance" (*i.e.* with no information on the realization of any variable affecting their *ex post* utility level), they would vote in its favor. This line of reasoning has been criticized because it seems to imply that economic agents should agree on the rules of the game before being born (or alternatively that they are born before being allowed to perform any trade within the model: see Peled, 1985). In fact, quite a number of political institutions, including constitutions, seem to exist precisely for this reason – the need to establish rules of the game of which all future generations will presumably approve (and abide by).

How does all this fit in with the "practical view" that the objective of debt management should simply be to minimize the cost of debt service? Are the two related in some simple fashion, in the sense that the objective of debt-servicing minimization is monotonically related to some proper social welfare function of the variety just discussed? In reality, the "practical view" belongs to the stage-wise approach to public financial policy mentioned above, as it implicitly assumes the path of deficits to be exogenous. Starting from this premise, it seems reasonable that the standard of efficiency for the government should simply be to get finance from the private sector at the best possible terms. One may be tempted to suggest that the objective of debt-service minimization and that of welfare maximization are bound to coincide. If the Treasury is to minimize the burden of debt servicing it will have to issue debt with characteristics tailored as closely as possible to the preferences of its holders, and this should presumably be beneficial for investors as well. We shall see below, however, that this is not generally the case, and that the basis for defending the "practical view" lies rather in the opportunity to reduce fiscal pressure on future taxpayers than in the benefits for current investors.

3   Optimal choice between debt and taxes

We can now turn back to the policy issues that currently confront the Italian government and see what kind of answers economic analysis is capable of giving. The first issue concerns the future path of fiscal deficits. With public debt approximately as large as national income, most popular discussions on this issue start from the premise that the current stock of debt is too high and that it should be reduced by generating substantial surpluses in the near future (though opinions differ as to whether this should be done by raising ordinary taxes and/or lowering expenditure, by levying a drastic wealth tax or by calling an outright default on public debt). Is this premise correct? In other words, does the currently high level of *per capita* debt *per se* justify calling for a restrictive fiscal stance – until debt is down to some "normal" level – or should one instead disregard the current level of the stock in deciding about future deficits?

To face this issue at the highest level of simplicity, I shall analyze it in models where there is no uncertainty. This rules out the choice between different types of debt (except that between different maturities), because in the absence of uncertainty all types of debt are perfect substitutes.

3.1   Smoothing cycles across generations

We have seen above that when the life of economic agents is finite (and they do not care about the welfare of their descendants), debt policy is capable of reallocating income across generations, so that choosing a path for debt and taxes requires an objective function with distributional weights on the welfare of current and future generations.

To see the implications of this approach to debt policy, consider an overlapping generations model with stationary population where the rate of interest is exogenously given, either by technology or by foreign capital markets (as in Chiesa 1986, upon which the discussion below is based). With the interest rate ($r \equiv R - 1$) given and constant, the lifetime utility level of each individual depends only on the present discounted value of his lifetime endowment: for simplicity, assume that people born at time t have an endowment w_t in the first period of their life and nothing in the second, and that they pay a lump-sum tax of size τ_t on their endowment (and none on the interest income they earn on their savings). Let us denote by $u(w_t - \tau_t, R)$ the indirect utility function of an individual born at time t (*i.e.* the maximum utility that he can get, given his endowment and the interest rate). The objective function of the government at time t is assumed to be increasing in the welfare of each generation's representative individual (although successive increases in the latter raise the objective function by decreasing amounts), and is additively separable across generations, with discount factor $\beta \equiv 1/(1 + \delta)$:

$$\sum_{i=0}^{\infty} \beta^i W(u(w_i - \tau_i, R)),$$

where $\partial W/\partial u > 0$, $\partial^2 W/\partial u^2 < 0$. $\quad\quad\quad\quad\quad\quad\quad\quad\quad\quad$ (1)

The planning horizon of the government extends from time 1 to infinity: its control variable is the sequence of taxes $\{\tau_1, \tau_2, \dots\}$, and all time 0 variables (including the initial *per capita* level of debt, B_0) are taken as given. Similarly, the future path of public spending $\{g_1, g_2, \dots\}$ is assumed to be exogenous, so that the optimal path of taxes will also define the optimal deficit at each date (for a given initial debt). The deficit at time t is in fact defined by:

$$B_t - B_{t-1} = rB_{t-1} + g_t - \tau_t, \quad\quad\quad\quad\quad\quad\quad (2a)$$

where B_t is the *per capita* level of debt at time t. Solving equation (2a) forward and imposing the transversality condition:

$$\lim_{i \to \infty} B_{t+i}/R^i = 0, \quad\quad\quad\quad\quad\quad\quad\quad\quad (2b)$$

one obtains the following expression for the government's budget constraint at time $t - 1$:

$$B_{t-1} = \sum_{i=0}^{\infty} \frac{\tau_{t+i} - g_{t+i}}{R^{i+1}}, \quad\quad\quad\quad\quad\quad\quad (2)$$

that, for $t = 1$, specializes to:

$$B_0 = \sum_{i=0}^{\infty} \frac{\tau_{i+1} - g_{i+1}}{R^{i+1}}. \quad\quad\quad\quad\quad\quad\quad (2')$$

Since the policy-maker starts its planning at $t = 1$, its decision problem is to maximize (1) subject to the intertemporal budget constraint $(2')$, and to the feasibility constraint:

$$\tau_i \leq w_i. \quad\quad\quad\quad\quad\quad\quad\quad\quad\quad\quad\quad (3)$$

The budget constraint $(2')$ requires the current value of public debt to equal the present discounted value of all future surpluses, while condition (3) restricts taxes not to exceed the income they are levied upon.
   The first order conditions for a maximum yield:

$$\frac{\partial W/\partial \tau_t}{\partial W/\partial \tau_{t+1}} = \beta R \equiv \frac{1 + r}{1 + \delta}, \quad \text{for } t = 1, 2, \dots \quad\quad (4)$$

It is reasonable to assume that the authorities discount the welfare of future generations at the rate of interest $(\delta = r)$, thus applying to intergenerational transfers the same opportunity cost that individuals face in intertemporal choices over their lifetime. When $\delta = r$, condition (4) implies that $\partial W/\partial \tau_t$ should be constant over time: for this to be the case, the argument of that function, *i.e.* the welfare of each generation $u(w_t - \tau_t, R)$, must be constant, which in turn requires that taxes be set so as to keep disposable income constant: $w_t - \tau_t^* = \bar{w}_d$, $\forall t^3$. The implied path of public debt can immediately be found by substituting the implied expression for taxes in the time $t - 1$ budget constraint given by (2):

$$
\begin{aligned}
B_{t-1} &= \sum_{i=0}^{\infty} \frac{w_{t+i} - \bar{w}_d - g_{t+i}}{R^{i+1}} \\
&= \sum_{i=0}^{\infty} \frac{w_{t+i} - g_{t+i}}{R^{i+1}} - \frac{\bar{w}_d}{r} .
\end{aligned}
\tag{5}
$$

The sum in the second step of (5) is the net worth of the private sector of the economy, on a *per capita* basis: the present discounted value of the future resources of the economy (the wealth of the nation) less that of the resources that will be appropriated by the government (the net worth of the public sector). Let us denote the annualized value of the total resources of the economy and of those appropriated by the government by w_t^p and g_t^p respectively:

$$
w_t^p \equiv r \sum_{i=0}^{\infty} \frac{w_{t+i}}{R^{i+1}} , \quad g_t^p \equiv r \sum_{i=0}^{\infty} \frac{g_{t+i}}{R^{i+1}}
\tag{6}
$$

that can be thought of as the permanent level of income and expenditure of the economy. Using (6), we can then rewrite (5) as:

$$
rB_{t-1} = w_t^p - g_t^p - \bar{w}_d
\tag{7}
$$

Noticing that the expression for the deficit in (2a) can now be written as:

$$
B_t - B_{t-1} = rB_{t-1} + g_t - (w_t - \bar{w}_d),
\tag{3'}
$$

and substituting from (7) for rB_{t-1}, the optimal deficit turns out to be:

$$
B_t^* - B_{t-1}^* = (w_t^p - w_t) + (g_t - g_t^p).
\tag{8}
$$

The fiscal rule implied by (8) has two noteworthy features: (i) the initial stock of *per capita* debt, B_0, does not play any role in the determination of the deficit – a higher B_0 merely shifts up the entire path of future levels of debt B_t^*; (ii) increases in public debt must be used to smooth out temporary shortfalls of income or temporary bulges in government expenditure. The deficit's anticyclical behavior with respect to income is reflected in the implied path of taxes, that must offset temporary deviations of private sector income from its permanent level, besides paying for the permanent component of expenditure and for interest on outstanding debt:

$$\tau_t^* = (w_t - w_t^p) + g_t^p + rB_{t-1}^* \tag{9}$$

A switch from tax to deficit-financing is thus the optimal response to an abnormally low level of private sector income or to an abnormally high level of expenditure (remember that here expenditure is taken to be exogenous), whereas on average taxes should be set to pay for the normal level of expenditure and interest on debt. Obviously, this implies that the average level of taxes at each date is *ceteris paribus* higher if the initial stock of debt is higher, since that raises the level of debt at each date and therefore raises the interest component rB_{t-1}^* in equation (9): taxes must be on average higher (and welfare will correspondingly be on average lower) to pay for the larger interest rate bill.

3.2   Smoothing cycles within generations

Although national income and public spending may display secular cycles that span over the entire lifetime of a generation, most macroeconomic fluctuations are much shorter-lived than that. The idea that income is much more stable across generations than over the lifetime of an individual is probably the implicit motivation for the traditional view that debt management should be used as a short-run stabilization device rather than as a vehicle for intergenerational redistributions: for instance Modigliani (1984) recommends "a procyclical behavior of the budget surplus, while ensuring a balanced budget over the cycle as a whole," so as to leave the stock of debt roughly unchanged across generations ("each generation should pay for itself, without encroaching on others," p. 4).

The proposal that debt management should be aimed at short-run stabilization runs into the problem that transfers within the lifetime of an individual are neutral, as seen in Section 2.2. But, it will be remembered, this neutrality result holds only if private capital markets are perfect: if they are not, intragenerational transfers are again effective. Let us then consider an amended version of the previous section's model to illustrate the possible use of deficits as an optimal "short-run" countercyclical device, in the presence of capital market imperfections.

Suppose that each generation receives income in *both* periods of its life (not only in the first period, as in the last section): let us denote the two endowments of generation t by w_{1t} and w_{2t+1} respectively. To concentrate only on *intragenerational* fluctuations in *income*, assume that: (a) the present discounted value of the lifetime income is the same for each generation, *i.e.* $w_{1t} + w_{2t+1}/R = k$ for all t (k being a constant) and (b) there are no fluctuations in public spending, *i.e.* g_t is fixed at g for all t.

However, the *distribution* of the total endowment across the two periods will in general be different for each generation. This would not matter if capital markets were perfect, since people could borrow or lend at the rate r ($\equiv R - 1$) so as to make their lifetime consumption plan invariant to the time distribution of the endowment: lifetime consumption and welfare would then only depend on the present discounted value of lifetime resources net of taxes, *i.e.* on $(k - \tau_{1t} - \tau_{2t+1}/R)$. Thus, if capital markets were perfect, the optimality condition found in the last section – equalizing the lifetime utility of all generations – is satisfied simply by levying on each generation the same total amount of taxes $(R\tau_{1t} + \tau_{2t+1} = rB_0 + g, \forall t)$, while the precise distribution of this total over the lifetime of each generation would be irrelevant. But the main point is that there is no scope for using deficits, because the need for short-run stabilization is eliminated by the workings of the market (and that for intergenerational redistribution is ruled out by assumption).

This will no longer be the case, instead, if there is a wedge between borrowing and lending rates on credit markets: suppose that, due to the inefficiency of the banking system, one can borrow only at a rate $r' > r$. In this case the distribution of the endowment *does* matter. Consider in fact a consumer who is a net lender and suppose one reshuffles his disposable income from the first to the second period of his life so as to turn him into a net borrower. Even if in the process the discounted value of his lifetime disposable income $(k - \tau_{1t} - \tau_{2t+1}/R)$ is kept constant, his consumption and welfare will be lowered by this reshuffling of the total endowment over time. The reduction in welfare will occur when first-period disposable income $(w_{1t} - \tau_{1t})$ falls below the amount of first-period consumption that would be chosen if the consumer could borrow at the rate r: this critical magnitude, to be denoted by c_{1t}^*, depends only on the present value of lifetime resources (discounted at rate r), *i.e.* $k - \tau_{1t} - \tau_{2t+1}/R$. Thus generations with low disposable income in the first period of their life $(w_{1t} - \tau_{1t} < c_{1t}^*)$ are *ceteris paribus* worse off than those whose disposable income is mostly concentrated in their youth $(w_{1t} - \tau_{1t} > c_{1t}^*)$. Since the standard of optimality for our government is the equalization of welfare across generations, this outcome is suboptimal.

The welfare of generations with first-period disposable income below c_{1t}^* is lower because they cannot get that level of first-period consumption except by borrowing, and they can only do this on unfavorable terms. If government policy could enable them to buy c_{1t}^* without borrowing, the welfare level would be the same for all generations, provided of course that the overall tax burden falling on each generation $\tau_{1t} + \tau_{2t+1}/R$ were also kept the same for all t. The optimal policy must thus satisfy two requirements: (i) it must effectively replicate the operations of a perfect capital market, letting people borrow on the same terms at which they can lend; (ii) it must impose the same tax burden on all generations. From the latter requirement, it is evident that, under the optimal scheme, lifetime disposable income $k - \tau_{1t} - \tau_{2t+1}/R$ is the same for all generations, and that therefore also the critical level of consumption c_{1t}^* is a constant – to be denoted hereafter by c_1^*.

A scheme that satisfies both the above requirements is the following: stabilize at c_1^* the first-period disposable income of all generations, by setting first-period taxes[4]:

$$\tau_{1t}^* = w_{1t} - c_1^*; \tag{10}$$

if $\tau_{1t}^* < 0$, *i.e.* if it is a transfer, finance it by issuing additional debt (if $\tau_{1t}^* > 0$, use the tax to retire debt). Then to avoid unnecessary transfers across generations, use second-period taxes τ_{2t+1}^* to retire the extra debt issued to finance the transfer and pay interest on it (or reduce τ_{1t+1}^* appropriately if $\tau_{1t}^* > 0$). Since obviously second-period taxes must also pay for current government spending and service the initial stock of debt B_0 (that will thus be passed over from each generation to the next), they must be set at

$$\tau_{2t+1}^* = -R\tau_{1t}^* + rB_0 + g. \tag{11}$$

Assuming that the government starts its scheme at time 1, so that B_0, the stock of debt at time 0, is given, and that second-period taxes on generation 0 are set at $\tau_{21}^* = rB_0 + g$,[5] it is easy to show that the optimal path of debt is simply:

$$B_t^* = B_0 - \tau_{1t}^* = B_0 + (c_1^* - w_{1t}) \tag{12}$$

i.e. the stock of debt fluctuates around the initial level B_0, increasing when the first-period income of the currently young falls below the threshold level c_1^*, and viceversa. The deficit correspondingly is:

$$B_t^* - B_{t-1}^* = -(w_{1t} - w_{1t-1}) \qquad (12')$$

i.e. it moves so as to precisely offset changes in first-period income. In conclusion, even though the precise path for the deficit differs from the previous case, it still displays the countercyclical behavior and the independence of the initial stock B_0 that were found above. The countercyclical behavior in this case is limited to correct income fluctuations spanning less than the life of a generation, and, as recommended by Modigliani, it does not cause intergenerational reallocations: these are not required here because income has been supposed to be stable across generations.

3.3   Smoothing the excess burden of taxation

Even when consumption plans are written over an infinite horizon and capital markets are perfect, there is a role for debt management if taxes can only be collected at a cost (be it a monetary cost to the government or a welfare cost due to deadweight losses), as shown by Barro (1979, 1984, 1985). Suppose that the collection costs at each date t (z_t) are homogeneous in both taxes and income, so that they can be written as a function of the ratio of the two, the average tax rate:

$$z_t = F(\tau_t, w_t) = \tau_t f(\tau_t/w_t) \quad \text{with, } F_1 > 0, F_2 < 0 = > f' > 0 \quad (13)$$

and the objective of the government is the minimization of the present discounted value of tax collection costs, as of time 0:

$$\underset{\{\tau_i\}}{\text{Min}} \ Z_0 = \sum_{i=0}^{\infty} \frac{z_i}{R^i} \qquad (14)$$

subject to the budget constraint (2′). The first-order conditions of the problem,

$$(\tau_i^*/w_i) f'(\tau_i^*/w_i) + f(\tau_i^*/w_i) - \lambda = 0 \quad \forall i \qquad (15)$$

require the optimal tax rate to be *constant* at all dates (λ is the Lagrange multiplier associated with the budget constraint). This result, that is due in this context to the homogeneity of the $z_t(\cdot)$ function, could also be obtained if the objective function of the government were the minimization of the welfare loss arising from tax distortions (under appropriate assumptions[6]), and thus the maximization of the welfare of the representative consumer.

Denoting the constant tax rate by $\bar{\tau}$, we can write the tax revenue raised at time t as $\tau_t^* = \bar{\tau} w_t$. Using the government budget constraint (2) and the definitions of "permanent" income w_t^p and "permanent" expenditure g_t^p in (6), we can write:

$$B_{t-1} = \sum_{i=0}^{\infty} \frac{\bar{\tau} w_{t+i} - g_{t+i}}{R^{i+1}} = \bar{\tau} \frac{w_t^p}{r} - \frac{g_t^p}{r} . \tag{16}$$

Substituting the tax rule $\tau_t^* = \bar{\tau} w_t$ and the expression for rB_{t-1} implied by (16) into expression (2a), we get the following expressions for the optimal deficit at time t:

$$B_t^* - B_{t-1}^* = \bar{\tau}(w_t^p - w_t) + (g_t - g_t^p), \tag{17}$$

while the corresponding value of taxes is:

$$\tau_t^* = \bar{\tau} w_t = \frac{w_t}{w_1^p} (g_1^p + rB_0), \tag{18}$$

where the expression for $\bar{\tau}$ has been found solving (16) for $t = 1$.

Thus, once more, the theory states that deficits must behave anticyclically with respect to income and absorb abnormal bulges in public spending. On the other hand, taxes should be set so that – aside from cyclical fluctuations – they will pay for permanent government expenditure (calculated as of time 1, the starting date of the optimal plan) and for real interest on the initial stock of debt. The optimal time path for the deficit, this time, is *not* completely independent of the initial stock of debt, as in the previous two cases: the sensitivity of the deficit to cyclical changes in income is in fact increasing in B_0, because so is the tax rate $\bar{\tau}$ (for the same reason, the deficit turns out to be increasing in the growth rate of income). However, it is still true that a higher initial level of debt does not imply that the government should hasten to bring the stock of debt down by running surpluses: quite to the reverse, it can be seen from (16) that the entire time path of debt is shifted *up* by an increase in B_0, since this induces a rise in $\bar{\tau}$.

The qualitative features of the optimal debt path are thus impressively similar, whether the reason for the non-neutrality of debt management lies in finite life, imperfect capital market or tax collection costs (or distortions) – and thus whether deficits are to be used for long-run stabilization, short-run stabilization or tax-smoothing. For the purposes of debt management in Italy today, what the theory tells us is that : (i) the current high level of debt does not *per se* require that the government should take a restrictive fiscal stance, running surpluses to reduce the debt; (ii) deficits should retain their anticyclical behavior (and taxes their procyclical behavior) with respect to income, and should also be used to absorb unusual deviations of spending from its permanent value; (iii) on average, taxes should be set high enough so as to pay for some measure of permanent government spending and of real debt service.

4   Optimal menu of debt issues

In a world of uncertainty and incomplete contingent markets the set of public financial policies that can produce real effects is far richer than in a world of certainty. By issuing state-contingent debt and using state-contingent taxes and transfers, the government can provide the private sector with new opportunities for risk-sharing, both among members of the same generation and across different generations. The precise set of effective financial policies obviously depends on the assets that the private sector is unable to provide, and thus on the unexploited opportunities for risk-sharing that exist in the economy. In this respect, Italian capital markets offer considerable potential for effective innovation in public financial policies, because their shortcomings in the allocation of risk are quite pervasive. The next section surveys the features and imperfections of Italian financial markets that are most relevant for the choice of assets to be issued by the Treasury.

4.1   Potential for effective innovation in the Italian debt menu

First, in Italy neither the corporate sector nor the government provide bonds indexed to the rate of inflation (except for the 1985 issues by the Treasury mentioned in section 1). *Second*, historically only housing and human capital have provided a hedge against inflation, although the decreasing degree of indexation of wages and pensions is gradually turning human capital into a less effective hedge. The real yield of equities has instead displayed a strong negative correlation with inflation (which may be due to a variety of factors, such as the association of the inflation of the 1970s with adverse real shocks and contractionary policy responses, the adverse effects of inflation on corporate tax liabilities, and irrational valuation by the stock market). *Third*, only a small fraction of the total stock of equity capital is listed on the stock market, with the result that the stock market offers a scarcely diversified menu of stocks, while most of the equity capital of the country is composed of the shares of family firms, where property coincides with control. *Fourth*, until May 1987, capital controls have largely prevented people from holding foreign assets to insure against exchange rate fluctuations[7]. The controls are currently being dismantled, but as of now households have not yet reallocated their portfolios towards foreign assets.

From the first two points, it is clear that government issue of indexed bonds would have real effects, offering protection against unexpected inflation that currently the market does not provide (even T-Bills can at most protect savers against *expected* inflation). Further, the negative correlation of the real return on stocks with inflation and the decreasing degree of wage indexation suggest that indexed bonds would probably pay an equilibrium real yield below that of nominal bonds (as shown by Fischer (1975) and Modigliani (1976)). Incidentally, governments are in general better equipped than private corporations for issuing indexed bonds, given that tax revenue is naturally indexed to the general price level (whereas the revenue of an individual firm is indexed to its product price, so that relative price variability can turn the private issue of such bonds into a risky business).

The fact that only a limited number of equities is listed and traded on the stock market opens the way to other non-neutral policy schemes. Presumably the households that own and control unlisted firms have portfolios that are highly unbalanced, being dominated by the risk characteristics of the profits of the family firm. These households would then pay a premium for an asset with returns negatively correlated with these profits, and the government could issue such an asset, provided one could identify a publicly-known variable reflecting the pattern of unlisted firms' profits. The Treasury could then either bear the implied risk directly, or hedge it by selling on the stock exchange an asset with returns negatively related to those of the first (and thus positively correlated with the profits of unlisted firms). If the Treasury were to hedge completely, it would essentially end up placing with the stock market some of the risk of the unlisted firms' stocks, while earning a profit in the intermediation (due to the fact that the owners of unlisted firms cannot raise equity capital *directly* from the public, presumably because of the fixed costs implied in listing their firms on the Exchange).

Finally, to the extent that households will not take immediate advantage of the removal of capital controls to diversify their portfolios, the government will retain the opportunity of capturing part of the portfolio shift towards foreign securities, issuing a whole array of foreign-denominated assets to the domestic market (which would merely represent an extension of the policy started with the issue of CTEs, the Treasury Certificates denominated in ECUs).

It thus appears that the issue of new types of debt by the Italian Treasury would be far from neutral in its effects. However, this should *not* be taken to imply that all these innovations in the menu of Treasury issues are to be recommended. Evaluating their welfare merits is far more difficult than assessing their non-neutrality, as witnessed by the fact that "there is as yet no satisfactory theory of what type of assets a government should issue" (Fischer, 1983, p. 243). In the next section I will attempt to provide, if not such a theory, an example that helps us to understand the effects of alternative choices that the Treasury can make in this area.

4.2   Choosing from the menu: a simple model

As noticed in Section 2.1, in general the design of optimal debt policy under uncertainty requires the use of *both* contingent debt and contingent taxes and transfers. Fischer (1983), for example, shows that optimal risk-sharing in an overlapping generations model cannot be implemented without the use of taxes and transfers (the welfare criterion being unconditional Pareto optimality). This implies that the private sector could not reach that allocation without government intervention – simply setting up a private financial intermediary. Here I will instead consider the more realistic case where taxes cannot be used as an instrument to achieve optimal risk-sharing, and must be taken as pre-determined in designing the menu of debt instruments. In choosing from the menu, the Treasury must then find the solution to a second-best problem.

Assume that taxes have been set so as to pay for government expenditure and for interest payments on the initial stock of debt, on the assumption that the latter were to be entirely covered with issues of safe debt. Thus, if the Treasury actually issued only safe debt, the budget would always be balanced. But suppose that the Treasury instead decides to cover part of its borrowing requirement by issuing another asset, characterized by non-zero covariance with the equity capital of the economy. One would expect that, if this covariance was negative, the asset would sell at a premium relative to safe debt, and this would *ceteris paribus* reduce the burden of debt servicing. But will the introduction of this other asset also raise investors' welfare? And what will be the implied dynamics of debt, considering that a portion of public debt will pay stochastic real returns?

The setup that I will use to address these questions is that of a simple overlapping generation economy with no population growth and risk-averse consumers, who live for two periods, receive a single endowment w when young and pay taxes τ (I will denote their after-tax income by $y \equiv w - \tau$). They can purchase three assets: a safe real asset, a risky asset issued by the private sector ("equities") and a risky asset issued by the government. The price of the safe asset is normalized to unity (each unit of it costs a unit of consumption). All three assets have a one-period maturity: the return on each of them can thus be thought of as its final value.

The return on safe real debt is a constant R ($\equiv 1 + r$), that can be regarded as set by foreign capital markets or by a linear production technology. Equities can be bought at unit price p_k and pay unit return $\tilde{R}_{kt} = \mu + \epsilon_t$, where μ is constant and ϵ_t is a zero-mean, serially uncorrelated normal disturbance with variance σ^2. The risky asset issued by the government is sold at price p_x and pays instead $\tilde{R}_{xt} = \mu + \lambda\epsilon_t$: its return is thus indexed to that of equities, with a correlation coefficient λ, and its expected payoff is μ, $i.e.$ the same as that of equities (with no loss of generality). The government decides both upon λ, $i.e.$ on the way the asset return should be indexed on the return on equities, and upon X, $i.e.$ the supply of the asset[8].

As for the price of equities, p_k, I propose two *alternative* assumptions: (i) that $p_k = \bar{p}_k$, an exogenous constant, implying that the supply of equities is infinitely elastic at that price (one must then impose $\mu > R\bar{p}_k$, or no positive amount of equity will be demanded in equilibrium); (ii) that the supply of equities be totally inelastic (a fixed amount $\bar{K}$), and that p_k be determined by market equilibrium. The first assumption is more suited to analyzing the long-run, when one would expect the supply of equities to have adjusted to demand shifts, bringing the equilibrium price of equities back in line with the replacement cost of capital $\bar{p}_k$ (that is equivalent to considering steady states, where Tobin's q is 1). The second assumption may be more appropriate for the short-run, when the adjustment of supply has not yet taken place. I will start with the long-run assumption (i).

To derive closed form expressions for asset demands involving the variances and covariances of returns, I suppose that the representative individual of each generation has an inverse exponential utility function, additive across periods (time subscripts are dropped for ease of notation):

$$\text{Max } U = - e^{-c_1} + R^{-1} E[- e^{-\tilde{c}_2}]$$

$$\text{s.t. } \tilde{c}_2 = K(\tilde{R}_k - Rp_k) + X(\tilde{R}_x - Rp_x) + R(y - c_1)$$

(19)

where c_1 and $\bar{c}_2$ denote consumption in the two periods of life, R^{-1} the discount factor (for simplicity set equal to the inverse of the return on the safe asset) and K and X the demand for equities and for risky public debt. Since all individuals belonging to the same generation are alike, there is no loss of generality in standardizing the population size to 1, and treating K and X as the aggregate asset demands. Since both $\bar{R}_k$ and $\bar{R}_x$ are normally distributed, so is second-period consumption $\bar{c}_2$, so that integrating in (19) yields:

$$U = - e^{c_1} + R^{-1}[- e^{-E(\bar{c}_2)+\frac{1}{2}\mathrm{Var}(\bar{c}_2)}]. \tag{20}$$

Maximizing with respect to c_1, K and X, we then get the three first-order conditions:

$$c_1 = E(\bar{c}_2) - \tfrac{1}{2}\mathrm{Var}(\bar{c}_2) \tag{21}$$

$$\mu - Rp_k = (K + \lambda X)\,\sigma^2 \tag{22}$$

$$\mu - Rp_x = (K + \lambda X)\lambda\sigma^2 \tag{23}$$

Now remember that, under assumption (i), the amount of equity held by the public, K, is endogenous, while its price, p_k, is exogenous. Using (22) and (23) in (21) and rearranging, we can express the optimal level of first-period consumption only in terms of the exogenous parameters y, R, μ, σ^2 and $\bar{p}_k$:

$$c_1 = \frac{1}{1 + R} [yR + (\mu - R\bar{p}_k)^2/2\sigma^2]. \tag{21'}$$

Thus, if p_k, the price of equities, is pinned down exogenously by the replacement cost of capital $\bar{p}_k$, consumption and saving are invariant to the mix of debt instruments issued by the Treasury (the size of X relative to total debt) and to the correlation of risky debt with equities (λ). Interestingly, using (21) in (20), one sees that the expected utility of investors is an increasing function of first-period consumption c_1, so that welfare is also unaffected by the financial policy of the Treasury.

But this does not imply that this policy is irrelevant: in fact, by choosing to issue risky debt whose return is negatively correlated with that of equities ($\lambda < 0$), the Treasury can reduce the average burden of debt servicing. As we shall see below, this will enable the government to retire debt gradually, if fiscal pressure is kept unchanged, and eventually to reduce the tax burden as well. In equilibrium, in fact, if $\lambda < 0$, the expected return on a unit of risky debt issued by the Treasury (μ) is below that on an equivalent amount of safe debt ($R\bar{p}_k$) – as is immediately evident using (22) in (23) to get the relationship between risk premia:

$$\mu - Rp_x = \lambda(\mu - R\bar{p}_k). \tag{23'}$$

where $\mu > R\bar{p}_k$ by assumption. Conversely, if the return on risky debt were positively correlated with that on equities ($\lambda > 0$), the government would have to pay a positive risk premium on that portion of its debt, thus increasing the burden of debt servicing and leading to a rising deficit (an explosive debt path), unless fiscal pressure was eventually raised.

In this case, then, the "practical view" that the government should try to minimize the burden of debt servicing seems fully vindicated. Its prescription has no adverse welfare effects on current generations of investors, and leads to prospective tax reductions on future generations – and thereby raises the expected value of any reasonable social welfare function. In fact, one could actually raise the welfare level of all generations (including the current one) by handing back to each one of them – in the form of tax rebates – part of the savings on debt servicing that on average this policy produces. Moreover, the "practical view" translates into a simple rule of thumb for the Treasury: issue debt with returns as inversely correlated with the "market portfolio" as possible, and issue as much of it as possible. For example, if the real return on the market portfolio is negatively related to inflation, the government should not simply issue safe (indexed) debt, but debt over-indexed to inflation; or, if the return on the market portfolio is dominated by the behavior of the stock market, the Treasury should issue debt with returns inversely related to changes in the stock market index.

One may ask: how can it be that the size of X does not matter? How can the economy absorb without problem any amount of risky debt issued by the Treasury? The answer is in equation (22): all variables in that equation are constant parameters except K, λ and X, so that it must be that $dK = -d(\lambda X)$. This means that when the correlation λ becomes more negative or risky public debt X rises (with $\lambda < 0$), the stock of equities held by the public also rises: due to its negative correlation with equities ($\lambda < 0$), risky Treasury debt raises the amount of risk-taking in the economy and thus leads to an expansion of the equilibrium stock of equities. What gets squeezed, then, is the share of the safe asset in total saving: in the limit, when $\bar{p}_k K + p_x X = y - c_1$, no safe asset is demanded – and beyond that limit, domestic investors start borrowing abroad at the safe rate of interest to invest in the mix of the two risky assets at home.

Let us now examine the model under the "short-run" assumption that the total stock of equities is fixed at $K = \bar{K}$, and the price p_k equilibrates the market. Noticing that first-period consumption $(21')$ can be rewritten as

$$c_1 = \frac{1}{1 + R} [yR + (\bar{K} + \lambda X)^2 \, \sigma^2]. \tag{21''}$$

it is immediate that consumption – and thus welfare – are increasing in λX: does this imply that the rule set out in the previous case (make λ as negative and X as large as possible) is now turned on its head? It would, if one could ignore the fact that issuing risky debt strongly correlated with equities raises, on average, the burden of debt servicing and thus sets debt on an explosive path – unless taxes rise, sooner or later. If however taxes must be raised in the future, it means that the welfare increase of the current generation would be at the expense of future generations.

To avoid neglecting this important effect, I propose to abandon for a moment the assumption that taxes are invariant to the Treasury policy of debt issues, and consider the choice of λ and X under the assumption that consumers are granted via lower taxes the entire (expected) saving $(Rp_x - \mu) X$ that the Treasury makes by issuing debt with $\lambda < 0$ – and conversely that they are charged via higher taxes the extra (expected) burden of debt servicing $(\mu - Rp_x) X$ that arises from $\lambda > 0$. Under this assumption, first-period consumption becomes:

$$c_1 = \frac{1}{1 + R} [yR + (\bar{K}^2 - \lambda^2 X^2) \, \sigma^2/2], \tag{24}$$

that is maximized for $\lambda X = 0$. Since expected utility is a monotone positive transformation of c_1, the optimal rule for the Treasury now becomes simply: just issue safe debt. The "practical view" that the Treasury should minimize the cost of debt servicing is defeated this time (it can be shown that maximizing $(Rp_x - \mu) X$, that is the objective consistent with this view, leads to setting $\lambda X = -\bar{K}/2$ rather than $\lambda X = 0$). It should be stressed, anyway, that in this model safe debt is safe *real* debt: thus, in an inflationary economy, the afore-mentioned rule translates into recommending the issue of indexed bonds.

Thus the optimal rule for the Treasury depends on the response of the supply of equities to their price (or, if one prefers, to the cost of raising equity capital). If this supply function is quite elastic, the government should issue risky debt with returns negatively correlated to the return on equities, otherwise issuing safe debt is the best strategy (unless one wants to unload the cost of the policy onto future generations via higher deficits). If it is correct to conjecture that the first assumption is more appropriate for the long run and the second for the short run, following the first of the two rules will impose costs on the current generation that may be balanced by gains further into the future.

Someone could object in general to the idea that the Treasury may index the returns on public debt to a stochastic variable, by arguing that this will increase the variance of debt service payments and thus the variance of the deficit (since realistically taxes could not be increased and lowered to absorb the changes in government outflows due to debt servicing). There are two answers to this argument: first, as a matter of fact, virtually the entire outstanding stock of public debt has stochastic *real* returns (all nominal debt has this property) and thus the implied *real* interest payments already contribute to the variance of the *real* deficit; second, there is no reason why the Treasury should not destabilize the time path of the real deficit if that paid well enough in terms of the overall objective function of the government, for instance by allowing a substantial reduction in the average size of the deficit.

Let us for instance consider what would happen to the dynamics of public debt in this model if, from time 0 onwards, the Treasury started issuing a constant amount X of risky debt with correlation coefficient $\lambda < 0$. Since the initial stock of debt is B_0 and $X < B_0$, the Treasury has to issue also some safe debt $D_t = B_t - p_x X$ (for $t \geq 0$) to cover its financing needs. Tax revenue is set at a constant level $\tau = rB_0 + g = r (D_0 + p_x X) + g$ per period, just enough to balance the budget if only safe debt were issued. The dynamics of safe debt are then described by:

$$D_t \equiv B_t - p_x X = (RD_{t-1} + \bar{R}_{xt} X - \tau + g) - p_x X$$
$$= RD_{t-1} + (\mu - Rp_x + \lambda\epsilon_t) X - rD_0 \qquad (25)$$

that can be solved to yield:

$$D_t = D_0 + \sum_{i=0}^{t-1} [- R^i(Rp_x - \mu) X + R^{t-1-i} \lambda\epsilon_{i+1} X]$$

$$= D_0 - \frac{R^t - 1}{R - 1} (Rp_x - \mu) X + \sum_{i=0}^{t-1} R^{t-1-i} \lambda\epsilon_{i+1} X \qquad (25')$$

i.e. safe debt at time t is the initial level *minus* the final value of the savings obtained by selling X units of risky debt (recall that with $\lambda < 0$, $Rp_x > \mu$). Obviously, these savings are such only in expected value: the presence of the ϵ_i's in the expression reminds us that there will be periods in which *ex post* the Treasury will lose, rather than save, through this scheme.

The fact that on average, however, the scheme saves the Treasury money is witnessed by the fact that the expected value of debt, as seen from time 0, is declining in t:

$$E(D_t) = D_0 - \frac{R^t - 1}{R - 1} (Rp_x - \mu) X \qquad (26)$$

but, since the process in (25) is non-stationary (for $R \geq 1$), the variance of debt is also increasing over time:

$$\mathrm{Var}(D_t) = \frac{R^{2t} - 1}{R^2 - 1} \lambda^2 \sigma^2 X^2 . \qquad (27)$$

These expressions also tell us that although a larger λ (in absolute value) and a larger X lead to larger average savings (by raising the term $(Rp_x - \mu) X$) and thus to more rapid retirement of debt, they also lead to larger swings in the level of debt at each date, because they raise the variance of the debt-servicing component of the deficit.

The fact that, under the proposed scheme, the process that generates debt is non-stationary may appear worrying: is there a sense in which the debt may explode, due to a series of adverse realizations of ϵ_t? Not really: it can be shown that, although the variance of debt is increasing over time, its expected value declines so fast that the probability that it will fall below any preassigned level increases over time. For instance, suppose one considers the probability that by time t all safe debt D_0 will have been retired: then as t is made larger and larger, it becomes more and more likely that by that time this event will have taken place[9]. Thus there is a well-defined sense in which the process can be trusted to reduce public debt, and thereby taxes on all successive generations.

Finally, it should be noticed that although in this simple model all assets have the same maturity, the model's results can be reinterpreted to throw some light also on the choice of the maturity structure of government debt. It is widely recognized in the empirical literature that the return covariance of public debt with equities differs systematically across maturities, and that these different covariances play an important role in the pricing of public debt instruments (Frankel 1985, Friedman 1978, 1981, 1985a, 1985b, Bodie, Kane and McDonald 1983). Selecting a certain maturity structure thus translates into choosing a certain correlation between the (average) return on public debt and equities, *i.e.* (in terms of the model above) a certain λ. For instance, if the return on long-term debt covaries more closely with that on equities than the return on short-term debt, reducing the proportion of long-term debt will be tantamount to lowering the parameter λ and should thus lead, *ceteris paribus*, to a lower burden of debt-servicing for the government – and to welfare effects that can be analyzed in the framework of the above model. For the same reason, however, the model is not a useful guide to the choice of the maturity structure if the differences between short- and long-term debt cannot be reduced to differences in their return covariances, and are to be measured along other dimensions (such as their ability to yield liquidity services to asset-holders or flexibility in debt management to the policy-maker).

5   Conclusions

I will now summarize the main implications for the future management of Italian public debt that can be drawn from the normative theories discussed in this chapter.

(i)   The fact that Italy's public debt has reached approximately the same size as its national product does not *per se* provide grounds for aiming at a reduction of the debt-income ratio to some target level. The tax burden implied by the existing stock of debt should be spread over the infinite future, rather than concentrated over a short time horizon to achieve such a target.

(ii)   This does not imply that the current level of debt has no implications for the setting of fiscal policy. To ensure solvency, in fact, taxes must *on average* be set at a level high enough to pay for the permanent level of government expenditure and for the real interest on debt: a larger initial debt level raises the real interest bill of the government, and thus increases the average tax burden at each future date. It is an interesting empirical issue to check whether meeting this solvency condition requires a change in the current fiscal policy regime.

(iii)   Deficits should have a countercyclical time profile relative to income (induced by procyclical movements in taxes), and should also be used to finance deviations of public spending from its permanent level.

(iv)   Given the strong negative correlation between the real yield on equities and inflation and the decreasing degree of indexation of labor income and pensions, debt indexed to the inflation rate would sell at a premium. More generally, this would be true for any public debt instrument with return negatively correlated with that of the market portfolio. Thus such an asset should be issued if the objective of the Treasury is to minimize the burden of debt servicing. On welfare grounds, the argument to proceed in this direction is less general. In the context of the model of Section 4.2, I have shown that this innovation raises welfare if the real yield on equities is unresponsive to changes in asset supplies – a reasonable assumption for the long run. The welfare gain essentially stems from the fact that by issuing assets of this kind the Treasury will *on average* realize savings on debt servicing, and thus will be able to reduce the tax burden on all generations.

NOTES

* I am grateful to the Conference participants, and particularly to John Flemming, Luigi Spaventa and Francesco Giavazzi, for giving me useful advice and pointing out some mistakes. I retain responsibility for all remaining ones.
1 See the introductory essay by Spaventa in this book for a more detailed account of this process.
2 The essay by Tabellini in this book extensively analyzes the changing relationship between the Central Bank of Italy and the Treasury.
3 To analyze the cases where $\delta \neq r$, notice that, since $\partial^2 W/\partial \tau_t^2 < 0$, the derivative $\partial W/\partial \tau_t$ is larger in absolute value when disposable income $w_t - \tau_t$ is lower: the marginal social cost of levying extra taxes on generation t is higher the lower the level of its disposable income. This implies that, if $r > \delta$, to have $\partial W/\partial \tau_t > \partial W/\partial \tau_{t+1}$ the optimal tax path must be such that $w_t - \tau_t^* < w_{t+1} - \tau_{t+1}^*$, *i.e.* disposable income will have a rising profile across generations: if pre-tax income is constant, taxes will decline and debt will rise over time. Conversely, if $r < \delta$, the authorities give a lower weight to the welfare of future generations, and will want current disposable income to fall over time ($w_t - \tau_t^* > w_{t+1} - \tau_{t+1}^*$): if pre-tax income is constant, tax pressure will be gradually increased and large deficits at early dates will be paid for by large surpluses later on: in this fashion the current generation will in effect be borrowing from future ones.
4 The essential point is that the first-period disposable income of generation t should be *at least* c_{1t}^*, not necessarily *equal to* c_{1t}^*: all schemes that satisfy the condition $w_{1t} - \tau_{1t} > c_{1t}^*$ will produce the same allocation, provided the lifetime tax burden $\tau_{1t} + \tau_{2t+1}/R$ is the same.
5 The assumption that $\tau_{21}^* = rB_0 + g$ means that the taxes paid by generation 0 cover both interest payments (rB_0) and public expenditure (g) made at time 1, thus covering the entire amount of time 1 deficit: as a result the stock of debt turned over from generation 0 to generation 1 is simply B_0, and the new stock of debt at time 1, B_1, will simply be equal to B_0 minus any taxes levied on generation 1 young ($B_1 = B_0 - \tau_{11}^*$). However, nothing of substance is lost by relaxing this assumption and leaving τ_{21}^* unspecified: at time 1 debt then is

$$B_1 = RB_0 + g - \tau_{21}^* - \tau_{11}^* = \alpha - \tau_{11}^*,$$

where $\alpha \equiv RB_0 + g - \tau_{21}^*$ is the initial level of debt (B_0) *plus* the portion of time 1 deficit not covered by the taxes of the old of generation 0 ($rB_0 + g - \tau_{21}^*$, *i.e.*

the additional debt turned over by generation 0 to generation 1). With this change in assumptions, it turns out that α is the stock of debt to be passed over from each generation to the next under the optimal policy scheme: α will play the same role as B_0 in the text. The optimal tax scheme will in fact entail replacing (11) with

$$\tau^*_{2t+1} = - R\tau^*_{1t} + r\alpha + g$$

and the optimal debt path will correspondingly be

$$B^*_t = \alpha - \tau^*_{1t} = \alpha - (c^*_1 - w_{1t}),$$

i.e. debt will fluctuate around the constant level α rather than B_0, otherwise keeping the same time pattern described in the text.

6 See Barro (1979), p. 944, footnote 7.

7 Households may want to do so, for example, if their consumption basket includes imported goods, whose price is affected by exchange rate movements.

8 As will appear more clearly below, the government finances the payment of the coupons R_{xt} on its risky asset by issuing more or less safe debt, *i.e.* by letting the deficit absorb the corresponding shocks in debt servicing (taxes are in fact assumed to be constant). For instance, if $\lambda < 0$, a negative realization of ϵ_t (a stock market crash) will force the government to issue extra (safe) debt to finance the payment of a high return R_{xt} on each unit of its risky debt. Obviously an important assumption here is that the safe rate of interest R is not affected by this additional issue of safe debt (one can imagine the government as borrowing at the safe rate of interest from a very large pool of saving, such as the international capital market). The reason why in this model the government can affect real outcomes by manufacturing such an asset from existing ones lies in the fact that people, having finite lives, cannot run the intergenerational insurance scheme effectively enacted by the government by providing an asset with return negatively related to those on equity.

9 Since the ϵ_t's are normally distributed with mean 0 and variance σ^2, the stock of safe debt at time t is also normally distributed with mean $E(D_t)$ and variance $\mathrm{Var}(D_t)$. Using the expressions in (26) and (27), the probability that by time t the entire stock D_0 will have been retired can be written as:

$$P(D_t < D_0) = \Phi\left(\frac{D_0 - E(D_t)}{\sqrt{\mathrm{Var}(D_t)}}\right)$$

$$= \Phi\left[\frac{\dfrac{R^t - 1}{R - 1}(Rp_x - \mu)X}{\left(\dfrac{R^{2t} - 1}{R - 1}\right)^{1/2}\lambda\sigma X}\right].$$

Upon differentiation, it turns out that the necessary and sufficient condition for $(d\Phi/dt) > 0$ is

$$\frac{R^t - 1}{R - 1}(Rp_x - \mu)X > 0,$$

which is always true if $Rp_x > \mu$, as will be the case if $\lambda < 0$.

REFERENCES

Barro, Robert J. (1974), "Are Government Bonds Net Wealth?" *Journal of Political Economy*, 82 December.

(1979), "On the Determination of Public Debt," *Journal of Political Economy*, 87 October.

(1984), "US Deficits Since World War I," paper presented at the Conference on "Growth and Distribution: Intergenerational Problems," Uppsala, Sweden, June.

(1985), "Government Spending, Interest Rates, Prices and Budget Deficits in the United Kingdom, 1730–1918," University of Rochester Working Paper, No. 1 March.

Bodie, Zvi, Alex Kane and Robert McDonald (1983), "Why Are Real Interest Rates So High?" NBER Working Paper No. 1141, June.

Chiesa, Gabriella (1986), "La politica ottimale del debito pubblico e del debito estero. Le implicazioni sulla risposta ottimale alla riduzione del prezzo del petrolio," *Giornale degli Economisti e Annali di Economia*, September.

Fischer, Stanley (1975), "The Demand for Index Bonds," *Journal of Political Economy*, 83, June.

(1983), "Welfare Aspects of Government Issue of Indexed Bonds," in *Inflation, Debt and Indexation*, edited by Rudiger Dornbusch and Mario Henrique Simonsen, The MIT Press.

Frankel, Jeffrey A. (1985), "Portfolio Crowding-out Empirically Estimated," *Quarterly Journal of Economics*, 100, Supplement.

Friedman, Benjamin M. (1978), "Crowding Out or Crowding In? Economic Consequences of Financing Government Deficits," *Brookings Papers on Economic Activity*, No. 2.

(1981), "Debt Management Policy, Interest Rates, and Economic Activity," NBER Working Paper No. 830, December.

(1985a), "The Substitutability of Debt and Equity Securities," in *Corporate Capital Structures in the United States*, edited by Benjamin M. Friedman, Chicago: University of Chicago Press.

(1985b), "Crowding Out or Crowding In? Evidence on Debt-Equity Substitutability," mimeo, December.

Hammond, Peter J. (1986), "On the Impossibility of Perfect Financial Markets," Stanford University IMSSS Economics Technical Report.

Levhari, David and Nissan Liviatan (1976), "Government Intervention in the Indexed Bonds Market," *American Economic Review*, Papers and Proceedings, 66.

Lucas, Robert E., Jr. and Nancy L. Stokey (1983), "Optimal Fiscal and Monetary Policy in an Economy without Capital," *Journal of Monetary Economics*, 12, July.

Modigliani, Franco (1976), "Some Economic Implications of the Indexing of Financial Assets with Special Reference to Mortgages," in *The New Inflation and Monetary Policy*, edited by Mario Monti, London: Macmillan.

(1984), "Comment on 'U.S. Deficits Since World War I' by Robert J. Barro", paper presented at the Conference on "Growth and Distribution: Intergenerational Problems," Uppsala, Sweden, June.

Peled, Dan (1985), "Stochastic Inflation and Government Provision of Indexed Bonds," *Journal of Monetary Economics*, 15, May.

Rawls, John (1971), *A Theory of Justice*, Harvard University Press.
Stiglitz, Joseph E. (1983), "On the Relevance or Irrelevance of Public Financial Policy: Indexation, Price Rigidities, and Optimal Monetary Policies," in *Inflation, Debt and Indexation*, edited by Rudiger Dornbusch and Mario Henrique Simonsen, The MIT Press.
Wallace, Neil (1981), "A Modigliani-Miller Theorem for Open Market Operations," *American Economic Review*, 71, June.

Discussion

JOHN FLEMMING

This is an admirably clear paper: clear as to the questions asked, the answers offered, and the method by which they are obtained.

In my own work in this area (see Flemming 1987a and 1987b) I have relied more on distorting taxes and less on overlapping generations than does Pagano. I also started by looking at the case for being concerned about the debt/income ratio and possible rationalization of a political determination to put it on a downward path. The problem of containing the debt is much less acute in the UK than in Italy and the maturity of our debt remains considerable not only in terms of the period to redemption but also of the period for which the interest rate is fixed.

It is quite difficult to think of good reasons for raising taxes now in order to lower them later (this is option (d) in Alesina's paper and is made even more difficult to justify if its consequences are assumed to be "deflation" as in Barry Eichengreen's comment. This difficulty is clearly related to the insight behind Robert Barro's tax rate smoothing propositions (and Pagano's section 3.3). This leads naturally to the notion that the debt ratio should fall in times of "peace" so that it can rise again in times of "war" – or the fiscal equivalent of old-style wars. Where transitions between "war" and "peace" are entirely predictable the problem is not very interesting – but the associated uncertainties of the more interesting cases play no role in Pagano's presentation.

Pagano presents three different models. In the first, overlapping generations are not concerned with each other's welfare thus breaking Barro's (1974) Ricardian equivalence. Lump sum taxes could, and should, be used for intergenerational redistribution, if endowments differ, or if for some reason the pattern of public expenditure is not either constant or separable in private welfare. Pagano restricts himself to the case in which the optimal redistribution involves equalizing the private consumption of all generations. This depends on an assumption that the government discounts future private utility at the interest rate.

167

Given a perfect capital market the allocation of consumption between any one generation's two periods of life is immaterial. It could however be affected by a private utility discount rate (say ϱ) which differed from the exogenous interest rate r. It is then not clear whether it is more natural that the government discount at $\delta = r$ than at $\delta = \varrho$. (In equation 19 in section 4.2, private utility is explicitly discounted at $r[R \equiv (1 + r)^{-1}]$ i.e. $\varrho = r$.) In the second model, capital market imperfection provides scope for welfare enhancing *intra*generational *inter*temporal redistribution. Note, however, that though this is still achieved with lump sum taxes they are cohort or age specific. The third model follows Barro (1974) in introducing convex "collection costs" as a proxy for the deadweight burden of distorting taxes. The tax rate should then be smoothed and in special cases constant.

This last model leads to three equations (Pagano's 16, 17 and 18) which I rewrite here:

$$B_{t-1} = \bar{\tau} \frac{w_t^p}{r} - \frac{g_t^p}{r} \tag{1}$$

$$B_t^* - B_{t-1}^* = \bar{\tau}(w_t^p - w_t^p) + (g_t - g_t^p) \tag{2}$$

and

$$\bar{\tau}_t^* = \bar{\tau}w_t = \frac{w_t}{w_1^p} (g_1^p + rB_0) \tag{3}$$

Pagano emphasizes that though B_0 enters equations (1) and (2) indirectly through $\bar{\tau}$, a higher B_0 shifts the whole path of B^* upwards and has no implications for its slope. This can be seen more explicitly if we consider the special case in which exhaustive government spending g and the tax base w ("income") grow steadily at the rates G_g and G_w respectively (clearly $G_g > G_w$ presents some problem if w is interpreted as national income and the economy is closed).

Then the values of permanent income and public expenditure are given by

$$w_t^p = w_t r/(r - G_w) \tag{4a}$$

$$g_t^p = g_t r/(r - G_g) \tag{4b}$$

whence, assuming $r > G_g, G_w$, (1) and (3) become

$$B_t = \bar{\tau} w_t (1 + G_w)/(r - G_w) - g_t(1 + G_g)/(r - G_g) \qquad (5)$$

and

$$\bar{\tau} = \frac{g_0}{w_0} \frac{r - G_w}{r - G_g} \frac{1 + G_g}{1 + G_w} + \frac{B_0}{w_0} \frac{r - G_w}{1 + G_w} \qquad (6)$$

From (5)

$$\frac{B_t}{w_t} = \frac{\bar{\tau}(1 + G_w)}{(r - G_w)} - \frac{g_0}{w_0} \frac{(1 + G_g)^t}{(1 + G_w)} \frac{1 + G_g}{r - G_g} \qquad (7a)$$

and

$$\frac{B_t}{g_t} = \frac{\bar{\tau} w_0}{g_0} \frac{(1 + G_w)^t}{(1 + G_g)} \frac{(1 + G_w)}{(r - G_w)} - \frac{1 + G_g}{r - G_g} \qquad (7b)$$

If the tax base, (income, w) grows faster than public expenditure ($G_w > G_g$) the term $(1 + G_g)/(1 + G_w)^t$ in (7a) tends to zero and B_t/w_t tends to $(1 + G_w)/(r - G_w)$ as t tends to infinity.

In the other case ($G_g > G_w$) the corresponding term in (7b) tends to zero while B_t/g_t tends to $- 1 + G_g$ – while B_t/w_t goes to $- \infty$.

Thus the sign of the asymptotic debt/revenue or debt/expenditure ratio depends crucially on the relative long-run growth rates of the tax base and expenditure, and is not sensitive to the initial conditions, which only determine the constant tax rate τ.

This is not very surprising: if the growth of expenditure exceeds that of the tax base ($G_g > G_w$) in the limit, current revenue contributes a negligible proportion of expenditure which must be financed by interest arising on a *negative* public debt which grows at the same rate (G_g) as expenditure. In the other case ($G_w > G_g$) public expenditure asymptotically absorbs a negligible proportion of revenue which must increasingly go to service the debt.

This may serve to reinforce the first and third of Pagano's conclusions on p. 162. The second is that the debt should cushion deterministic swings in revenue at given tax rates, or in revenue requirements. Stochastic models, in which the enlarged deficit may more naturally be described as a policy response, are only slightly more complicated and broadly confirm this conclusion. They do, however, provide scope for arguments of the kind that if it were necessary to raise revenue to service an enlarged debt that would do more damage than a reduction of similar size would do good (and this becomes increasingly true as the maximum feasible revenue is approached); therefore a risk-averse government would have a bias towards a falling debt ratio – even though it would allow the ratio to rise in fiscal bad times.

Given the non-monetary models of this paper, non-contingent bonds are implicitly indexed to the price level. Moreover as there are no external shocks to the public finances (wars, famines) the scope for contingent bonds is very limited.

Pagano considers introducing an instrument whose return is negatively correlated with that on equities. I have several reservations about this analysis. I would prefer a more explicit general equilibrium model in which the production technology and the source of the randomness of equity returns were fully specified. Is equity, or capital, the relevant market portfolio? What about human capital, GNP or consumption? Finally, cost savings from a lower mean yield on government debt are said to be used to (stochastically) reduce the debt. How long does this process continue? It cannot go on for ever without violating the budget constraint. It can only stop if taxes are cut or expenditure raised. Why not operate the rule for doing this from the start?

A penalty for formulating questions clearly is that one's discussant can check whether they have been answered. Pagano asks a question about the maturity of debt which he does not address directly. The fact that his models do not introduce either productive capital or money and inflation, which might enable one to endogenize real and nominal interest rates and corresponding yield curves, is a major obstacle but, as he points out, the previous analysis may be extensible to this case.

The United Kingdom has a long tradition of maintaining the substantial maturity of its debt. In part this reflects the pattern of demand from long-term investing institutions such as pension funds. This demand, however, has not typically been so strong that long-term funding could easily be justified as minimizing service costs. Another consideration is that to allow the maturity of the debt to shorten complicates its management and the conduct of monetary policy by increasing the turn-over of the debt. More important probably is the feeling that a shorter debt is more liquid, more nearly monetized, and more likely to be spent with inflationary consequences.

The evidence for these fears is, however, not clear cut. On the one hand both theoretical and empirical specifications of demand functions typically use current values of wealth without an additional liquidity factor. On the other hand problems of availability and accuracy of data have lead many studies to rely on liquid assets rather than comprehensive wealth.

If one's concern is with inflation, it is nominal wealth that matters and the shorter the borrowing to finance a given deficit the greater the increase in nominal wealth is likely to be. This is for several reasons. Firstly, if the yield curve is upward sloping, and the short-term debt is expected to be rolled over, the tax liability to finance it is reduced. Secondly, shorter non-indexed debt is a closer substitute for money, the velocity of which is likely to rise, raising all nominal prices, if the money supply is held fixed.

These arguments are, of course, inconsistent with Stiglitz' financial irrelevance results but these are, as Pagano points out, extensions of the Barro "equivalence theorem" which implies that no public sector debt adds to private sector wealth. If the assumptions for that result, including capital market perfection and dynastic altruism, are relaxed the arguments above can be sustained.

A separate consideration yet more difficult to introduce into this kind of model is a concern for the structure of the financial liabilities of firms. They may move shorter when the maturity of government debt rises and vice versa and a shorter liability structure may be interpreted as a weakening of balance sheets. (See, for example, B.M. Friedman 1987.)

A rather different reason for concern about the maturity of nominal debt relates to revaluation effects and the adjustment of debt service costs for the effect of inflation in eroding the real value of the principal. Suppose that the short- (and long-) term real interest rates is a constant (r) so that the short nominal rate $S = r + \pi$. Then if the debt D is all short the real cost of service is $rD = SD - \pi D$ and the inflation adjustment to the nominal interest bill is indeed πD. Suppose now that the debt consists of perpetuities. Under the simplest expectations hypothesis of the yield curve and rational expectations the real cost of service is still rD where D is valued at market prices, but the nominal service cost is LD where L is the nominal long rate and differs from S if the inflation rate is expected to change. Thus $rD = LD - (\pi + L - S)D$ and the inflation adjustment has to incorporate not only the current rate of inflation π but also its expected evolution reflected (on our special assumptions) in the long-short nominal interest differential $L - S$.

This is not merely a problem of statistical adjustment but becomes an operational difficulty if the authorities' inflation expectations differ from those of the markets. Consider a government which has long nominal debt outstanding and is determined to reduce inflation faster when the markets expect it to. Such a government would see long nominal debt as being more costly than short. For reasons mentioned above, however, a resort to shorter instruments could easily fuel inflation fears and raise all rates. This may be another reason for indexation to the price level – over and above those advanced by Pagano.

In the case of both indexed and nominal debt there is another issue. Where it is recognized that there may be shocks to public finance, as on the outbreak of a war, there will, in a closed economy, generally be an impact effect on the capital/labor ratio as men join the army or labor supply is affected by tax rate changes. The changed factor proportions will affect the short-run real interest rate directly and long-run rates rather differently.

There is thus an impact on citizens' wealth which may interact with their labor supply decisions. Thus a long-term bond may have some of the features of a contingent bond and this property may enable a higher level of welfare to be achieved.

REFERENCES

Barro, R.J. (1974), "Are Government Bonds Net Wealth?" *Journal of Political Economy*, 82, December.
Flemming, J.S. (1987a), "Debt and Taxes in War and Peace: the Case of a Small Open Economy," in *Private Saving and Public Debt*, edited by M. Boskin, J.S. Flemming and S. Gorini. Oxford: Blackwell.
  (1987b), "Debt and Taxes in War and Peace: The Closed Economy Case," in *The Economics of Public Debt*, edited by K. Arrow and M. Boskin, for the IEA. London: Macmillan.
Friedman, B.M. (1987), "New Directions in the Relativity Between Public and Private Debt," NBER Working Paper No. 2186 March.

Discussion

LUIGI SPAVENTA

Marco Pagano's rigorous and lucid paper offers an important contribution to the debate on debt management, especially with reference to the Italian case. He uses economic theory and models to provide meaningful answers to two sets of questions. The first arises when a government inherits a large stock of debt from the past: does the size of *past* debt affect the government's choice as to the optimal path of *future* deficits, so that the government should first aim at reducing the debt to some target level? The second set of issues regards the menu of debt instruments to be issued, with two objectives in mind: the minimization of the cost of debt for the State (the "practical view," as Pagano calls it) and welfare maximization. Many questions receive relevant answers from Pagano's analysis; some others are left unanswered.

As for the first problem, Pagano examines cases in which financial policy is effective, either because it reallocates income across generations, or because agents are subject to a liquidity constraint and can only borrow at an interest rate higher than that at which the government can, or because taxes can only be collected at a cost. In all three cases Pagano's story starts at $t = 0$, with an arbitrary stock of debt B_0 inherited from the past: as from that date the government, subject to its intertemporal budget constraint, embarks upon an optimal plan defining the path of future deficits and taxes. Under perfectly acceptable assumptions as to the objective functions of the government in the three cases, it is shown that in general deficits should behave anticyclically, with respect to income and procyclically, with respect to fluctuations of public expenditure around its permanent level, *and* that this optimal behavior is independent of the initial stock of debt (or at least does not require that such stock be brought down to some lower level).

The conclusion that the feasibility and the outcome of optimal policies are unaffected by the initial level of outstanding debt is indeed remarkable. Spendthrift governments of the past can be blamed for having

173

deviated from optimal behavior, but not for having made life difficult for their successors, no matter how high the level of debt which the successors inherited.

As it turns out, however, it is *not* true that Pagano's model yields this unqualified conclusion. It is not, because, at the outset, Pagano introduces a feasibility constraint and then forgets about it. The constraint is that taxes should not exceed the income they are levied upon, on the assumption that only endowments, and not interest income, are taxable: once it is brought to bear, the initial level of debt becomes relevant. Thus, consider Pagano's first model, dealing with reallocation of income across generations. The optimal path of taxes, his equation (9) is:

$$\tau_t^* = (w_t - w_t^p) + g_t^p + rB_{t-1}^*$$

where the first term on the right is the deviation of income from its permanent level and the second is the permanent component of public expenditure. It is readily seen that the constraint that taxes should not exceed the tax base (Pagano's equation (3): $\tau_i \leq w_i$) sets a limit to the initial stock of debt compatible with a *feasible* optimal path of taxes. Such a limit is defined by:

$$B_{t-1} \leq \frac{w_t^p - g_t^p}{r}$$

The initial debt should not exceed the difference between the present discounted values of the future streams of the economy's resources and government's expenditure (as follows from the definitions of w^p and g^p in equation (6) in the paper).

Note however that the feasibility of the optimal plan would be unaffected by the initial level of debt, if the constraint prescribed that taxes should not exceed the entire gross disposable income, and not just the endowments, *i.e.*: $\tau_i \leq w_i + rB_0$. Feasibility is always insured now, as the constraint only requires $g_t^p \leq w_t^p$. This is a corollary of the proposition that, when gross disposable income is considered, the existence of an upper bound to debt growth is a sufficient, but not a necessary condition for the respect of the intertemporal budget constraint in a model with rational agents[1].

But even in this case the initial level of debt becomes relevant again (and all the more relevant in Pagano's case), if the maximum burden of taxation society is ready to bear is (as is likely to be) less than 100 percent. Now the constraint is $\tau_i \leq \alpha_1 w_i + \alpha_2 rB_{i-1}$ with $\alpha_1 < 1$, and $\alpha_2 = \alpha_1$ in the above case and $\alpha_2 = 0$ in Pagano's case. Then the maximum initial stock of debt compatible with the optimal plan becomes:

$$B_{t-1} \leq \frac{\alpha_1 w_t^p - g_t^p}{(1 - \alpha_2) r}$$

if we neglect cyclical fluctuations of income and set $w_t^p = w_t$.

Admittedly, the numbers can be quite large: but not as large as in Pagano's case. Thus, merely by way of example, consider some numbers relating to the Italian case. Keeping the ratio to GDP of non-interest expenditure net of non-tax and contributions revenues and net of seignorage from growth and money creation constant at its 1986 level (approximately 34 percent) and setting $\alpha = 0.45$ (with an increase of over 10 points from its current value), the maximum level of the debt ratio compatible with the feasibility of an optimal plan would range from 2.75, with a real interest rate of 4 percent, to 1.8, with a real interest rate of 6 percent. Conversely, keeping the non-monetary debt ratio constant at its 1986 level (0.72) would require an increase in the tax burden between 2.4 and 3.8 points. Note that the ex-post real cost of debt was about 5.5 percent in 1986.

I have only considered Pagano's first model: but the condition that the initial stock of debt should not exceed a maximum level for an optimal plan to be feasible is readily established for his other two models as well[2]. There is thus a sense in which governments wishing to undertake an optimal financial plan may have to worry about the level of the debt they inherit from the past and may wish to achieve a once-and-for-all reduction of such level in order to insure the feasibility of the optimal path of taxation.

In his analysis of the optimal choice of debt instruments Pagano shows that the cost of debt could be reduced by innovations, such as indexed bonds insuring a constant real yield, foreign denominated bonds, or assets with a yield negatively correlated to that of equity capital. In Pagano's view, the first possibility, besides reducing the cost of debt, is always beneficial on welfare grounds. He carefully models the third possibility and shows that it unequivocally "raises the expected value of any reasonable social welfare function" in the long run, while this may not be the case in the short run. On the whole, he has much to say in favor of the "practical view" that the cost of debt could be reduced by suitable innovations in the menu of debt instruments and that this target should be pursued by public policy.

If this is the case (as I am inclined to believe, along with Marco

Pagano), we are left here with another unanswered question. Why, at least in Italy, have practitioners of debt policy (the monetary authorities) not practiced the "practical view," if it is beneficial on welfare grounds as well as reducing the cost of the debt? Is it a case of irrationality (or malevolence) on the part of the authorities or are the models used inadequate to capture their motivations and their behavior?

I am unable even to suggest a satisfactory answer. But it may be worth while mentioning two reasons behind the resistance of the Italian authorities to go beyond financial indexation on short-term nominal rates. The first is the view, based on Latin American and other experiences, that other forms of indexation represent a surrender to inflation, coupled with the feeling that it was politically impractical to index financial assets while attempting to reduce wage indexation. The second is the fear that, insofar as indexation reduces *nominal* interest payments, this would provide a tempting possibility to governments and Parliaments (unaware of inflation accounting) to use the apparent improvement in the budget for raising *real* non-interest expenditures. Right or wrong, this is the "practical view" which has so far prevailed.

NOTES

1 See B.T. McCallum (1984), "Are Bond-Financed Deficits Inflationary? A Ricardian Analysis," *Journal of Political Economy*, Vol. 92. For a discussion of the implications of indefinite debt growth on the path of taxation, see L. Spaventa (1987), "The Growth of Public Debt: Sustainability, Fiscal Rules, and Monetary Rules," *Staff Papers*, International Monetary Fund, Vol. 34.

2 In the second model the condition is

$$B_0 \leq \frac{w_{1t}R + w_{2t+1} - g}{r}$$

while in the third model the condition is identical to that of the first model.

5 Capital controls and public finance the experience in Italy*

ALBERTO GIOVANNINI

1 Introduction

The current policy debate in Italy is, appropriately, focusing on the government debt and the constraints it imposes on macroeconomic and monetary policy. This paper studies aspects of the linkage between public finances and capital mobility with special attention to the Italian experience. Its purpose is to provide a framework that can be used to analyze the effects of the recent liberalization of international capital flows on public finances, and to discuss more generally the appropriate forms of regulation of international capital flows. The paper stresses the importance of international capital flows triggered by changes in taxes in different countries, which have largely been ignored in the macroeconomic literature. Furthermore, it shows that the "public finance" approach to the regulation of international capital flows can provide a coherent framework for evaluating alternative policies.

To organize ideas, section 2 presents a theoretical model that illustrates the macroeconomic implications of tax evasion through international capital flows. The model borrows heavily from Giovannini (1987b), and analyzes capital controls in the presence of other unavoidable distortions, represented by capital-income taxes. Section 3 discusses the historical experience: surprisingly, during the interwar period balance-of-payments crises were often associated with strains in the tax system and could have been motivated by the desire of wealth holders to avoid taxes, both present and prospective. Section 4 deals with current policy questions. First, it summarizes the experience in the post-Second World War period. Especially during the 1970s, the problems of monetary control in an open economy with an exchange-rate target provide the most appropriate justification for the regulators' attitude towards capital controls. Next, the "public finance" approach is applied to evaluate three common justifications for capital controls. The section

177

is concluded with a discussion of the issues raised by the recent liberalization of capital flows in Italy.

2   Capital mobility as tax evasion: a macroeconomic analysis

In this section I study a version of the model of government debt of Diamond (1965), where, as in Persson (1985), domestic residents trade in goods and assets with the rest of the world.[1] Unlike these models, I take the case where lump-sum taxes are not available: only income from financial assets is taxed. This is also analyzed by Diamond (1970), though in the context of a closed economy.

The model is designed to analyze the macroeconomic consequences of capital flight to evade domestic taxes. If foreign assets' income is tax-free, either by law or because the law cannot be enforced, any tax increase on domestic assets' income will be met by an attempt by domestic residents to shift towards foreign securities.[2] This flight of capital will affect the wage rate, savings, and welfare. Whether these capital flows are legal or not is irrelevant for the results in this section, as long as domestic residents can avoid paying taxes on income from foreign assets. Perhaps most realistic is a case where income from foreign assets is taxable, but cannot be detected. This condition characterizes countries with relatively underdeveloped financial and tax systems, where the purchase of foreign assets is not always recorded by the authorities.[3]

It is well known that capital controls impose distortions on the relative prices faced by a country's savers and investors. Thus the standard argument against capital controls is economic efficiency: we should avoid as much as possible the distortions arising when the market mechanism is not permitted to work freely. This argument, however, relies on the very restrictive assumption of no other inefficiencies in the economy. In the presence of unavoidable distortions, eliminating controls on international capital flows can actually be undesirable from the viewpoint of the whole economy.[4] Therefore the "economic efficiency" argument needs to be modified to take into account distortions.[5] This section evaluates the case for capital controls as second-best solutions in the presence of unavoidable distortions, that originate from the need to finance government spending.

Consider an economy where people live two periods. In the first period of their life, they inelastically supply labor, earning a wage w, which they allocate to consumption and savings for their retirement in the second period, as in the life-cycle model of Modigliani and Brumberg (1954). Per-capita consumption of the young born at time t is denoted by c_{1t}, and consumption of the old born at t is c_{2t+1}. Population grows at the rate n:

total population at t, N_t, equals $(1 + n)^t N_0$. In this economy there is only one good, that can be traded with the rest of the world. Current-account surpluses or deficits are financed at the world real interest rate r^*, which I assume exogenous and constant. A given foreign interest rate means that the rest of the world requires a certain rate of return on investments in the domestic country. Foreign residents do not pay taxes to the domestic government; an alternative assumption is that all taxes paid by foreign residents to the domestic government are instantaneously and costlessly rebated through an international tax treaty. Even in the absence of distortionary taxes, it is well known that the competitive equilibrium in this model is not necessarily dynamically efficient. In the analysis that follows, I avoid the problems arising when competitive equilibria are Pareto-inefficient by assuming that $r^* > n$.

Every period, the young purchase titles of ownership to the domestic capital stock from the old, and bonds from the government; they also trade foreign bonds with the rest of the world.[6] The old receive interest income from their domestic assets and pay taxes on it. They receive interest from – or pay interest to – the rest of the world, depending on the debt position of the country. They sell government bonds back to the government, and titles of ownership to the domestic capital stock to the young. In addition, they settle the principal payments with the rest of the world. The net receipts from these operations provide for consumption.

The consumption, saving, and portfolio allocation problem of the young is formally stated as follows:

$$\text{MAX } U(c_{1t}, c_{2t+1}) \tag{1}$$

subject to:

$$w_t - c_{1t} = s_t \tag{2}$$

$$s_t = (1 + n)[k_{t+1} + d_{t+1} + f_{t+1}] \tag{3}$$

$$c_{2t+1} = (1 + n)[k_{t+1}(1 + r_{t+1}(1 - \tau_{t+1})) + d_{t+1}(1 + r^d_{t+1}(1 - \tau_{t+1})) + f_{t+1}(1 + r^*)] \tag{4}$$

where all the lower case letters stand for per-capita quantities. d denotes holding of government debt, k is the per-capita capital stock (or capital-labor ratio), and f denotes (positive or negative) holdings of foreign assets. r is the rate of return on domestic capital. I assume that interest on government debt, r^d, is taxed, although, as I will show below, perfect substitutability among all assets makes this assumption irrelevant. The factor $(1 + n)$ in equations (3) and (4) is present since the stocks of assets at time $t + 1$ are purchased with the savings of the young at t. The aggregate accumulation equation is:

$$S_t = K_{t+1} + D_{t+1} + F_{t+1} \tag{5}$$

dividing both sides by N_t, equation (3) is obtained. The solution of problems (1)–(4) implies that, in every period, the after-tax returns on domestic and foreign assets have to be equal in equilibrium:

$$r_t(1 - \tau_t) = r^* \tag{6}$$

$$r_t^d(1 - \tau_t) = r^* \tag{7}$$

and implies the following condition for the optimal lifetime consumption plan:

$$U_1(c_{1t}, c_{2t+1}) = (1 + r^*)U_2(c_{1t}, c_{2t+1}) \tag{8}$$

Substituting (8) into (2)–(4) I obtain the savings function: $s(w_t, r^*)$. Optimal consumption is then substituted in (1) to get the indirect utility function, $V(w_t, r^*)$.

Output is produced with a neoclassical constant-returns-to-scale production function, using capital and labor, $Y(K_t, N_t)$. Per-capita output is $y(k_t)$. A competitive output supply industry ensures that the return to capital is equal to the marginal productivity of capital, $r = y'(k)$, and that per capita wages are equal to $y(k) - y'(k)k$. Cost minimization and constant returns to scale imply the following factor-price frontier:

$$w_t = \Phi(y'(k_t)) \tag{9}$$

I now turn to the government budget constraint. The increase in government debt is equal to the excess of interest expenses over tax revenues:

$$D_{t+1} - D_t = r_t^d(1 - \tau_t)D_t - \tau_t K_t r_t \tag{10}$$

Dividing both sides of (10) by N_t and using (6) and (7) we can express the budget constraint as follows:

$$d_{t+1}(1 + n) = (1 + r^*)d_t - \tau_t r^* k_t/(1 - \tau_t) \tag{11}$$

Equation (11) proves that, in this model, taxing interest payments on government debt has no effects on budget deficits. This result is a direct implication of the absence of uncertainty. Under perfect foresight, utility maximization makes all assets perfect substitutes. Changes in tax rates on any assets bring about an equal change in their equilibrium returns, and this maintains the equality of after-tax yields. This result would of course also apply to the case where different assets are taxed at different rates. Thus the effects of taxing government securities on the government budget depend entirely on the degree of substitutability of government securities and other assets.

2.1   The macroeconomic consequences of capital flight

The general equilibrium effects of capital flight can be illustrated by studying the consequences of an increase in government debt originating, for example, from a lump-sum transfer to the young. In this model the dynamic effects of changes in fiscal policy are straightforward to compute[7] and stability conditions are always met. However, since the full description of the dynamics does not add substantially to the main argument in this section, I omit it, and concentrate only on steady states, characterized by constant stocks of per-capita government debt, $\bar{d}$.[8]

An increase in public debt is associated with higher taxes, insofar as the taxing capacity of the government is not exhausted, and government revenues go up with an increase in the tax rate. These higher taxes trigger capital outflows, that continue until the after-tax rates of return on domestic and foreign investments are equalized.[9] The main effect of an increase in government debt is to crowd out the domestic capital stock through tax evasion.[10] The change in the domestic stock of capital affects the real wage, savings and the current account.

The long-run cumulative response of the current account to a change in the stock of government debt is obtained by solving the model, and computing the derivative of the net foreign asset position of domestic residents with respect to the steady-state government debt.[11]

$$\frac{df}{d\bar{d}} = (r^* - n) \frac{1 - k|y''| \dfrac{s_w}{1 + n}}{k|y''| - \dfrac{r^* \tau}{(1 - \tau)}} - 1 \qquad (12)$$

where s_w is the partial derivative of the savings function with respect to the wage rate. Under the assumption that a higher tax rate increases tax revenues, the denominator on the right hand side of (12) is positive. If savings are given, an increase in the stock of government debt leads investors to substitute it for foreign assets. This is the interpretation of the -1 term on the right hand side of (12). Capital flight, however, decreases the desired stock of domestic capital, and therefore reduces the fall in foreign assets in response to higher government debt. This last effect is mitigated by the lowering of the wage rate and savings, caused by a lower stock of capital: hence the first term in (12).

To compute the steady-state welfare effect of an increase in government debt, I differentiate the indirect utility function, after substituting for the change in the real wage arising from the general-equilibrium response of domestic investment.[12]

$$
\frac{dV}{d\bar{d}} = \frac{\partial V}{\partial w}\frac{dw}{d\bar{d}} = - V_w \frac{(r^* - n)\,k\,|\,y''(k)\,|}{\left(k\,|\,y''(k)\,| - \dfrac{\tau}{1-\tau}r^* \right)}
\tag{13}
$$

The $(r^* - n)$ term in equation (13) indicates that, when the interest rate equals the rate of growth of population, changes in the stock of government debt do not require any increase in steady state taxes, since the interest bill is exactly covered by the issue of new debt that is necessary to keep per-capita holdings of government securities constant. When $r^* = n$, changes in the stock of government debt affect welfare only in the transition to the new steady state. The second term in the denominator of (13) stands for the second-order excess burden associated with distortionary taxation: see, for example, Atkinson and Stiglitz (1980, p. 368). In the presence of tax evasion, distortions in the intertemporal terms of trade are absent. An increase in debt and taxes crowds out the capital stock and lowers welfare through distortions in the production side of the economy.

In order to assess the welfare costs of tax evasion through capital flight we need to compare the country studied above to one where this form of tax evasion is prevented by capital controls. Capital controls can be a prohibition of international borrowing and lending, or a tax on net income from foreign assets. The two restrictions are not equivalent in this model, because of the presence of two imperfections: the difference between the world interest rate and the "biological" rate of interest and the distortionary tax on income from capital. A prohibition of international lending and borrowing does not appear to be a realistic form of capital controls, since constantly balancing current accounts are never observed in practice.[13]

I analyze here the case where income from foreign assets is taxed at the same rate as income from domestic assets.[14] This restriction eliminates all incentives to substitute domestic with foreign assets for the purpose of tax evasion.[15] When all income from domestic and foreign assets is taxed at the same rate, the budget constraint of domestic residents needs to be changed as follows:

$$c_{2t+1} = (1 + n)[k_{t+1}(1 + r_{t+1}(1 - \tau_{t+1})) \\ + d_{t+1}(1 + r^d_{t+1}(1 - \tau_{t+1})) + f_{t+1}(1 + r^*(1 - \tau_{t+1}))]$$
(4')

Furthermore, portfolio equilibrium implies that the return on capital equals the foreign rate of interest, and the rate of interest on domestic government securities:

$$r_t = r^*$$
(6')

$$r^d_t = r^*$$
(7')

Condition (6'), together with the first order condition from cost minimization of firms, fixes the capital stock and the wage rate independently of changes in fiscal policy. Savings decisions are now determined by the after-tax real rate of interest:

$$U_1(c_{1t}, c_{2t+1}) = (1 + r^*(1 - \tau_{t+1}))U_2(c_{1t}, c_{2t+1})$$
(8')

Solving equation (8') and using the budget constraint, yields the following savings equation: $s(w_t, r^*(1 - \tau_{t+1}))$.

Finally, the government budget constraint becomes:

$$d_{t+1}(1 + n) = (1 + r^*(1 - \tau_t))d_t - \tau_t r^*(k_t + f_t)$$
(11')

What are the effects of changes in the stock of government debt when capital flight for tax evasion is avoided? Consider first the response of net foreign assets:

$$\frac{df}{d\bar{d}} = - \left[1 + \frac{\dfrac{s_r}{(1 + n)}(r^* - n)}{k + \bar{d} + f - \dfrac{\tau r^* s_r}{(1 + n)}} \right]$$
(12')

The denominator in (12') is positive under the assumption that the government revenues are an increasing function of the tax rate. The increase in the tax rate associated with the higher steady-state government debt lowers the after-tax real interest rate faced by domestic residents, but leaves the real wage unaffected. If the elasticity of savings to the real interest rate is non-negative, the increase in foreign indebtedness after an increase in government debt is larger in the case where tax evasion is prevented. Therefore avoiding tax evasion can have undesirable effects on a country's net external debt. From a policy perspective, however, the relevant magnitude is *gross* international indebtedness, since the assets of those who have exported capital to evade taxes cannot be seized. The experience of Latin American countries in this respect is instructive.[16]

The welfare effects of changes in the government debt are computed here first by obtaining the long-run, general-equilibrium response of the tax rate to a change in $\bar{d}$, and then by differentiating the indirect utility function:[17]

$$\frac{dV}{d\bar{d}} = -r^* \frac{\partial \tau}{\partial \bar{d}} V_r = - \frac{(r^* - n) V_r}{k + \bar{d} + f - \dfrac{\tau r^* s_r}{(1 + n)}} \qquad (13')$$

A comparison of equations (13') and (13) reveals the basic difference between a regime with capital controls and the case of capital flight for tax evasion. When domestic residents are taxed on all assets at the same rate, changes in taxes affect the intertemporal terms of trade, but leave the productive sector of the economy unaffected. In the presence of tax evasion, changes in taxes generate distortions in the productive sector of the economy, but leave the intertemporal terms of trade unaffected.

Therefore, once all general-equilibrium effects of capital flight for the purpose of tax evasion are taken into account, the case for or against capital controls is not clearcut. The analysis, however, can highlight the different types of distortions present under the two regimes. In the presence of tax evasion, increases in tax revenue bring about distortions on the production side; on the other hand, when tax evasion through capital flight is eliminated, changes in tax revenue are associated with distortions of the intertemporal rate of substitution.[18]

Which of the two types of distortions is less desirable from society's viewpoint remains an empirical question. There is, however, a reason to believe that changes in the intertemporal terms of trade like those that would be empirically observed in the presence of government debt – in a regime where all asset income is taxed at the same rate – would have a smaller welfare effect than the changes in factor productivities caused by capital flight: this presumption comes from the empirical evidence suggesting that the intertemporal elasticity of substitution in consumption is extremely low (see Hall 1985, for example).[19]

2.2 The inflation tax

In this section I sketch an extension of the model to study the effects of an inflation tax. When governments have the option to monetize current deficits, it is often asked whether capital flight makes it "harder" to raise a given amount of tax revenue, and thus compels authorities to make a heavier use of the inflation tax.

To study these questions, I need assumptions about the way money enters into the economy. The hypothesis is that real money balances enter in the utility function of consumers. In the case where income from foreign assets is not taxed, the maximization problem of an individual born at time t becomes

$$\text{MAX } U(c_{1t}, c_{2t+1}) + v(m_{t+1}) \tag{14}$$

s.t.: $$p_t(1 + n)(k_{t+1} + d_{t+1} + f_{t+1}) + h_{t+1}(1 + n) = p_t(w_t - c_{1t}) \tag{15}$$

$$(1 + n)[k_{t+1}(1 + r_{t+1}(1 - \tau_{t+1})) + d_{t+1}(1 + r_{t+1}^d(1 - \tau_{t+1})) \\ + f_{t+1}(1 + r^*)] \\ + (1 + n)m_{t+1} = c_{2t+1} \tag{16}$$

where m and h are per-capita real and nominal money balances, respectively, and p_t is the price level. Equation (15) reveals that money is acquired by the young (from the old and from the government) to carry wealth from one period to the next. Although money is completely dominated by productive capital as a store of value, its utility services specified in equation (14) justify its coexistence with real assets in private portfolios. Including money in the utility function is equivalent to specifying a transactions technology that makes it less costly to use money – instead of other assets – for payments.

Since there is only one good in the model and perfect price flexibility, the "Law of One Price" holds: normalizing the foreign price level to 1, p_t becomes the nominal exchange rate. The first-period budget constraint in real terms is obtained dividing both sides of (15) by p_t:

$$(1 + n)(k_{t+1} + d_{t+1} + f_{t+1}) \\ + m_{t+1}(1 + \pi_{t+1})(1 + n) = w_t - c_{1t} \tag{17}$$

where $\pi_{t+1} = p_{t+1}/p_t - 1$. Solution of (14), (16) and (17) yields the following savings function and indirect utility function:

$$s(w_t, r^*, \pi_{t+1}), V(w_t, r^*, \pi_{t+1})$$

together with the portfolio equilibrium conditions and money demand equation:

$$r_{t+1}(1 - \tau_{t+1}) = r^* \tag{18}$$

$$r^d_{t+1}(1 - \tau_{t+1}) = r^* \tag{19}$$

$$h_{t+1}/p_{t+1} = m(w_t, r^*, \pi_{t+1}) \tag{20}$$

The partial derivative of the savings function with respect to the rate of inflation is ambiguous, since the rate of inflation has a role analogous to that of the real interest rate; on the other hand, indirect utility is a decreasing function of the rate of inflation. Money demand can be shown to be an increasing function of the wage rate and a decreasing function of the rate of inflation. The partial derivative with respect to r^* is ambiguous: if however $[U(\cdot) + v(\cdot)]$ is of the family of functions satisfying the gross-substitutes property, money demand is decreasing in r^*.[20]

Government budget deficits are financed by both issuing bonds and printing money. Letting uppercase letters denote the aggregates of the corresponding lowercase letters, and using equations (18) and (19), I obtain the government budget constraint:

$$(H_{t+1} - H_t)/p_{t+1} + D_{t+1} = (1 + r^*)D_t - \tau_t K_t r^*/(1 - \tau_t) \tag{21}$$

Equation (21) is expressed in per-capita terms as follows:

$$m_{t+1}(1 + n)\mu_t/(1 + \mu_t) + d_{t+1}(1 + n) = (1 + r^*)d_t - \tau_t k_t r^*/(1 - \tau_t) \tag{22}$$

where μ is the rate of growth of the aggregate money stock.

To close the model we need assumptions about the exchange-rate regime. Under flexible exchange rates, the monetary authority chooses the path of the money stock (and consequently μ) while the nominal exchange rate p is determined by market forces. Under managed exchange rates the path of p is chosen by the monetary authority, and the nominal money stock passively accommodates the money demand equation: I study here the latter regime. This eliminates the indeterminacies associated with floating exchange rates, and arising from the fact that money demand depends on both the level and the rate of change of the exchange rate.[21]

Would the government tend to inflate more in the presence of capital flight than in a regime of capital controls?[22] Consider, as in the previous analysis, the long-run effects of an increase in the stock of government debt when only income from domestic assets is taxed, as opposed to the case where all income from assets is taxed. In the former case, an increase in income taxes lowers the wage rate but leaves the real interest rate relevant for savings decisions unaffected. In the latter case, the wage rate is unaffected, whereas the intertemporal terms of trade decrease. The money demand equation (20) shows that a decrease in the wage rate, other things being equal, lowers money demand; on the other hand, a decrease in the intertemporal terms of trade increases demand for money. This implies that under capital controls a lower rate of inflation is needed to raise a given revenue by money creation, when income taxes are raised.

Thus demand for money shifts downward whenever domestic residents can substitute away from domestic assets for the purpose of avoiding taxes on domestic assets' income. This result is a general one, and has been noted in the context of other money-demand models. Dornbusch and Giovannini (1987), for example, argue that inward shifts in the demand for money function are the most likely effects of liberalization of international capital movements in developing countries. These shifts occur mainly because of substitution away from domestic demand deposits towards foreign currency deposits. The model in this section provides some microeconomic justifications for this claim. Money demand increases with capital controls because the return on the alternative asset is lower in the presence of controls. This observation suggests that countries with capital controls need a lower inflation rate to generate a given tax revenue.

2.3   Dynamic inconsistency

The model presented above is solved under the assumption that the government does not seek to optimize tax collection over time. The increase in government debt was implicitly assumed to be exogenous. This assumption overlooks one important aspect of the interaction between the government and private savers: once wealth is accumulated, taxation of wealth has a relatively low social cost, since its supply is inelastic (the stock of accumulated wealth is given).

The government has the incentive to raise a capital levy on the stock of accumulated wealth, whenever the capital levy is not anticipated by the public. As shown by Kydland and Prescott (1977), Fischer (1980) and Calvo (1987), reneging on any given announced sequence of taxes is in general the optimal ex-post policy. The public's knowledge of the government's incentives to tax accumulated wealth can give rise to an additional justification for capital flight. If the government cannot seize assets of domestic residents held abroad, investors who recognize its incentives would seek to purchase foreign assets up to the point where the government is prevented from exercising the option to tax accumulated wealth. Thus the dynamic inconsistency of government tax policies is an additional motivation for capital flight.

3   Capital controls in Italy: the public finance connection

In this section I provide a historical overview of Italian restrictions on international capital flows. The discussion starts with the interwar period, since the basic structure of regulations affecting capital flows in the post-Second World War period is inherited from the interwar years.

Wealth holders' fears of heavy taxation or expropriation, and public concern that capital flight illegally conceals large riches from taxation and takes them away from more productive activities at home, are recurring themes in popular debates on the issue of international capital controls in Italy. One objective of this section is to determine whether these "public emotions" are justified, i.e. whether international capital flows triggered by changes in current or anticipated taxes are significant from a macroeconomic perspective.

To "prove" the empirical importance of capital flows for tax evasion or tax avoidance is however an extremely difficult task, for a number of reasons. First, as I have argued in section 2, international capital flows that avoid domestic taxes are in many cases illegal, and therefore hard to detect in the data. This problem is compounded by the absence of complete balance-of-payments statistics for Italy in the interwar period. Second, an assumption used in the model of section 2 is that wealth holders diversify portfolios to attain the highest return. Therefore the avoidance of current and future taxes is only one of the motivations for capital flight, the other being expectations of exchange-rate changes.[23] The period I survey in this section is characterized, at times, by extreme political instabilities, during which expectations of future – possibly confiscatory – taxes were likely to be accompanied by expectations of exchange rate devaluations. In these cases, isolating the tax effects is even more problematic.

Notwithstanding these difficulties, the hypothesis that capital flight for fear of taxation did occur in several instances cannot be rejected outright by a first analysis of the events in the 1920s and 1930s.

Table 5.1 GNP and government debt: 1914–25

	GNP (million Italian lire)	Debt (million Italian lire)	Debt/GNP (%)	Floating debt (% total debt)	Consolidated (% total debt)
1914	24044	15766	65.6	5.9	62.9
1915	28137	18695	66.4	14.8	53.1
1916	40479	23857	58.9	17.0	41.6
1917	56389	33694	59.8	26.8	50.7
1918	58893	48402	82.2	34.0	49.1
1919	81276	60213	74.1	42.8	39.1
1920	123900	74496	60.1	29.8	58.1
1921	116100	86482	74.5	36.4	51.3
1922	124100	92856	74.8	39.0	47.9
1923	135500	95544	70.5	37.1	46.7
1924	143000	93163	65.1	35.1	47.9
1925	179600	90848	50.6	30.4	49.1

Sources: GNP: Mitchell (1978).
Debt: Confalonieri and Gatti (1986).

3.1   The 1920s

At the end of the First World War Italy, like other European countries, was plagued by high inflation and high (by historical standards) government debt. The unexpectedly long war had heavily drained the capacity of the government to tax its own citizens, and its ability to finance deficits in the domestic bond markets. The maturity structure of the very high stock of government debt, as shown in Table 5.1, was progressively shifted towards short term notes. The share of current spending financed by taxes went from 94 percent in 1914 to 30 percent in 1918.[24] Furthermore, the monetization of government debt had increased dramatically: the state's advances from the banks of issue rose from 734.9 million lire in December 1914, to 8076.6 million lire at the end of 1922. These, in addition to a large increase of Treasury notes, accounted for a sevenfold increase of circulation from the end of 1914 to the end of 1920.[25]

Government spending in the immediate postwar period was kept high by a system of grain subsidies, subsidies to agricultural cooperatives and to steel producers, that were meant to cope with the increase in unemployment and social unrest associated with the transition from a war economy.

Since during the war the number and types of taxes multiplied, "the fiscal situation in Italy in 1919 was little short of chaotic."[26] In addition, the immediate need to increase revenue prompted authorities to pursue

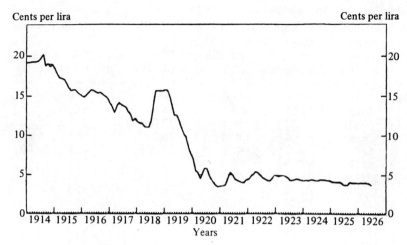

Figure 5.1   Lira exchange rates on New York, 1914–26.
Source: Reproduced from McGuire (1926).

the imposition of a capital levy. The capital levy was publicly debated in Italy throughout 1919: despite wide opposition in Parliament, it was passed in November 1919 with the support of a Liberal-Socialist coalition. The tax was imposed on property valued at the least 50,000 lire, at rates ranging from 4.5 percent to 50 percent. After the imposition of the capital levy, another important measure affecting wealth holders was passed: all private citizens had to register securities they owned. This measure – inspired by the same principle as that of the capital levy, that hidden wealth has to be dragged out into the open – received formidable resistance both within and outside Parliament.

Figure 5.1 and Table 5.2 report data on the lira exchange rate. The lira was not part of the gold standard before the war.[27] The steady depreciations in the early war years prompted the government to constitute the National Institute for Foreign Exchange in December 1917. This body was given the monopoly of foreign exchange transactions and was assigned the task of managing fluctuations of the lira exchange rate through direct market interventions. As shown in Figure 5.1, the war successes of 1918, coupled with a series of loans from the governments of the United States and Britain for the purpose of foreign exchange support,[28] were associated with a sharp improvement in the exchange rate between the second half of 1918 and the beginning of 1919. In March 1919, however, the Foreign Exchange Institute's open market activities were discontinued. Its monopoly of all foreign exchange transactions was ended two months later: at that time the lira exchange

Table 5.2 The lira exchange rates: 1914–24
(monthly averages, percent of par)

	US$	Pound Sterling	SF	FF
1914: June	100	100	100	100
December	102	103	102	103
1915: June	115	113	111	109
December	127	123	124	112
1916: June	123	121	121	108
December	132	130	135	117
1917: June	138	135	143	124
December	160	157	190	145
1918: June	176	173	231	161
December	122	120	130	116
1919: June	155	148	151	125
December	252	199	242	122
1920: June	326	266	309	134
December	552	396	441	170
1921: June	383	300	339	162
December	438	373	440	177
1922: June	388	355	382	177
December	384	363	376	144
1923: June	422	400	392	138
December	446	399	402	121
1924: June	446	395	407	121

Source: Bachi (1925).

rate collapsed dramatically until the second half of 1920. As Table 5.2 shows, the lira exchange rate in New York, for example, went from 122 percent of par in December 1918 to 552 percent of par in December 1920.

Why did the lira collapse in 1919–20? By most contemporary accounts, the lira was clearly overvalued in 1918, thus explaining at least part of the depreciation in the following year. According to Young (1925, p. 374), however, in the years following 1919–20 the lira was below its purchasing parity level. Similar conclusions are reached by Toniolo (1980), whose calculations suggest a 74 percent cumulative real depreciation of the lira between 1918 and 1920: the lira was 42 percent above its purchasing power parity in 1918, and ended 31 percent below the purchasing parity level in 1920.

Another very likely cause of the collapse of the lira is capital flight. As we mentioned above, discussions on the imposition of a capital levy dominated public debate throughout 1919. Savers were further threatened by the securities registration laws. McGuire (1926, p. 99) holds the view that the capital levy *caused* capital flight:

> The chief consequence of the experiment was to stimulate the exportation of capital, and to sharpen the determination of the propertied classes in the country to have done with the succession of coalitions shifting the administrative control of the country from one to the other and disclaiming responsibility for chaotic financial conditions.

Bachi (1925, p. 165), discussing the period from 1918 to 1920, offers the same interpretation:[29]

> ... the disturbances in the economic and political life of the country ... caused in several instances considerable hoarding of notes, while in several other instances substantial amounts of notes and checks were taken abroad either for foreign speculation in Italian currency or because of fear of extraordinary taxation, political disturbances, etc.

The political disturbances mentioned by Bachi were certainly additional, powerful incentives to transfer wealth abroad. The years 1919–20 were dubbed the "red two-years"[30] after the political turmoil, and the episodes of occupation of factories and of farmland by workers and peasants.

Direct quantitative evidence on the actual size of capital flight in 1919–20 is however very hard to obtain. The only estimates I was able to find are reported by Toniolo (1980, p. 94): in the fiscal years 1919–20 and 1920–21 published purchases of foreign securities in Italy shot up to 77 and 148 million lire, respectively, to fall back down to 30 and 11 million lire in the following two fiscal years.[31] Data on central banks' balance sheets indicate that over the years from 1919 to 1921 the combined foreign assets and reserves at the three banks of issue fell by 900 million lire:[32] by comparison, reserves at the three banks of issue increased by 692 million lire in 1916–18 and 150 million lire in 1922–24. However, since the corresponding current account deficits for the three groups of years were 23,187 million lire in 1916–18, 23,327 million lire in 1919–21 and 3,583 million lire in 1922–24, information about reserves needs to be supplemented with data on official capital flows and trade credits, if one is to estimate capital flight. Finally, the depreciation of the lira in 1919–20 is so dramatic, that the volume of capital flight consistent with asset holders' portfolio equilibrium could plausibly be relatively small.

The capital levy did not solve all the problems of Italian public finances. The task of reforming the administration of the tax system was assigned to Alberto Dè Stefani, the finance minister in the first Mussolini government.[33] As shown in Table 5.1, following Dè Stefani's reform, the ratio of debt to GNP decreased significantly, and the maturity com-

Table 5.3 GNP and government debt: 1927–38

Year	GNP (million Italian lire)	Debt (million Italian lire)	Debt/GNP (%)
1927	162200	85596	52.8
1928	164200	88287	53.8
1929	163300	88932	54.5
1930	143900	89876	62.5
1931	124400	93178	74.9
1932	117000	97268	83.1
1933	109500	98868	90.3
1934	108900	104230	95.7
1935	121200	107269	88.5
1936	126600	109407	86.4
1937	156700	125613	80.2
1938	165900	133565	80.5

Sources: GNP: Mitchell (1978).
Debt: Confalonieri and Gatti (1986).

Table 5.4 The current account balance: 1927–38
(millions of lire unless otherwise specified)

Year	Imports	M/Y (percent)	Exports	X/Y (percent)	Visible balance	Invisible balance	Current account
1927	20375	12.6	15519	9.6	− 4919	4223	− 696
1928	21920	13.3	14444	8.8	− 7432	4180	− 3252
1929	21303	13.0	14767	9.0	− 6505	4103	− 2402
1930	17347	12.1	12119	8.4	− 5220	3700	− 1520
1931	11643	9.4	10210	8.2	− 1386	3154	1768
1932	8268	7.1	6812	5.8	− 1383	2155	772
1933	7432	6.8	5991	5.5	− 2644	2076	− 568
1934	7675	7.0	5224	4.8	− 2378	1751	− 627
1935	7790	6.4	5238	4.3	− 2874	1284	− 1590
1936	6039	4.8	5542	4.4	− 1701	1962	261
1937	13943	8.9	10444	6.7	− 4384	2392	− 1992
1938	11273	6.8	10497	6.3	− 2281	1734	− 547

Source: Mitchell (1978). See also Ercolani (1969).

position of the debt considerably improved. Dè Stefani's career in the government, however, ended with his resignation in 1925, after the developments in the foreign exchange markets. The sharp deteriorations – starting in 1924 – of the lira exchange rate, and a stock-exchange boom, prompted the finance minister to impose strict regulations on securities trading. These regulations were received with great outrage by the financial community and – according to contemporary newspapers – increased speculative outflows. As a result, Dè Stefani imposed a series of strict controls on international capital flows, including the prohibition of purchases of foreign bills, and the prohibition of lira loans to nonresidents.[34]

3.2   The 1930s

In the 1930s controls on international capital flows in Italy underwent major changes for the second time.

The measures taken by Dè Stefani were lifted by finance minister Mosconi in 1928, the year after Volpi's exchange rate stabilization. The period of relatively free international capital flows, however, lasted only until 1931. Nine days after the devaluation of sterling, the finance minister delivered instructions to commercial banks to contain as much as possible their foreign exchange position, which was to be monitored, case by case, by the Bank of Italy.[35]

The events of the four following years are reflected in Tables 5.3 and 5.4. The exchange rate revaluation and debt consolidation of 1927 had large contractionary effects, which were magnified by the world depression and the restrictive trade moves of industrialized countries, begun by the US Smoot-Hawley tariff of June 1930. As a result, the number of unemployed tripled from about 300,000 in 1929 to about 1 million in 1933, and the price level fell considerably. Table 5.3 shows that the fall in nominal GNP from 1928 to 1934 almost doubled the debt/GNP ratio, which reached 95.7 percent in 1934.

Table 5.4 illustrates the contraction in international trade: imports and exports as a fraction of GNP almost halved between 1929 and 1934. From the beginning of 1932 Italy had entered a number of barter agreements with trading partners that regulated all imports and exports in following years.

Direct controls of imports and exports did not solve the balance of payments problem. As argued by various authors,[36] capital flight explains the sizeable losses of reserves at the Bank of Italy from the beginning of the 1930s. Guarneri (1953, p. 345) reports that the loss of gold reserves at the Bank of Italy from 1927 to 1934 amounted to 7198 million lire, given a stock of 12105 millions on 31 December 1927. Table 5.5 contains estimates of net capital flows from 1929 to 1936, obtained from central bank reserves – the same data reported by Guarneri – and the current account balance, after netting out changes of holdings of

Table 5.5 Estimates of capital flows: 1929–36
(millions of lire)

Year	Financial assets changes	Reserve changes	Capital flows
1929	− 460.949	− 729.572	1211.479
1930	436.108	− 717.017	1239.091
1931	− 10.001	− 1827.690	− 3605.690
1932	4.678	− 652.546	− 1419.860
1933	− 15.321	252.641	805.320
1934	15.960	− 1513.450	− 870.496
1935	6.353	− 2488.560	− 892.216
1936	− 124.240	626.966	241.726

Sources: Changes in financial assets are taken from line 4 of the asset side of the balance sheets of Banca d'Italia, Banco di Napoli and Banco di Sicilia reported in Table 2 of De Mattia (1967, volume I, tomo I). Changes in reserves are from lines 3.b + 3.c of the same table. The estimate of capital flows is obtained by subtracting from the sum of the first two columns the current account balance, from Ercolani (1969).

foreign financial assets by the central bank. The four years that stand out with sizeable negative net capital flows are 1931–32 and 1934–35. In 1931–32 the net capital outflows are as much as double the size of current account surpluses; in 1934–35 they are comparable in size to the current account deficits.

What was behind capital flight in the 1930s? As in 1919, the overvaluation of the lira after the currency reform certainly contributed to speculative flows, together with the devaluations of sterling (1931) and the dollar (1933). But also in this case capital flight could have been caused by the fear of higher taxes in the near future. First, public finances were rapidly deteriorating. Second, everybody expected even larger budget deficits: in the spring of 1934 the fascist government clearly hinted its colonial ambitions.[37] Events after 1934 demonstrated that these hypothetical fears of wealth owners would have been completely justified. The government first imposed extremely severe controls on all forms of foreign asset holdings and foreign exchange transactions, then raised a series of income and wealth taxes to finance the colonial wars in Africa.

At the end of May 1934 new foreign exchange regulations were introduced, which forbade foreign exchange operations and all financial transactions with nonresidents unless they were linked to industry and commerce. Export of banknotes was also forbidden. Commercial banks were required to report to the Bank of Italy their foreign exchange position, and were forbidden to extend any lire credit to nonresidents, including discounts of lire bills, without the authorization from the ministry of finance. In December 1934 capital controls were further tightened. All incorporated businesses were obliged to offer – and, if requested, to sell – all credits vis-à-vis nonresidents. All Italian citizens had to declare all their assets abroad. A National Institute of Foreign Exchange was created, with the task of collecting all export proceeds, including IOUs, for allocation to domestic importers. The state monopoly of foreign exchange transactions was thus re-established.[38] Special sanctions against infractions of capital controls – like under- and over-invoicing – were stiffened.[39] The emphasis of the new regulations was to forbid everything in the field of foreign exchange, unless it was explicitly allowed by the law.[40]

In 1935 a special tax on income from bearer securities was established, the rate being 10 percent, and later 20 percent. In October 1936 the lira was realigned to its 1927 dollar parity: it was thus devalued by 41 percent. At the same time a loan was floated, and had to be compulsorily bought by all real estate owners. Later, an extraordinary real estate tax was created to service this same loan. In the following years more taxes were imposed: in correspondence to the lira devaluation, an extraordinary 10 percent levy on the capital of all incorporated businesses;[41] in 1938 a securities turnover tax; in 1939 a general capital levy of 0.5 percent. During the Second World War years the government implemented a number of additional taxes on wealth and capital income.

3.3   Interpreting the interwar experience

The evolution of public finances and capital controls in the 1920s and 1930s contains many features brought up by the model in section 2. Although the magnitude of capital flight in response to wealth taxes, securities' registration laws, and financial assets' income taxes cannot be accurately estimated, the preceding discussion contains enough elements to draw some general lessons from the interwar years.

A combination of weak public finances, an inefficient and under-developed tax system, and political instability had disruptive effects on international capital flows in the interwar years. Inefficiencies of the domestic tax system can offer incentives to transfer wealth abroad because of the "tax arbitrage" opportunities, and because compliance to the tax law is difficult to enforce. In addition, international financial transactions can easily go unrecorded, thus affording anonymity to wealth-holders. Finally, as discussed in section 2, under unstable political and public-finance conditions, the fear of a tax levy provides another powerful incentive to transfer wealth abroad. Domestic financial instabilities, and the effects of a misguided currency stabilization in the second half of the 1920s, justified expectations of an exchange rate devaluation in the 1930s, which also explains the large capital outflows observed in the beginning of the 1930s.

What is the legacy of the interwar years? One inheritance from the 1930s is the system of capital controls that has worked in Italy until very recently, and that has not yet been overhauled by comprehensive new laws. That system was created at a time of severe foreign exchange shortages caused by the autarchic economic policies of the fascist regime, and effectively prevented wealth owners from escaping an unprecedented increase in taxes on wealth and assets' income. The basic feature of the system is the monopoly of all foreign exchange transactions assigned to the central bank. A second likely inheritance from the 1920s and the 1930s is a chronically defensive attitude on the part of Italian wealthholders, justified by the experiences of those years. This attitude is revealed, for example, by the strong resistance against any proposal to register ownership of financial assets, and the comparatively small resistance to increases in withholding tax rates. A case-by-case analysis of these biases in investors' behavior could uncover significant aggregate social costs.

4   Current policy questions

4.1   Policy: the post-Second World War experience

During most of the post Second World War period, the main task of Italian monetary authorities has been to reconcile given constraints on domestic credit expansion – largely associated with the requirement of financing government budget deficits – with exchange-rate targets. Faced with these dilemmas, policymakers chose to maintain a regulatory environment for foreign exchange transactions whose basic principles had been inherited from the interwar years. Foreign exchange can only be obtained from the appropriate government agency (Ufficio Italiano Cambi (UIC), or the banks that act as agents of UIC), and must be sold back to it when obtained from nonresidents, unless other options are explicitly authorized. Table 5.6, reproduced from Micossi and Rossi (1986), summarizes the exchange restrictions in Italy in the 1970s and early 1980s.[42]

Table 5.7 provides an overview of a 20-year period during which the relationship between the central bank and the Treasury has changed

Table 5.6 Exchange restrictions during 1972–86

Permanent	Emergency
All residents	
a. Inconvertibility of lira banknotes:	a. Foreign exchange transactions:
b. Investments and loans:	– dual foreign exchange market.
– loans to be authorized.	– compulsory deposit on "current"
– deposit on purchase of foreign	purchases.
assets.	– tax on all purchases.
c. Holdings of foreign assets:	
– purchase of short term assets	
prohibited.	
– purchase of nonlisted securities	
prohibited.	
Firms	
a. Forward cover:	a. Holdings of foreign exchange:
– non trade-related prohibited.	– holding period limited.
– trade-related permitted for	b. Leads and lags:
limited maturity.	– terms of settlements limited.
	– foreign currency financing
	required.
	– observance of contractual
	maturities required.
	c. Payments for imports:
	– compulsory non-interest
	bearing deposit.
Banks	
a. External position:	a. Foreign-currency financing of
– net asset position prohibited.	residents:
– ceiling on gross foreign assets in	– introduction of a ceiling.
lire.	b. Net forward position against
b. Net position in foreign currency:	lire:
– to be balanced daily.	– lowering of ceiling.
c. Forward position against lire:	
– to be balanced daily with	
nonresidents.	
–ceiling on positions with	
residents.	

Source: Reproduced (in part) from Micossi and Rossi (1986).

significantly.[43] The whole period is characterized by a steady increase in government deficits and debt. The 35 percent debt/GDP ratio of 1966–68 is close to the lowest reached in Italy in the entire post-Second World War period. From that level, and starting at the end of the 1960s, deficits

Table 5.7 Government deficits and their financing: 1966–86

	1966–68	1969–74	1975–86
Deficit (percent of GDP)	4	6	13
Debt (percent of GDP)	35	40	63
Central Bank (percent of PSBR)	35	81	17
Long Term Bonds (percent of PSBR)	66	15	47

Source: The two top lines of the table are computed from IMF, *International Financial Statistics.* The bottom lines are computed from Banca d'Italia, *Bolletino.*

and debt have increased at an accelerating rate: the debt/GDP ratio is currently about 88 percent (according to the latest revision of national accounts, correcting for the large estimated "underground economy"). In the 1960s government bonds were used extensively to finance budget deficits, as confirmed by the first three years in the table, but they were almost completely replaced by monetary financing in the inflationary years at the beginning of the 1970s. In the following years, when a large government securities market developed, and when the Bank of Italy progressively freed itself from the constraint to provide automatic financing to the Treasury, monetary financing decreased significantly.[44]

Foreign exchange regulations were relaxed in the early 1960s, in accordance with the articles of the Treaty of Rome, and the OECD Code of Liberalization. This liberal attitude of monetary authorities was justified by the general conditions of price stability and fast growth that characterized the postwar period, until the end of the 1960s. Government deficits were financed by long-term bonds and Treasury bills, whose prices were maintained relatively stable by the central bank's interest-rate pegging policies,[45] and by substantial direct financing from the central bank.

In 1969, in response to an increase in inflation, increased wage pressures, and capital flight, the central bank abandoned the policy of interest-rate pegging. In the following years the state of the Italian economy rapidly deteriorated. On the one side, government deficits and debt increased significantly; on the other side there were the external shocks: the collapse of the Bretton Woods system, and the oil price increases.

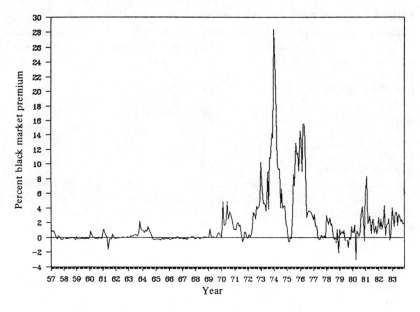

Figure 5.2   The black market premium (parallel dollar rate relative to inflation).
Source: Pick's Currency Yearbook, and IMF.

Figure 5.2 shows the premium of the black market dollar exchange rate. It shows the substantial pressure in the foreign exchange markets in the early 1970s. Balance of payments crises in 1972, 1973, and 1976 prompted the authorities to tighten foreign exchange restrictions significantly.[46] In 1972 lira banknotes were declared unconvertible. In 1973 residents were required to provide an interest-free deposit equal to 50 percent of the value of all new portfolio investment;[47] at the same time a two-tier foreign exchange market was instituted in 1973, but lifted in 1974. In 1974 interest-free deposits at the central bank were required for the equivalent of 50 percent of the value of all imports.[48] In 1976 exporters were required to surrender foreign exchange to the monetary authority only 7 days after receipt. In addition, all purchases of foreign exchange, for whatever purpose, were subject to a tax in October 1976. All trade financing had to be denominated in foreign currency. Finally, criminal law was applied to infractions of foreign exchange restrictions. At the same time, a generalized system of credit controls was extended to all the banking system.[49]

Most of the stringent restrictions of the mid-1970s were progressively lifted in the following years, with an interruption in 1981, when the interest-free deposit vis-à-vis payments to nonresidents was reinstated until the beginning of 1982. The interest-free deposit on foreign investments has been progressively decreased in size and has been eliminated in May 1987.

4.2   Were capital controls appropriate? The "Inconsistent Trinity" justification

The experience of the 1970s brings up another important link between public finances, capital mobility, and capital controls. The need to monetize large budget deficits compelled Italian monetary authorities to maintain high rates of domestic credit growth relative to the rest of the world, thereby triggering allegedly destabilizing capital flight. Padoa Schioppa (1982) suggests that the Italian policymakers' decision to impose capital controls in the postwar period, and especially in the 1970s, was motivated by the attempt to reconcile the "inconsistent trinity" of "monetary policy independence," international capital markets integration, and nominal exchange-rate targets. This general motivation is frequently supported by three arguments which I report and discuss below:

(a)   Since short term capital flows adjust instantaneously, while the current account responds slowly to external imbalances, capital controls "buy time" to domestic policymakers.

This argument can be illustrated by considering a country where the monetary authority, for exogenous reasons, needs faster growth of the domestic money stock than the rest of the world.[50] With perfect international capital mobility, domestic monetary expansions are immediately offset by capital outflows, given the world interest rate and world prices. Therefore, if the monetary authority has a constant exchange rate target, with perfect capital mobility it can only achieve the world inflation rate. On the other hand, capital controls allow a divergence of the domestic rate of inflation from the foreign one, at least for limited periods of time. As the real exchange rate appreciates foreign exchange reserves are drawn out by (supposedly slow to respond) current account deficits. When reserves are exhausted, either the original expansionary policies are reversed – to restore foreign exchange reserves – or the exchange rate is depreciated. In the first case the original inflation rate target is abandoned, while in the second case the original exchange rate target is abandoned.

Clearly this argument provides no justification for capital controls, since it does not explain why constant exchange rate targets should have intrinsic value. Monetary authorities could establish a "crawling peg" that accommodates a higher domestic inflation rate, thereby avoiding real-exchange-rate appreciations and current-account deficits, that are inevitably followed by large discrete depreciations or reversals of the original policy.[51]

(b) With perfect capital mobility monetary disturbances have substantial real effects. Capital controls minimize these real effects.

This is the "sand in the wheels" argument of Tobin (1982), that was recently forcefully restated by Dornbusch (1987).[52] When goods markets adjust slowly and asset markets adjust rapidly, monetary disturbances lead to disproportionate fluctuations in asset prices, that end up having important real effects on relative prices. In the Mundell-Fleming model with sticky prices, capital mobility and floating exchange rates, monetary disturbances lead to large nominal exchange rate responses, and large real exchange rate movements. Under fixed exchange rates, changes in domestic credit affect real interest rates.

The implicit justification for this view is that the first-best policy – eliminating the distortions associated with sticky prices – is unattainable. Capital controls are a candidate for second-best policy. As Frankel and Rodriguez (1982) show, less-than-perfect capital mobility limits the phenomenon of overshooting: thus there is a presumption that capital controls might limit the destabilizing impact of money supply changes on real variables.[53]

This argument, however, does not take into account the complications arising from expectations. As stressed by the asset-market literature, the nature of policy shocks is of crucial importance for their effects on real variables. In general, steady and predictable monetary policies, even in the presence of sticky prices, are likely to reduce – but not completely eliminate – the undesirable real effects of goods markets' imperfections.[54]

(c) Fluctuations in asset prices like the exchange rate and interest rates are often dictated by speculative phenomena, independent of "fundamentals." Capital controls limit financial market instability.

The view that asset markets are vulnerable to "speculative bubbles" that push asset prices away from their "fundamental" value has a long tradition in economics. Recent work has proved that, even endowing economic agents with very long foresight and consistent behavior, these speculative phenomena cannot in principle be ruled out.[55] Furthermore, in some cases, these "bubble paths" are inferior outcomes in terms of the welfare of economic agents. Once again, capital controls might be a way to avoid aberrant fluctuations in financial markets. Here too, however, it is not clear what type of controls would be most efficient. Obstfeld and Rogoff (1983) show that some fractional backing of the currency is enough to rule out speculative hyperinflations. Similarly, Diamond and Dybvig (1986) argue that a lender of last resort can help to avoid runs in an economy with financial intermediaries providing liquidity services. The effectiveness of both these institutions hinges on their credibility with the public: direct controls, like those imposed in Italy in the 1970s, are an easy device for assuming this credibility problem away.

In summary, the "inconsistent trinity" justification for capital controls must rely on the assumption that exchange rate targets bring about some kind of positive externality. None of the arguments reported above, however, explains why exchange rate targets are desirable.

Clearly, exchange-rate targets were not trusted by the authorities as a means of eliminating speculative bubbles, otherwise capital controls would have been unnecessary. A more plausible justification for exchange-rate targets is the "imported discipline" argument of Giavazzi and Pagano (1986) and Giavazzi and Giovannini (1987). These authors show that central banks can achieve lower, and socially preferable, rates of inflation by pegging the exchange rate to a low inflation country, and periodically adjusting the peg, to correct for the losses in competitiveness. With perfect capital mobility, however, these policies are associated with extreme interest rate volatility around realignment dates: capital controls might eliminate the disruptive effects of domestic interest rate volatility, by severing the link between domestic interest rates and exchange-rate expectations.[56] These models do not, of course, explain Italy's decision to join the Bretton Woods system. They do, however, highlight one motivation for joining the European Monetary System in 1979, and the value of exchange rate pegs.

4.3 Questions raised by the recent liberalization

The desire of the authorities and the pressure of the public to remove exchange restrictions is in part explained by the improvement in the general political environment in the country, as well as by the successful disinflation of the 1980s. Figure 5.3 shows the inflation tax relative to the one in the United States (the lira was tightly pegged to the dollar in the 1950s and 60s) and in West Germany.[57] The figure indicates a dramatic

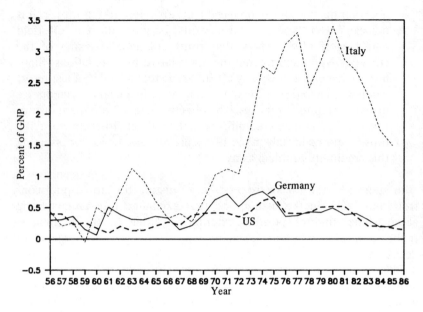

Figure 5.3 The inflation tax in Italy, the US and Germany.
Source: IMF.

decrease in the use of the inflation tax, although it is still three times as large as that in the US and West Germany.[58]

The current trend towards freer international capital flows raises two broad issues. The first is the choice of an exchange rate regime. Although inflation has slowed down significantly in the recent past, Italy has not yet reached Germany's inflation rate. Therefore, even at the present time, the Bank of Italy's job of keeping the lira within the EMS bounds[59] would become much harder in the presence of free international capital flows. In addition, doubts about future inflation are intensified by the state of public finances. As Cividini, Galli and Masera (1986) show, even under the most optimistic scenarios, Italy will not be able to grow out of its government debt. This implies higher taxes in the future. Unless extraordinary taxation – like debt repudiation – is used, increased monetization of government deficits will most likely be resorted to.[60] Under an exchange rate regime like the EMS, solving the government debt problem seems necessary for Italy to afford a lasting integration of its own financial markets with the rest of Europe.

The second issue concerns taxation of foreign assets' income. Section 2 indicates that, in general, all incentives to allocate portfolios internationally in response to differences in tax rates give rise to undesirable distortions, and should be eliminated. Unfortunately, while capital controls are being removed, there has been little concern for providing an efficient and internationally balanced system of taxation of capital assets. At the EEC level nothing guarantees the uniform taxation of capital income among member countries, because of differences in the tax treaties signed individually by the various member countries.[61] A harmonization of withholding tax regimes is not likely to be achieved soon. EEC members, however, could still afford integrated financial markets, as long as each country could make sure that its own residents pay the same taxes on all investment income, at home and abroad. At present, this condition is only in part met by the Italian system, where the income tax on foreign assets is withheld at the time payments are received by Italian banks.[62] For example, there are no provisions against tax deferment: since withholding taxes are levied when income from foreign assets is repatriated, and not when income is earned, investors in foreign securities can borrow at zero interest all taxes owed to the Italian government, as long as they delay repatriation of foreign assets' income.[63] The creation of a tax system neutral with respect to the geographical location of financial assets should be the top priority of Italian regulators embarking on an effort to liberalize international capital controls.

NOTES

* I would like to thank the staff of the Research Department of the Bank of Italy for generously helping with data and analyses on the Italian economy. Giorgio Basevi, Rudi Dornbusch, Francesco Giavazzi, Herakles Polemarchakis, Maurice Obstfeld, Antonio Pedone, Richard Portes, Lars Svensson, Gianni Toniolo, and Charles Wyplosz offered many useful suggestions. All remaining errors in the paper are mine.

1 See also Dornbusch (1985a) for an overlapping-generations model in an open economy.

2 Strictly speaking, the term "evasion" should be used only when the purchase of foreign securities after an increase in taxes on income from domestic securities is not allowed by the law. Below I use the term evasion to denote both the legal and the illegal transactions.

3 At the present time, Italian residents can purchase foreign financial assets through commercial banks. The income from these assets is taxed at a rate higher than that on domestic assets. The model discussed in this section is relevant for present-day Italy if, notwithstanding these regulations, illegal asset transactions with foreign residents are still important, or other forms of tax evasion are possible. These questions are discussed in section 4.

4 This is, of course, just an implication of the general concept of second best due to Lipsey and Lancaster (1956).

5 For this reason, research has recently focused on the specific distortions that might make capital controls desirable. See, for example, Tornell (1986) and Velasco (1987).

6 Assuming that foreign bonds can be issued by domestic residents to domestic residents does not affect the results in any way.

7 See, for example, Persson (1985).

8 The different intertemporal welfare effects of changes in fiscal policy under different tax regimes are briefly mentioned below.

9 In the model, the adjustment of domestic investment is of course instantaneous: consumers substitute foreign for domestic assets before investment is actually carried out.

10 This result is of interest since in a small country, changes in government debt do not normally crowd out the domestic capital stock. See Persson (1985) and Giovannini (1987a). Changes in the steady-state capital stock in response to changes in fiscal policy can also arise when different goods are needed for investment (Obstfeld 1987), or when labor is supplied elastically.

11 Substitute the savings equation into (3) and differentiate, together with the arbitrage relation (6), the government budget constraint (11), and the factor-price frontier (9), after imposing $d_t = \bar{d}$. The result is equation (12).

12 The utility loss for the increase in government debt and taxes is, as expected, larger than in the case where the government can raise lump-sum taxes on the young. With non-distortionary taxes the utility loss is $dV = - V_w(r^* - n)d\bar{d}$: see Persson (1985).

13 Although specific forms of quantitative restrictions are adopted by many countries.

14 Thus, when the net asset position vis-à-vis the rest of the world is negative, interest payments are tax-deductible.

15 In this regime changes in fiscal policy do not give rise to any distortions in the production side of the economy. Imposing a zero current account restriction brings distortions into the production side. The real interest rate and the capital stock have to adjust and generate the changes in savings required to absorb changes in the stock of government debt.

16 See, for example, Dornbusch (1985b).

17 Since the stock of capital is exogenous, for any given tax rate a rise in d is exactly offset by a fall in f. Therefore – from (11') – a change in steady-state d does not affect taxes when $r^* = n$.

18 The intertemporal welfare effects of a lump-sum transfer to the young financed with a permanently higher level of government debt are as follows. In the case where foreign-source income is not taxed, the young generation at the time of the transfer experiences a welfare gain (the transfer) but no loss, since the intertemporal terms of trade are unaffected by the change in the future tax rates. Future generations face a loss of wage income, but, of course, no changes in the intertemporal terms of trade. In the case where all income from assets is taxed at the same rate, the young generation at the time of the transfer experiences a gain in welfare represented by the transfer, and a loss, associated with the change in the after tax real interest rate. Future generations experience losses caused by the change in the intertemporal terms of trade. For an analysis of intertemporal welfare economics in finite-horizons models, see Calvo and Obstfeld (1987).

19 Notice, however, that zero interest elasticity of savings does not imply that the indirect utility is insensitive to the real interest rate. With separable, isoelastic utility, the partial derivative of the indirect utility with respect to the real rate of interest decreases as the elasticity of intertemporal substitution decreases.

20 Notice, for future reference, that the relevant interest rate in (20) is the *after tax* rate.

21 A multiplicity of equilibrium exchange rate paths cannot be ruled out. Each of these competitive equilibria is characterized by a different initial exchange rate, and is in general associated with different levels of consumption, investment, and so on. See Geanakoplos and Polemarchakis (1986) for an analysis and some solutions to the indeterminacy problem in closed economies.

22 When the government can use two different forms of taxation the question of their optimal combination arises. This question is not addressed here.

23 Fanno (1939, p. 31), in his analysis of "abnormal" international capital flows, stresses the role played by capital levies and other forms of wealth taxation.

24 Clough (1964, p. 96); also reported by Eichengreen and Giavazzi (1984).

25 Clough (1964).

26 McGuire (1926).

27 The currency was not convertible into gold at a fixed rate.

28 Young (1925).

29 Since contemporaries perceived the problem of capital flight in 1919 as serious, the lifting of the monopoly of foreign exchange transactions in May of that year and further liberalizations of capital flow in 1921 are somewhat puzzling. As suggested above, one possible explanation is that Italy was following other European allies in the liberalization of capital flows; another justification might be the authorities' mistrust of the effectiveness of these measures against capital flight, at a time when other countries were lifting their own controls.

30 "Il biennio rosso."

31 These figures are taken from Ministero delle Finanze (1925). Toniolo himself states that these figures certainly underestimate the size and importance of capital flight in 1919–20.

32 The three banks of issue were the Banca d'Italia, the Banco di Napoli and the Banco di Sicilia. Their balance sheets have been published by De Mattia (1967).

33 A description of Dè Stefani's years in the finance and treasury ministries is in Toniolo (1980).

34 McGuire (1926) suggests that the capital flight could not easily be stemmed by the Italian capital controls of 1925 since all other European countries were free of these regulations at the time.

35 Guarneri (1953).

36 See, for example, Guarneri (1953), Catalano (1969), Schneider (1936), and Clough (1964).

37 On 18 March 1934 Mussolini made the following public proclamation: "The historical objectives of Italy have two names: Asia and Africa."

38 In May 1935 the "Sovrintendenza allo Scambio delle Valute," which became later "Ministero degli Scambi e delle Valute" was formed, and headed by Felice Guarneri.

39 On 9 May 1935 a new law established that all titles to foreign assets had to be deposited in custody at the Bank of Italy.

40 Baffi (1959) and Bollettino Economico (1984) suggest that the general criteria underlying these regulations survived well beyond the Second World War: "Along with the ruin wrought by war, this control apparatus was inherited by the first democratic Governments of Italy." (Baffi 1959).

41 In November 1938 the levy was extended to unincorporated businesses at a rate of 7.5 percent.
42 See Micossi and Rossi (1986) for a detailed description of the Italian foreign exchange legislation.
43 For a description of the experience and an interpretation of the data, see Spaventa (1984).
44 In 1975 the Bank of Italy stopped buying all government securities at the Treasury auctions. In July 1981 the central bank relinquished its commitment to act as a residual buyer at Treasury auctions.
45 See Fazio (1979). The latter could be held in the form of reserves by commercial banks. It should be stressed, however, that the policy of pegging interest rates was not achieved primarily through open market operations. It was instead largely obtained by means of administrative controls and rationing practices. See Padoa Schioppa (1985).
46 In 1972 the lira joined the European "snake," but left it the following year. In 1974 the government signed a stand-by loan with the IMF.
47 Also, residents receiving foreign exchange were required to surrender it to the exchange authority within 30 days from the date of receipt (this limit was previously six months).
48 Except oil, investment goods, and the like.
49 See Fazio (1979), Spaventa (1984) and Padoa Schioppa (1985).
50 In our case expansionary monetary policies are required to finance government budget deficits.
51 As suggested by the recent US experience, real exchange rate and trade balance fluctuations might impose significant real costs to domestic industries.
52 ". . . throwing sand into the wheels is no longer sufficient. But why stop there and not use rocks?," Dornbusch (1987), p. 17.
53 See also the papers on the working of dual exchange-rate systems, surveyed by Dornbusch (1986).
54 In these models, higher steady-state inflation rates bring about real effects (losses) caused by the very transactions imperfections that give rise to sticky prices.
55 See, for example, Brock (1975) on speculative hyperinflations with infinite horizons and perfect foresight. The argument there could easily be transposed to exchange rates. Kareken and Wallace (1981) discuss indeterminacies in flexible exchange rates models populated by investors with finite horizons.
56 See Wyplosz (1986) for a discussion of capital controls and speculative attacks under fixed exchange rates.
57 The inflation tax is computed by multiplying the yearly percentage change of the GNP deflator by the real stock of high powered money (reserve money in *International Financial Statistics*). The result is divided by real GNP. The 1985 observation for Italy is computed using the consumer price index instead of the GNP deflator.
58 The inflation rate in Italy is about double that in the US and Germany.
59 Notwithstanding the flexible arrangement that Italy presently enjoys: the bilateral fluctuation band for the lira is 12 percent.
60 Historically, exceptional tax needs are met with higher inflation, since the costs of additional income tax revenue are normally high.
61 See Ancidoni (1987).
62 Residents are required by law to deposit all their holdings of foreign securities with Italian commercial banks.

63 The US Internal Revenue Code devotes a whole section (Subpart F) to provisions against this form of tax deferment.

REFERENCES

Ancidoni, G (1987), "La tassazione e i mercati finanziari," mimeo, Bank of Italy.
Atkinson, A.B. and J.E. Stiglitz (1980), *Lectures in Public Economics*. New York: McGraw Hill.
Bachi, R. (1925), "Position of the Currency and Currency Reform in Italy," in *European Currency and Finance* by J.P. Young. Commission of Gold and Silver Inquiry, US Senate. Washington, DC: Govt. Printing Office.
Baffi, P. (1959), "Monetary Developments in Italy from the War Economy to Limited Convertibility," *Banca Nazionale del Lavoro Quarterly Review*.
Banca d'Italia (1984), *Bollettino Economico*, February.
Brock, W.A. (1975), "A Simple Perfect Foresight Monetary Model," *Journal of Monetary Economics*, 1.
Calvo, G.A. (1987), "The Volatility of Government Debt," mimeo, University of Pennsylvania.
Calvo, G.A. and M. Obstfeld (1987), "Optimal Time-Consistent Fiscal Policy with Uncertain Lifetimes," mimeo, University of Pennsylvania.
Catalano, F. (1969), *L'economia Italiana di Guerra*. Milan.
Cividini, A., G. Galli and R.S. Masera (1986), "Vincolo di bilancio e sostenibilità del debito: analisi e prospettive," mimeo, Bank of Italy.
Clough, S.B. (1964), *The Economic History of Modern Italy*. New York: Columbia University Press.
Confalonieri, A. and E. Gatti (1986), *La politica del debito pubblico in Italia*. Bari: Laterza.
De Mattia, R. (1967), *I bilanci degli istituti di emissione Italiani: 1845–1936*. Roma: Banca d'Italia.
Diamond, D. and P. Dybvig (1986), "Banking Theory, Deposit Insurance, and Bank Regulations," *Journal of Business*, vol. 59, n. 7, January.
Diamond, P.A. (1965), "National Debt in a Neoclassical Growth Model," *American Economic Review*, 55.
(1970), "Incidence of an Interest Income Tax," *Journal of Economic Theory*, 2.
Dornbusch, R. (1985a), "Intergenerational and International Trade," *Journal of International Economics*, 18, n. 1/2, February.
(1985b), "External Debt, Budget Deficits and Disequilibrium Exchange Rates," in G. Smith and J. Cuddington, eds., *International Debt and the Developing Countries*. Washington, D.C.: The World Bank.
(1986), "Special Exchange Rates for Capital Account Transactions," *World Bank Economic Review*, vol. 1, no. 1.
(1987), "Exchange Rate Economics: 1986," *Economic Journal*, 97, n. 385, March.
Dornbusch, R. and A. Giovannini (1987), "Money in the Open Economy," mimeo, M.I.T., July.
Eichengreen, B. and F. Giavazzi (1984), "Inflation, Consolidation or Capital Levy? European Debt Management in the 1920s," mimeo, Harvard University.
Ercolani, P. (1969), "Documentazione statistica di base," in *Lo sviluppo economico in Italia*, edited by G. Fuà. Milano: Franco Angeli.

Fanno, M. (1939), *Normal and Abnormal International Capital Transfers.* Minneapolis: University of Minnesota Press.

Fazio, A. (1979), "La politica monetaria in Italia dal 1947 al 1978," *Moneta e Credito*, September.

Fischer, S. (1980), "Dynamic Inconsistency, Cooperation and the Benevolent Dissembling Government," *Journal of Economic Dynamics and Control*, 2.

Frankel, J.A. and C.A. Rodriguez (1982), "Exchange Rate Dynamics and the Overshooting Hypothesis," *IMF Staff Papers*.

Geanakoplos, J.D. and H.M. Polemarchakis (1986), "Walrasian Indeterminacy and Keynesian Macroeconomics," *Review of Economic Studies*, 53.

Giavazzi, F. and M. Pagano (1986), "The Advantage of Tying One's Hands EMS Discipline and Central Bank Credibility" CEPR Discussion Paper No 135, October.

Giavazzi, F. and A. Giovannini (1987), "Models of the EMS: Is Europe a Greater Deutsche-Mark Area?", in *Global Macroeconomics: Policy Conflict and Cooperation*, edited by R. Bryant and R. Portes. London: MacMillan.

Giovannini, A. (1987a), "The Real Exchange Rate, the Capital Stock, and Fiscal Policy," *European Economic Review.*

(1987b), "Taxation and International Capital Mobility," mimeo, Columbia Business School, August.

Guarneri, F. (1953), *Battaglie economiche tra le due guerre.* Milano: Garzanti.

Hall, R. (1985), "Real Interest and Consumption," NBER Working Paper n. 1694, August.

Kareken, J.H. and N. Wallace (1981), "On the Indeterminacy of Equilibrium Exchange Rates," *Quarterly Journal of Economics*, 92, n. 2.

Kydland, F.E. and E.C. Prescott (1977), "Rules rather than Discretion: The Inconsistency of Optimal Plans," *Journal of Political Economy*, 3.

Lipsey, R. and K. Lancaster (1956), "On the General Theory of the Second Best," *Review of Economic Studies.*

McGuire, C.E. (1926), *Italy's International Economic Position.* New York: Macmillan.

Micossi, S. and S. Rossi (1986), "Restrictions on International Capital Flows: The Case of Italy," mimeo, Bank of Italy, September.

Ministero delle Finanze (1925), *Alcuni indici dell'entità e dell'orientazione del capitale Italiano investito in valori esteri*, Roma.

Mitchell, B.R. (1978), *European Historical Statistics 1750–1970.* New York: Columbia University Press.

Modigliani, F. and R. Brumberg (1954), "Utility Analysis and the Consumption Function: An Interpretation of Cross-Section Data," in *Post Keynesian Economics* edited by K.K. Kurihara. New Brunswick, N.J.: Rutgers University Press.

Obstfeld, M. (1987), "Fiscal Deficits and Relative Prices in a Growing World Economy," mimeo, University of Pennslyvania, May.

Obstfeld, M. and K. Rogoff (1983), "Speculative Hyperinflation in Maximizing Models: Can We Rule Them Out?" *Journal of Political Economy*, 91, n. 4, August.

Padoa Schioppa, T. (1982), "European Capital Markets Between Liberalization and Restrictions," Speech to the Second Symposium of European Banks, June.

(1985), "Quantitative Policy and Monetary Control: The Italian Experience," Conference in Honor of Franco Modigliani, September.

Persson, T. (1985), "Deficits and Intergenerational Welfare in Open Econo-mies," *Journal of International Economics*, 19, n. 1/2, August.

Schneider, H.W. (1936), *The Fascist Government of Italy*. New York: Van Nostrand.

Spaventa, L. (1984), "The Growth of Public Debt in Italy: Past Experience, Perspectives and Policy Problems," *Banca Nazionale del Lavoro Quarterly Review*, February.

Tobin, J. (1982), "A Proposal for International Monetary Reform," in *Essays in Economics: Theory and Practice*. Cambridge, MA.: MIT Press.

Toniolo, G. (1980), *L'Economia dell'Italia fascista*. Roma-Bari: Laterza.

Tornell, A. (1986), "Capital Controls, Welfare and Reputation," mimeo, Massachusetts Institute of Technology, November.

Velasco, A. (1987), "Time Inconsistency in an Open Economy: Lack of Credibility and the Usefulness of Capital Controls," mimeo, Columbia University, March.

Wyplosz, C. (1986), "Capital Controls and Balance of Payments Crises," *Journal of International Money and Finance*, vol. 5, June.

Young, J.P. (1925), *European Currency and Finance*. Commission of Gold and Silver Inquiry, US Senate. Washington, DC: Govt. Printing Office.

Discussion

MAURICE OBSTFELD*

The central theme of Alberto Giovannini's wide-ranging paper is that capital flight is caused by private attempts to escape taxation by moving assets abroad. Currency depreciation, which holds center stage in recent theoretical accounts of balance of payments crises, is one form of taxation, but only one. As Giovannini reminds us, the capital flight seen at several points in Italian history, as well as in 1981 France and elsewhere, often reflects more general fears. In a crisis, domestic residents trying to switch out of vulnerable domestic assets can do so in the aggregate only by obtaining the one means of payment foreigners are willing to accept: foreign exchange. The result is a sharp drop in the home central bank's international reserves or (under floating) a sharp depreciation of the home currency.

The paper consists of three parts, an analysis of open-economy fiscal issues, a review of Italian experience, and a discussion of the cases for and against capital-account liberalization in Italy today. Below, I focus on the fiscal-policy effects explored by Giovannini, and then return briefly to a second-best case for capital controls that may be valid when the government cannot make credible precommitments.

Taxation in open economies: intertemporal dimensions

Giovannini uses an overlapping-generations model to study two regimes, a "capital-flight" regime in which interest on foreign assets is untaxed (or untaxable) and a "capital-controls" regime in which foreign and domestic assets are taxed at the same rate. The characterization of the two regimes in terms of fiscal arrangements is somewhat controversial. For example, in the "capital-flight" regime, must consumption of foreign income take place abroad, perhaps at some cost to the consumer? Such issues are left aside. The major questions that are addressed concern the effects of the increased taxes that finance an increase in the steady-state public debt.

212

Future consumption

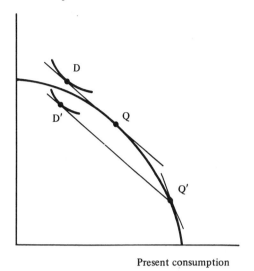

Present consumption

Figure 5.4   An investment tax raises the first-period current account surplus.

Giovannini observes that interest taxation is essentially an investment tax when foreign assets are not taxed along with domestic assets, and a consumption subsidy when they are. The first conclusion requires also that foreigners holding assets located domestically face the interest tax on domestic assets. Otherwise arbitrage would prevent domestic interest rates from rising above the world level, and domestic firms would simply borrow abroad at the world interest rate.[1] Given these assumptions, however, it is interesting to explore the differential effects of the two fiscal regimes in an alternative model that underlines Giovannini's conclusions but allows a simple diagrammatic argument. For this purpose I use the standard two-period Fisherian model, as set out, for example, in Chapter 7 of Krugman and Obstfeld (1988).

A two-period model

Figure 5.4 shows the effects of the investment tax on an economy that is an exporter of first-period consumption, i.e., one with a current-account surplus in period 1. The economy faces a budget line with absolute slope $1 + r^*$, which is the price of present consumption in terms of future consumption; the laissez-faire equilibrium entails production at point Q and consumption at point D. A tax on domestic assets' interest raises the

Future consumption

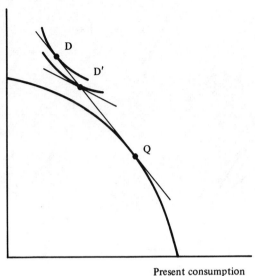

Present consumption

Figure 5.5   A subsidy to present consumption lowers the first-period current account surplus.

required marginal product of domestic capital, moving production to Q' and consumption to D'.

Clearly, welfare is lower compared with the undistorted situation. In addition, the first-period external surplus must *rise*. Because the tax discourages investment, production of first-period consumption goods is higher; however, consumption of those goods must fall, since consumers face unchanged intertemporal prices and have lower wealth. The same argument shows that the current account rises as well in the case of a first-period external borrower.

Figure 5.5 shows the case in which domestic and foreign assets are taxed uniformly, so that it is consumer prices, rather than producer prices, that change. As Giovannini points out, welfare is lower than under laissez-faire in this case too, and it is unclear whether the addition of foreign-asset taxation to domestic-asset taxation raises or lowers it. It may happen that taxation of foreign assets raises national welfare when the initial situation already involves taxes on home-asset holders.

Notice that the first-period current-account surplus always falls (or the deficit widens) as a result of a general tax on asset income. Tax proceeds are rebated to the public, and the tax on interest makes future consumption relatively more expensive but leaves production unchanged.

The role of seignorage

Relatively few papers have addressed the links between capital-account restrictions and seignorage. The intertemporal tradeoffs facing a government in this case are, however, quite complex. Suppose that exchange rate adjustments are sufficiently frequent that the exchange rate regime may be thought of as a crawling peg. In such a setting, capital controls make money demand inelastic in the short run, so that an increase in domestic-credit growth has a large positive effect on seignorage. Over the longer term, though, higher inflation causes reserve losses as the economy moves to a lower long-run level of real monetary balances. Since reserve losses lower national income – they deplete the nation's stock of interest-bearing foreign assets – money demand falls by more in the long run than the interest elasticity of money demand alone would indicate. So it is possible that capital controls, while enhancing the inflation tax's revenue-generating powers in the short run, reduce those powers in the long run.

Credibility and capital flight

Recent papers by Calvo (1987), Eaton (1987), and myself (1986) have focused on situations in which financial crises may result from self-fulfilling fears of certain government actions. For example, a government may have to impose distorting taxes to meet budgetary obligations if capital flight takes place; capital flight, in turn, may result from the threat of these fiscal measures. Two equilibria of such models are (1) the capital-flight equilibrium, in which capital outflows themselves bring about "surprise" taxation, and (2) the (generally Pareto-superior) no-capital-flight equilibrium.

In cases where equilibrium (1) is relevant, capital controls can sometimes raise welfare by preventing self-generating crises and thus enforcing equilibrium (2). This possibility adds another potential argument for capital controls to Giovannini's list. Obviously, however, controls are a second-best device. First-best would be a binding government renunciation of the fiscal measures expected by the markets.

NOTES

* Financial support from the National Science Foundation and the Alfred P. Sloan Foundation is acknowledged with thanks.
1 Further, in a more general setting than that of the paper's model, domestic residents must be able to borrow as well as lend in foreign financial centers at the world interest rate r^*, provided the proceeds are consumed abroad.

REFERENCES

Guillermo A. Calvo (1987), "Servicing the Public Debt: The Role of Expectations," Mimeographed, University of Pennsylvania, July.

Jonathan Eaton (1987), "Public Debt Guarantees and Private Capital Flight," *World Bank Economic Review*, 1, May.

Paul R. Krugman and Maurice Obstfeld (1988), *International Economics: Theory and Policy*. Boston: Little, Brown and Company.

Maurice Obstfeld (1986), "Rational and Self-fulfilling Balance-of-Payments Crises," *American Economic Review*, 76, March.

Discussion

CHARLES WYPLOSZ

The paper by Alberto Giovannini raises three interesting issues. First, are capital flights primarily triggered by fear of taxation? Second, is there an optimal structure of asset taxes in the open economy? Third, how is the European Monetary System (EMS) to survive once financial deregulation is achieved, as has been agreed upon for the 1992 horizon?

The central idea of the paper is that fears of asset taxation are the main motivation behind capital flights. To support his view, Giovannini presents a theoretical model and reviews the interwar experience in Italy. One major implication is that capital controls may not be welfare reducing since capital flight reflects a tax-related distortion: as is well-known, in such a second-best situation, further distortions may indeed be a superior policy response. In my comments I discuss some aspects of the paper and present my own views concerning the current emphasis of banning capital controls within the EMS.

Giovannini's view that capital flights are always related to fears of taxation is interesting, particularly because it stands in contrast with most of the literature which emphasizes instead fears of depreciation. It might seem then that we have two different explanations of capital flight, and that these two hypotheses ought to be tested against one another. The problem is that the two hypotheses are not mutually exclusive. A depreciation is a levy on domestic assets, so that both hypotheses boil down to the reasonable view that speculative outflows are indeed always related to fear of capital losses, be it due to outright taxes or to an inflation tax and the associated depreciation. Indeed, and this is shown in the second part of Giovannini's paper, unless foreign assets held by residents are taxed exactly as domestic assets, any asset tax increase will lead to an equal exchange rate depreciation. This is why it may be impossible to test the author's hypothesis in any meaningful way.

The theoretical model of asset taxation in the open economy is interesting in its own right. It is an innovative approach to the issue of

217

capital controls as it focuses on their real economy implications. Of course, it is not a model to deal with the other aspect of capital controls and capital flight, that related to fears of depreciation and speculative attacks during a balance of payments crisis. Giovannini is right to point out that existing distortions (here the missing intergenerational markets of overlapping generations models) imply that distortionary taxes may be, under certain circumstances, welfare improving. I believe that the trade-off between the required return on capital and the intertemporal rate of substitution for private saving is a real issue. I also agree with the author's intuition that the latter mechanism is less serious than the former, so that taxing foreign assets as domestic ones is a valid objective. In this connection, two remarks may be useful.

First, such measures may be generalized in all countries without international agreement. There is no logical need that tax rates be equalized across countries if non-resident holdings are not taxed in the country where the asset is being issued. This is the more so as the existence of offshore markets would make such a principle self-defeating. The real difficulty, and this is the second remark, is to enforce compliance to taxation of foreign assets, which would require that foreign assets be held at home and reported. This can be done, as is currently the case in several countries (Italy and France are two examples that I know of), by requiring that such assets be deposited in banks or other recognized institutions. There remains the possibility that assets may be kept abroad. There is no fool-proof system as taxation goes and evasion will always exist for anything which can be taxed (labor, goods, assets, etc). But, in this case, it is likely to remain within acceptable bounds. The reason is that it does not make sense to keep assets permanently abroad as this would preclude ever enjoying their returns, or would impose in most cases a reasonably high cost to travel there and collect (and enjoy) interest.

A significant section of the paper is devoted to an historical overview of the Italians' experience with capital flight. I am certainly not qualified to assess Giovannini's characterization of that experience. It is clear however that the author cannot claim that his proposed explanation of capital flight is supported by the events that he describes. First, of course, because it is an informal account. Second, because it is quite apparent that all major events reported here show that massive capital flight coincides with exchange rate crises. This would rather suggest that inflation and depreciation represents a very attractive substitute (or often complement) to straight capital levies or other forms of taxation. In other words, I see this section as showing that the two alternative hypotheses (capital flight as a response to expectations of taxes rather than of depreciation) are not separate, and in the Italian case not distinguishable. I also see the evidence as indicating that the structural effects of capital flight and capital controls are likely to be relatively limited as they arise mainly during intermittent crisis periods, and may not therefore be at work long enough to be a sizeable magnitude. Put another way, such issues arise during difficult times where major policy errors and other disturbances create major inefficiencies, of which capital flight is merely a consequence. While Giovannini may well be right that, in these periods, capital controls may be second-best solutions, the first-best response of dealing with the major disturbance is most often an open policy option.

Of course, during more normal periods, there is still a very important and current issue: the effect of financial market integration (as officially planned for 1992) on the functioning of the EMS. Giovannini brings up the "inconsistent trinity" argument put forward by Padoa-Schioppa (1982) and Wyplosz (1986a). This argument asserts that only two of the three following situations may co-exist:

an exchange rate target, as in the EMS,
monetary policy independence, i.e. the ability to choose any steady-state rate of inflation,
free capital mobility.

The reason for the inconsistent trinity follows from the theory of balance of payments crises (see Krugman 1979, Obstfeld 1984, Flood and Garber 1984 and Wyplosz 1986b). This theory asserts that, in the anticipation of a devaluation, a country's reserves would be wiped out by the virtually unbounded volume of speculative capital susceptible of being mobilized under free capital mobility. Deprived of reserves, monetary authorities would have to abandon *any* fixed parity, temporarily at least.

The implication is that one of the three components of the "inconsistent trinity" must be abandoned. Which one in Europe? A first candidate is the EMS. Despite all its shortcomings, the EMS has brought about a significant reduction in the unexpected volatility of exchange rates, as shown by Rogoff (1984). In particular, the EMS has been successful in avoiding the kind of medium-run overshootings and currency misalignment which many non-EMS currencies have undergone in recent years.[1] Because sustained misalignments, eventually eliminated if not reversed, imply costly (because temporary) reallocations of productive resources, the EMS has played a useful role. This is why I believe that it should be retained.

A second possibility would be to aim at a complete convergence of inflation rates, to the point where realignments would become unnecessary. Attractive as it may look, this objective raises a number of formidable questions. To whose inflation rate should all rates converge? There seems to be a fundamental asymmetry which implies that the EMS tends to force convergence towards the lowest inflation rate, namely that of Germany. There is no proof that this is a Pareto superior solution and, consequently, that such large countries as Italy and France should welcome it.[2]

Another problem is that the loss of monetary independence implies the abandonment of seignorage as a source of government income. For countries stuck with high outstanding public debt, such as Italy, this is a most serious issue. It might raise fears of an eventual consolidation of the public debt. Alternatively, the other EMS countries might "buy in" Italy by acquiring its debt. I very much doubt that such a prospect is a viable one. So we are left with the uneasy conclusion that the complete removal of restrictions of capital movements is unwise within the current EMS arrangements. A possibility is that some form of capital controls be maintained. Many forms of controls exist and further work is needed to assess their respective costs and benefits. They include taxes as advocated by Tobin and Dornbusch, two-tier exchange markets and quantitative restrictions.

Another possibility has been suggested to me by Vittorio Grill during the conference. The point is that the largest amount of funds which can be mobilized in a speculative attack against a currency is the money base. By definition this exceeds the country's exchange reserves by the amount of the domestic credit component of the base. Hence a possible modification of the EMS: a formal agreement would guarantee automatic availability to each central bank of credit by other central banks of a volume of exchange *in excess* of the credit component of its base. Under such a scheme, speculation can never succeed against a currency and becomes useless. This represents a huge amount of credit, and conditions (term, interest, etc . . .) need to be worked out, but it may be able to break through the iron rule of the "inconsistent trinity."

The only other possibility that I can think of consists in avoiding discrete jumps at the time of realignments. For this to be the case, the actual exchange rate must simply slide within its margin of fluctuation. A necessary condition is that the margins of fluctuations before and after any realignment overlap, i.e. that the size of the realignment be smaller than the width of the band. This, in turn, requires either small but relatively frequent realignments, or larger bands. Any alternative chips away at the notion that the EMS is a close approximation to a fixed exchange rate regime: the former by bringing it closer to a crawling peg system, the latter by allowing more flexibility.

NOTES

1 The Italian lira is an important exception. The lira seems to have appreciated by some 10 percent since it last reached an "equilibrium" level before joining the EMS. This apparent overvaluation may have two explanations. According to the first one, the overvaluation is a conscious policy choice of the Italian monetary authorities as a way of speeding up the disinflationary process. The second explanation rests on the fact that productivity gains have been higher in Italy than elsewhere, so that there would actually be no overvaluation. In any case, this is not a consequence of the EMS as realignment negotiations typically hinge upon purchasing power parity rules.
2 This issue is explored formally in Begg and Wyplosz (1987).

REFERENCES

Begg, D. and C. Wyplosz (1987), "Why the EMS? Dynamic Games and the Equilibrium Policy Regime," in *Global Macroeconomics*, edited by R. C. Bryant and R. Portes, London: MacMillan.
Flood, R. P. and P.M. Garber (1984), "Collapsing Exchange Rate Regimes: Some Linear Examples," *Journal of International Economics*, vol. 17, August.
Krugman, P. (1979), "A Model of Balance-of-Payments Crises," *Journal of Money, Credit and Banking*, Vol. 11, August.
Obstfeld, M. (1984), "Balance-of-Payments Crisis and Devaluation," *Journal of Money, Credit and Banking*, Vol. 16, May.
Padoa-Schioppa, T. (1984), *Money, Economic Policy and Europe*, EEC, chapter VII.
Rogoff, K. (1984), "Can Exchange Rate Predictability be Achieved without Monetary Convergence? Evidence from the EMS," International Finance Discussion Paper No. 245, July.
Wyplosz, C. (1986a), "Capital Flows Liberalization and the EMS. A French Perspective," INSEAD Working Paper No. 86/40, December.
(1986b), "Capital Controls and Balance of Payments Crises," *Journal of International Money and Finance*, Vol. 5, June.

6 Public debt and households' demand for monetary assets in Italy: 1970–86*

C. ANDREA BOLLINO and NICOLA ROSSI

1 Introduction

On the basis of the most recent flow-of-funds accounts, the Italian households' net wealth is estimated to have reached, by the end of 1985, about 2,500 trillions of lire, having kept closely in line with the evolution of households' disposable income (Table 6.1)[1]. Indications are that, as in other European countries, a large proportion of total wealth is held by households in the form of real assets (dwellings, agricultural land and consumer durables), although the share of dwellings in real wealth tends to be greater in Italy than in other countries. In comparison with other European countries, however, the financial liabilities of Italian households represent a relatively small component, totalling only about 6 percent of gross financial assets and showing a tendency to decrease over time.

Since the mid 1970s, the allocation of households' net wealth appears to have been characterized by two major trends. First, as far as the composition of total wealth is concerned, the real component has shown, towards the mid-1980s, a sizable decline in coincidence with the sharp drop in the relative value of dwellings. Second, among financial assets, there has been a substantial shift from M2 money (currency in circulation, plus bank and postal deposits) to government securities. The latter component increased from nearly 3 percent of financial wealth in 1975, to more than 13 percent in 1980, and to over 25 percent in 1986. At the same time, the M2's share declined by nearly 20 percentage points, to 39 percent in 1986. The substitution away from currency and deposits was taking place almost entirely in the first half of the 1980s, since, in the late 1970s, most of the increase in the share of government securities was at the expense of non-government medium- and long-term securities whose share more than halved from nearly 8 percent in 1975 to less than 3 percent in 1980.

Table 6.1 Composition of Italian households' net wealth (percentages)

	1975	1980	1985	1986
Real assets	72.1	73.9	65.4	...
of which: Dwellings	81.0	80.8	83.2	
Land	9.8	9.2	5.5	
Durables	9.2	9.9	11.3	
Financial assets	30.4	28.1	36.7	...
of which: Notes and coins	6.8	5.4	3.8	3.4
Bank deposits	44.5	45.2	34.1	30.0
Postal deposits	8.2	8.0	5.6	5.5
Treasury bills	0.1	8.6	12.7	10.7
Deposits and savings certificates of SCI	2.6	1.6	2.3	2.1
Treasury credit certificates	—	2.3	12.0	11.4
Other govt. securities	3.1	2.3	2.1	3.3
Other securities	8.2	2.7	2.7	2.5
Italian shares and participations	5.3	7.0	9.5	13.5
Foreign assets	1.4	1.0	1.0	1.1
Actuarial reserves and severance pay provisions	19.8	15.5	11.6	16.5
Other assets	0.1	0.5	2.4	
Financial liabilities	2.6	2.0	2.2	...
of which: Bank loans	39.9	56.4	53.5	56.6
SCI loans	56.5	37.8	32.4	31.2
Other liabilities	3.7	5.9	14.1	12.2
Net wealth/Disposable income	4.4	4.6	4.4	...

Note: "Other assets" include banker's acceptances, atypical securities, Bank of Italy cashier's cheques and cheques. "Other liabilities" include bad debts on loans of banks, insurance companies and social security institutions and, from 1984 onward, non-bank consumer credit.
Source: Banca d'Italia (1986a and 1987).

To put the whole discussion in the right perspective, notice that developments in the allocation of financial wealth reflect most of the features which have characterized and, to a lesser extent, still characterize the Italian financial structure. The crucial point is that, historically, Italian sectoral financial balances have consistently shown a pattern characterized by households' financial surpluses approximately balancing the public sector's increasing deficits. The corresponding need for a high degree of financial intermediation, coupled with the limited development of the Italian capital market, has paved the way for a predominant role for credit institutions in the process of financial intermediation. The high and variable rates of inflation of the mid-1970s and the consequent collapse of the bond market strengthened further the phenomenon of over-intermediation by the banking system, leading to the absorption of the economy's financial assets into bank deposits.

In the second half of the 1970s the explosion in the public sector borrowing requirement, the outburst of inflation (and the consequent unavailability of the bond market to finance the deficit), and the evolution of monetary policy (Caranza and Fazio 1983) fostered the unprecedented growth of short-term and floating rate securities, such as Treasury Bills (*Buoni Ordinari del Tesoro*, BOT) and Treasury Credit Certificates[2] (*Certificati di Credito del Tesoro*, CCT), that started to be accumulated in households' portfolios. Subsequently, the continuous growth of public debt, and monetary policies aimed at encouraging its absorption by the household sector (as reflected in the positive *ex-post* real interest rates prevailing since 1982) further encouraged financial investment, particularly in government securities.

Developments such as these raise a number of important issues. First, it would be legitimate to ask whether the "effective" stock of money should also include, besides deposits and currency, other financial instruments (with appropriate weights) such as short-term government securities. Second, continuing debt-financed government deficits raise the question of whether (and to what extent) government debt drives up the rate of return on capital, therefore crowding out interest sensitive private sector spending (in particular, residential investment and investment in new productive capacity). Third, the Italian inflationary experience calls for an assessment of the responsiveness of the demand for government securities to the inflation rate, for this impinges on the complete bond refinanceability of inflation induced interest service. This, in turn, is related to the issue of the appropriate measurement of fiscal deficits.

In addition, it is often suggested that relative price movements cannot be invoked as the only explanatory factor for such dramatic shifts in the composition of households' wealth. Shifts in monetary aggregates "unaccounted for" by interest rate behavior are frequently pointed out and attributed to the role played by financial innovations, in particular if they lower transactions costs for asset purchases and sales, or lead to the appearance of previously unavailable assets.[3] Undoubtedly, such innovations have taken place extensively in the Italian financial markets in recent years and the recent popularity of mutual funds, repackaging assets to yield different services, provides the last such example. However, the mere recognition of the existence of specific innovations is only a starting point: it remains to be understood, also in quantitative terms, how they affect agents' behavior.

From an empirical viewpoint, the available econometric evidence in Italy is still scanty. The only available references on the allocation of (financial) wealth are Modigliani and Cotula (1973), Cotula and others (1984) and Banca d'Italia (1986b). In all cases, however, the whole private non-bank sector is considered. In view of this, the main purpose of the present paper is to provide additional empirical evidence regarding household demand for monetary assets.

The traditional way of attacking the problem, following the standard discrete-time theory of risk averse portfolio choice, and under well known assumptions, would be to regress actual portfolio shares held by households against some measure of expected returns exploiting (more or less completely) the information deriving from portfolio optimization theory. As a result, a number of important questions depending on the parameters in investors' asset demands could be tentatively answered (see Friedman 1978 and 1985, Roley 1982 and Frankel 1985, among others).

The status of this kind of empirical exercise is, however, not entirely undisputed. Friedman (1985) frankly reports the discouraging results of applying maximum likelihood methods to estimate investors' behavior using data on the aggregate portfolio of US households. Frankel and Dickens (1983) test the hypothesis of mean-variance optimization and statistically reject it. The poor empirical performance of traditional portfolio models is not an unexpected result, given the central import- ance of time-varying investors' risk perceptions in governing how market-clearing expected returns respond to changes in asset supplies, and considering also the restrictive representation of aggregate prefer- ences used in applied work.

A possible alternative would be to infer investors' unobservable perceptions of asset risks from actual after-tax return data, and then to apply the standard theory of risk-averse portfolio allocation to recover the relevant parameters of investors' asset demands. However, even abstracting from the issue of measurement of expected rates,[4] this line of research appears to be largely unfruitful in the Italian case, because of the lack of an adequate data base. In fact, long-term holdings data do not contain market valuation changes, quarterly data for equity holdings are not available, and the evaluation of tangible assets such as real estate and consumer durables is still somewhat doubtful.

In the light of these comments the paper focuses on households' short-term demand for assets in a "money in the utility function" context. Along with some recent literature (Diewert 1974, Donovan 1978, Barnett 1980 and 1981, Ewis and Fisher 1984 and 1985, Husted and Rush 1984, Serletis and Robb 1986 and Poterba and Rotemberg 1986), the paper assumes the households' objective function to be defined over non-durable consumer goods, labor services and the services of consumer durables and monetary assets. Given standard (but not unquestionable, intertemporal and intratemporal) separability assumptions, derived demand functions for financial assets are specified and estimated. Among the important advantages of working with explicit portfolio models involving utility maximization there are testable within- and cross-equation restrictions corresponding to meaningful representation of preferences, which can be used to improve the overall efficiency of estimation. Furthermore, it is quite natural to incorporate into this framework recent advances in the literature on functional forms, thereby introducing more flexibility into the analysis.

As is well known, this approach "is a reduced form approach which models, restricts, and characterizes the results of the consumer's decisions without the need to consider the explicit structure of the decision. While the true utility function does not contain money, a derived utility function containing money generally can be acquired" (Barnett 1981). However, it is not an uncontroversial approach. Its critics dislike the idea that money yields utility directly and point out that rate of return dominated assets are held because they reduce transaction costs, which should be explicitly modeled. The implicit modeling upon which the utility approach is based is not necessarily an alternative, though, to the explicit modeling used in the transaction demand approach. Indeed, recent research (Feenstra 1986) has shown that, under specific assumptions, there exists a functional equivalence between treating real balances as an argument of the utility function and entering money into liquidity costs as a part of the budget constraint.

Admittedly, some of the applied literature mentioned above can, in principle, be criticized on the grounds that the consumer's portfolio allocation problem tends to be modeled as one of choosing expenditures (i.e., opportunity cost times the quantity held) on liquidity services, and hence on different assets, while the opportunity cost of these assets is a random variable at the time when the consumer allocates his portfolio. This difficulty is avoided in the recent work of Poterba and Rotemberg (1986). Building up on Hansen and Singleton (1982), they estimate the parameters of a representative consumer's utility function from the first-order condition of the maximization problem. This line of research though, presents a number of serious problems. Its critics (Deaton 1986, among others) have underlined the danger of its application to aggregate data. Furthermore, its empirical implementation is limited to specific functional forms which unduly restrict preferences and, therefore, have been dismissed by empirical demand analysis a long time ago.[5] In the light of these remarks, this paper follows the standard practice and neglects the uncertainty of asset returns.

In order to focus on the details of demand for services on monetary assets, the paper ignores the upper (intertemporal) stage of the consumer's optimization problem, i.e. the allocation of consumer's resources among broad categories (consumption goods, labor and monetary services). In this framework four main issues are addressed. First, we specify and present estimates of the parameters of the technology allowing households to combine financial instruments available on the market and derive a non-marketed good such as "liquidity services." These estimates imply a whole pattern of substitution among financial assets and allow one to study the effects of changes in interest rates on asset holdings.

Second, we allow short-term and floating rate government securities such as BOTs and CCTs to provide liquidity services and present an indirect test of this contention. The inclusion of government securities in the liquidity generating technology is by no means unusual (see Barth, Kraft and Kraft 1977, Ewis and Fisher 1984 and 1985, and Poterba and Rotemberg 1986) and it appears to be suitable (at least as a working hypothesis) in the Italian case, where both short-term debt and medium-term debt (indexed to the short-term interest rate) are widely regarded as being easily marketable. In this respect, a more traditional risk-return framework should not necessarily be preferred and could instead be usefully confined to the choice between long-term debt, equities (amounting together to some 15 percent of households' financial wealth) and tangible assets.

Third, as in Barnett (1980) and Barth, Kraft and Kraft (1977), we exploit the concept of "committed quantities" and model the dynamic process governing the system of asset demand equations with a general procedure consistent with the "habit formation" hypothesis.

Finally, assuming that financial innovations can be classified as affecting one or more of the relevant coefficients (Judd and Scadding 1982), but not necessarily the preference parameters, we adopt a flexible functional form and model the elasticity of substitution between assets as a time varying quantity. At the same time, we test a number of interesting restrictions on preferences and we attempt to detect the presence of structural changes in the coefficients of the monetary aggregator implicit in the technology generating the demand for assets.

The paper is structured as follows. Section 2 introduces the theoretical framework and discusses a specific functional form for the households' objective functions. Section 3 presents the estimation procedure and the empirical results. Section 4 uses the estimated parameters to provide empirical evidence on the structure of the households' demand for monetary assets. Finally, section 5 concludes the paper, underlying some policy implications.

2   Theoretical background

Drawing on Diewert's (1974) seminal paper as well as on the subsequent work of Donovan (1978) and Barnett (1978, 1980, and 1981), some of the recent literature on assets demand has incorporated many of the concepts and techniques of modern consumer theory. Exploiting recent advances in duality theory, systems of asset demand equations have been derived from household models of utility-maximizing behavior by applying the concept of the rental price of a durable good to the case of financial assets.

Formally, given the appropriate separability assumptions (Barnett 1981), the optimization problem of the representative household can be cast in terms of the following one period minimization:

$$\min_{m} C(v_{1t}, \ldots, v_{It}, u) \quad (i = 1, \ldots, I; t = 1, \ldots, T). \quad (1)$$

Define:

$$\Sigma_j v_{jt} m_{jt} = M_t \quad (2)$$

where $m_t = (m_{1t}, \ldots, m_{It})$ is an I-vector of quantities of monetary assets (i.e., stocks deflated by some general price index p_t) held in period t and assumed to generate proportionately liquidity services; their rental prices (Jorgensonian user costs) are given by the I-vector $v_t = (v_{1t}, \ldots, v_{It})$. Hence, M_t represents total expenditure on liquidity services, while $C(.)$ is a cost function defining the minimum cost of reaching a given level of utility u at a given price vector v, and is assumed to satisfy the usual regularity conditions.

For the i-th asset,

$$v_{it} = [(R_t - r_{it})/(1 + R_t)]p_t \quad (3)$$

which denotes the discounted interest foregone by holding a lira's worth of that asset. In (3) R_t is the expected one-period holding (including realized or unrealized capital gains or losses) nominal yield available on a benchmark asset, that is an asset accumulated to transfer wealth between multiperiod planning horizons rather than to yield liquidity services during the current period. Notice that, from the agent's viewpoint, R_t contains all relevant premia available in the market for foregoing the services provided by monetary assets. Furthermore, r_{it} is the expected one-period holding nominal yield of the i-th asset.[6,7]

Despite its theoretical nicety, the empirical application of this approach must face the problem of giving an appropriate definition to the benchmark asset. The available literature has usually singled out a particular financial asset such as equity holdings (as in Poterba and Rotemberg 1986) or long-term corporate bonds (as in Husted and Rush 1984 and Donovan 1978), or, in each period, the asset yielding the highest rate of return (as in Serletis and Robb 1986 and Ewis and Fisher 1984 and 1985). In the present paper we identify it with long-term corporate bonds and tangible assets (dwellings).

To provide a sufficient degree of flexibility, we consider, for (1), the following functional form:

$$\log c(u, v) = \log(M_t - \Sigma_j \mu_j v_{jt})$$
$$= (1 - u) \log a(v) + u \log b(v) \qquad (4)$$

where

$$\log a(v) = \alpha_0 + \Sigma_k \alpha_k \log v_k + \tfrac{1}{2} \Sigma_k \Sigma_j \gamma^*_{kj} \log v_k \log v_j \qquad (5)$$

$$\log b(v) = \log a(v) + \beta_0 \Pi_k v_k^{\beta_k} \qquad (6)$$

with

$$\Sigma_k \alpha_k = 1, \ \Sigma_k \gamma^*_{kj} = \Sigma_j \gamma^*_{kj} = \Sigma_k \beta_k = 0.$$

Bollino (1987) shows that equations (4)–(6) generalize Deaton and Muellbauer's (1980) Almost Ideal (A. I.) demand system, by introducing overhead costs or committed quantities (that is, the μ_i's) into the original cost function belonging to the Piglog class. In terms of the primal problem, equation (4) implies that utility is generated by the net quantities $(m_i - \mu_i)$'s. Alternatively, equation (4) can be understood as the counterpart of a budget constraint defined in terms of expenditure net of committed expenditure consumed independently of current rates of return or expenditure on monetary services. In other words, the agent must bear a fixed (overhead) cost before obtaining any utility from liquidity services.

The μ_i's provide an immediate and theoretically coherent, well known way of introducing dynamics into the system. Since Pollak (1970), it has been recognized that past decisions are an important determinant of present allocation patterns, in order to characterize both short-run and long-run agent preferences. In the present context we adopt a general specification (known as "dynamic translating" since Pollak and Wales 1981 and already present in Barnett 1980) which permits some preference parameters to vary with past choices allowing a "habit formation" interpretation. In particular, we define

$$\mu_{it} = (\bar{\mu}_i + \lambda_i p_{t-1} m_{i,t-1})/p_t \tag{7}$$

The "dynamic translating" procedure is general in that it is not functional form dependent and can be applied to any demand system which represents the static maintained hypothesis.[8]

Reverting to equations (4)–(6), by Shephard's lemma the following share equations can be obtained:

$$w_i = (\mu_i v_i/M) + [1 - (\Sigma_j \mu_j v_j/M)]$$

$$\{\alpha_i + \beta_i \, log\,[(M - \Sigma_j \mu_j v_j)/V] + \Sigma_j \gamma_{ij} \, log \, v_j\} \tag{8}$$

$$log \, V = \alpha_0 + \Sigma_k \alpha_k \, log \, v_k + \tfrac{1}{2} \Sigma_k \Sigma_j \gamma_{kj} \, log \, v_k \, log \, v_j \tag{9}$$

where

$$w_i = v_i m_i/M, \quad \text{and} \quad \gamma_{ij} = \tfrac{1}{2}(\gamma_{ij}^* + \gamma_{ji}^*).$$

Equations (8) and (9) define a system of demand equations summing up to total expenditure on liquidity services, homogeneous of degree zero in rental prices and total expenditure, symmetric in the substitution matrix if the following restrictions are satisfied:

$$\Sigma_i \alpha_i = 1; \; \Sigma_i \gamma_{ij} = \Sigma_i \beta_i = 0 \qquad \text{(Adding-up)}$$

$$\Sigma_j \gamma_{ij} = 0 \qquad \text{(Homogeneity)}$$

$$\gamma_{ij} = \gamma_{ji} \qquad \text{(Symmetry)}$$

Unfortunately there is no way of imposing, by means of simple parametric restrictions, the negative semidefiniteness of the substitution matrix.

Following Deaton and Muellbauer's (1980) suggestion, in order to simplify the estimation procedure, $log\ V$ will be approximated as follows:

$$log\ V^* = \Sigma_j w_j\ log\ v_j \tag{10}$$

on the grounds of the consideration that, if rental rates move together, then $log\ V$ would be quite insensitive to the choice of weights.

3   Estimation and empirical results

In the empirical application we consider quarterly Italian time series[9] of five categories of financial assets for the period 1977.3–1986.4 inclusive.[10] The five aggregates are: "Notes and Coins, and Demand Deposits," "Savings Deposits," "Postal Deposits and Deposits and Savings Certificates of Special Credit Institutions," "Treasury Bills" and "Treasury Credit Certificates."

A number of points regarding the treatment of the data should be made. First, since 1984 Italian investors have been given the opportunity to invest even small amounts in a block of generically defined securities managed by investment funds. Presumably, the substantial increase in investment fund resources led to a corresponding reduction of the direct demand for securities by savers, crowding out in particular the direct demand for CCTs which, by the end of 1986, amounted to about 40 percent of mutual funds asset holdings. Since the amount of available information is certainly insufficient to allow a separate treatment of investment fund units, it was decided to allocate this component of household financial wealth *pro quota* to CCTs. While this procedure is at best a rough approximation, it substantially improves the forecasting performance of the model (as we should expect under reasonable assumptions), while leaving unaltered other features of the estimates.

Second, in the light of the previous discussion, R is defined as a weighted average of the one-period holding nominal yield available on long-term corporate bonds and the real assets rate of return, with weights given by the actual weights of those assets in total wealth normalized to sum to unity.

Third, with the exception of long-term assets, all rates of return are defined as actual, net of taxes, one period holding nominal yields. Capital gains and losses are tentatively taken into account for long-term assets computing returns as in Banca d'Italia (1986b).[11]

Fourth, a premium accounting for the difficulties encountered in evaluating the rate of return on real assets is estimated by scanning and then added to R. It turns out to equal 6 percent on a yearly basis.

Table 6.2 Parameter estimates under the homogeneity and symmetry constraints (1977.3–86.4)

	$i = 1$	$i = 2$	$i = 3$	$i = 4$	$i = 5$
$\bar{\mu}_i/100$	− 0.417	− 0.883	− 0.085	− 0.029	− 0.015
	(0.202)	(0.436)	(0.048)	(0.098)	(0.037)
λ_i	0.280	0.622	0.514	0.651	0.921
	(0.131)	(0.136)	(0.101)	(0.054)	(0.048)
α_i	0.397	0.625	− 0.036	0.239	− 0.224
	(0.073)	(0.079)	(0.040)	(0.070)	(0.071)
β_i	− 0.028	− 0.020	0.019	− 0.028	0.057
	(0.016)	(0.018)	(0.009)	(0.015)	(0.020)
γ_{i1}	0.201				
	(0.016)				
γ_{i2}	− 0.115	0.162			
	(0.026)	(0.027)			
γ_{i3}	− 0.042	− 0.029	0.077		
	(0.008)	(0.007)	(0.012)		
γ_{i4}	− 0.038	− 0.016	− 0.001	0.047	
	(0.011)	(0.010)	(0.003)	(0.017)	
γ_{i5}	− 0.007	− 0.002	− 0.005	0.008	− 0.006
	(0.004)	(0.004)	(0.002)	(0.003)	
$\hat{\sigma} \times 100$	0.264	0.305	0.121	0.277	0.190
dw	1.73	2.16	1.42	2.16	2.25

Note: $i = 1$: Notes and coins and demand deposits; $i = 2$: Savings deposits; $i = 3$: Postal deposits and savings and credit certificates of SCI; $i = 4$: Treasury bills; $i = 5$: Treasury credit certificates.

The parameters of the system (7), (8) and (10), estimated by Full Information Maximum Likelihood, are presented in Table 6.2 along with some summary statistics.[12] Most of the coefficients in Table 6.2 are significant, based on individual tests, and the overall fit seems satisfactory. Three of the β_i's are significantly different from zero, thereby pointing to a *prima facie* violation of the commonly accepted hypothesis of a liquidity generating technology independent of scale.[13] Nine out of ten free γ_{ij}'s are also significantly different from zero and testify a substantial price responsiveness of agents. As we would expect (given their relationship with adjustment speeds) the λ_i's are all significantly different from zero and of increasing magnitude as we move from short to longer term assets. The Durbin-Watson statistics, although not entirely appropriate in the present context, do not suggest dynamic misspecification of the system.

Tables 6.3, 6.4 and 6.5 report a sequence of tests of theoretical

Table 6.3 Likelihood ratio tests

	r	Ψ	Ψ_1	Ψ_2
Homogeneity $[H_0: \Sigma_j \gamma_{ij} = 0 \ (\forall i)]$	4	11.6	5.5	7.5
Symmetry $[H_0: \gamma_{ij} = \gamma_{ji} \ (\forall i \neq j)]$	6	7.6	—	—
Overhead cost $[H_0: \bar{\mu}_i = \lambda_i = 0 \ (\forall i)]$	10	263.4	249.9	187.3
Constant overhead $[H_0: \bar{\mu}_i = 0 \ (\forall i)]$	5	43.2	36.3	30.7
Habit formation $[H_0: \lambda_i = 0 \ (\forall i)]$	5	148.6	141.7	105.7
Quasi-homotheticity $[H_0: \beta_i = 0 \ (\forall i)]$	4	14.6	9.1	10.4
Restricted Price Response $[H_0: \gamma_{ij}=0 \ (\forall i, j)]$	10	73.0	59.5	51.9

interest. In Table 6.3 Ψ identifies the usual likelihood ratio test, and r the number of constraints. In addition, when appropriate, we also report the degrees of freedom corrected likelihood ratio statistics Ψ_1 (Pudney 1981) and Ψ_2 (Meisner 1979). Apart from checking whether the data are consistent with the assumption of utility maximizing behavior, the hypothesis of no overhead costs, of quasi-homotheticity and of restricted price response are also tested for statistically. The results are of considerable interest in that some of the hypotheses that have usually been assumed to characterize asset demand systems tend to be rejected by the data. Homogeneity and symmetry cannot be rejected on the basis of the available evidence. The assumptions of zero committed quantities and of no habit formation are strongly at variance with the data while the standard assumption of quasi-homotheticity[14] is only mildly so. The same conclusion can be drawn from the test for restricted price responses which is obtained by letting all γ_{ij}'s equal zero, thereby reducing the Almost Ideal demand system to a slightly underparametrized member of the same family belonging to the Forgeaud-Nataf (1959) class in which demands are a function of real total expenditure and the relative own price alone. As Deaton (1976) has shown, this would imply an approximate proportionality between expenditure and price elasticities which is usually regarded as a rather implausible behavior in applied demand analysis. On the contrary, the data suggests that flexibility is a basic

Table 6.4 Weak separability tests

	r	Ψ
Reference year: 1978		
[H_0: $u(u_1(M2), u_2(BOT, CCT))$]	6	7.0
[H_0: $u(u_1(M3), u_2(CCT))$]	6	17.1
Reference year: 1980		
[H_0: $u(u_1(M2), u_2(BOT, CCT))$]	6	6.3
[H_0: $u(u_1(M3), u_2(CCT))$]	6	19.6
Reference year: 1982		
[H_0: $u(u_1(M2), u_2(BOT, CCT))$]	6	5.7
[H_0: $u(u_1(M3), u_2(CCT))$]	6	27.0
Reference year: 1984		
[H_0: $u(u_1(M2), u_2(BOT, CCT))$]	6	5.6
[H_0: $u(u_1(M3), u_2(CCT))$]	6	21.1
Reference year: 1986		
[H_0: $u(u_1(M2), u_2(BOT, CCT))$]	6	7.3
[H_0: $u(u_1(M3), u_2(CCT))$]	6	17.1

ingredient in modeling asset demand price responses and these restrictions are soundly rejected.

Table 6.4 presents an indirect test of the hypothesis of weak separability of a money aggregate with respect to a government securities aggregate, in the uncommitted technology.[15] The test, which is a Wald test basically testing the implications of the Leontief-Sono condition, is conditional on a given portfolio allocation and therefore it was computed for every other year since 1978. As it turns out, throughout the period the marginal rates of substitution between the components of M2 money do not seem to depend on short-term and floating rate government securities and therefore an M2 aggregate can be meaningfully defined. Given the nature of CCTs, an M3 aggregate (i.e., M2 plus T-bills) is instead never appropriately defined.

As an additional check on the performance of the model, Table 6.5 reports the result of estimating the model excluding the observations for one or two years at the beginning or at the end of the sample period and then computing the structural stability test proposed in Anderson and Mizon (1983). In all cases the hypothesis of a stable model structure cannot be rejected at conventional significance levels, if proper account is taken of the tendency of these tests to reject the null in small samples. Interestingly, though, parameter stability tends to fail by the end of the period if mutual funds holdings of government bonds (mostly CCTs) are not merged with households' holdings of the same asset.

Table 6.5 Parameter stability tests

	r	Ψ	Ψ_2
Sample excludes:			
I. First year	16	21.6	15.3
First two years	32	29.1	20.7
Last two years	32	70.1	49.8
Last year	16	27.5	19.6
II. First year	16	21.9	15.6
First two years	32	30.9	22.0
Last two years	32	81.0	57.6
Last year	16	42.7	30.4

Note: Overall sample: 1977.3–86.4. This means that excluding the first year from the sample implies estimation over the sub-period 1978.3–86.4, excluding the last year implies estimation over the sub-period 1977.3–85.4, and so on. Section I denotes stability tests performed including mutual funds holdings of government bonds into CCTs, while section II excludes them.

In conclusion, these results tend to reinforce the contention that casting the analysis in terms of more general, flexible models, may capture some of the complexities of the available empirical evidence. In particular, it seems that, during the period under study, financial innovations have not necessarily implied structural breaks, that is, changes in the parameter characterizing the underlying representation of consumer preferences.

4   The structure of Italian households' demand for monetary assets

Having estimated and tested the model, we can now use its parameters to study the composition of households' portfolios and the effects of changes in interest rates on asset holdings. It should be noted that in the present case analytical solutions for the long run preferences are not available. Therefore, it proved necessary to revert to dynamic simulations. These were performed, first, by computing the long-run portfolio structure based on the levels of total short-term financial wealth and interest rates at the end of 1986. Subsequently, each rate of return was shocked by one percentage point in order to trace and assess the pattern of price responses, *for a given total short-term financial wealth*.[16]

Considering the long-run, fully adjusted portfolio structure implied by the rate differentials at the end of 1986, it is interesting to notice that the share of postal deposits and BOTs would remain approximately

Table 6.6 Effects of a one point change in selected rates of return (reference year 1986, percentage points)

	Quarter	Money	BOT and CCT
Rate of return: Demand and Savings Deposits			
	0	0.80	− 0.97
	4	2.19	− 2.62
	LR	2.98	− 3.54
Rate of return: Demand Deposits			
	0	0.17	− 0.20
	4	0.27	− 0.32
	LR	0.29	− 0.35
Rate of return: Savings Deposits			
	0	0.60	− 0.73
	4	1.88	− 2.25
	LR	2.71	− 3.22
Rate of return: Postal Deposits			
	0	− 0.04	0.05
	4	− 0.34	0.51
	LR	− 1.03	1.23
Rate of return: BOTs and CCTs			
	0	− 1.53	1.84
	4	− 3.98	4.75
	LR	− 4.97	5.91
Rate of return: CCTs			
	0	− 1.17	1.41
	4	− 4.69	5.61
	LR	− 8.19	9.74

Note: Price responses are computed for a given level of total short-term financial wealth.

unchanged. On the contrary, the share of CCTs over total assets would be substantially larger (up 6 percentage points, or, equivalently, 50,000 billions of lire), at the expense of bank deposits. In other words, there are reasons to believe that the substitution away from bank deposits would continue, given the present rates.

Since the theoretical framework adopted in this paper allows for time varying elasticities, Table 6.6 presents price responses evaluated at the end 1986 variable levels. For reasons of simplicity and comparability, price responses are presented in terms of the two most relevant aggregates, that is, M2 money and short-term and floating rate government securities.

Price responses in Table 6.6 should be understood as the percentage change in the demand for the relevant financial aggregate following a one point change in the rate of return of the j-th asset. Responses are recorded in the same quarter in which the change in the rate of return takes place (quarter 0), one year after (quarter 4), and in the long run (or five years after, LR).

Comparing these to the corresponding responses evaluated at different points in time (not reported here because of space limitations), it is possible to appreciate the advantage of working with models flexible enough so as to accommodate time varying responses while keeping the underlying structure of preferences constant.

To start with, in 1986 a one point change in the rates of return on (both demand and savings) bank deposits would have led in equilibrium to a 3 percent increase in M2 money (corresponding to about 13,000 billions of lire), and a 3.5 percent decrease in short-term government securities. As expected, agents would shift from short-term government securities to deposits in order to "produce" liquidity services efficiently. It is worth noting that performing the same calculations for the year 1980 implies quite different price responses, reflecting a different portfolio structure. M2 money would have increased by less than 2 percent with short-term and floating rate government securities decreasing by more than 7 percent.

This result hides important differences in the price responsiveness of different financial instruments. In particular, if the rates of return on demand and savings deposits are increased separately, an entirely different picture emerges. In fact, changes in the former rate only imply a reallocation inside M2 money: demand deposits rise by nearly 3 percent in equilibrium and savings deposits fall by more than 4 percent with the demand for government securities only marginally decreasing. On the contrary, changes in the latter rate lead to a reshuffling of the entire portfolio: BOTs and CCTs decrease by more than 2 and 3 percent respectively, demand deposits fall by almost 1 percent, while savings deposits rise by more than 6 percent.

An even stronger pattern of interactions is implied by a one point change in the rate of return on short-term government securities. Recalling that CCT rate is linked to the BOT rate, such a change would lead in equilibrium to a 6 percent increase in the stock of these securities (corresponding to nearly 20,000 billions of lire), and a slightly less than 5 percent decrease in M2 money. Again, the reference period is crucial in evaluating these responses. In 1980, a one point change in the rate of return of BOT and CCT would have produced in the long run a meagre 2.5 percent increase in the demand for bank and postal deposits, while, in the light of the then limited market dimension, the demand for BOTs and CCTs would have increased by nearly 10 percent.

Once more these figures hide asset specific effects. Consider for example a one percent increase in the CCTs spread over the BOTs rate. This would lead, with respect to the previous case, to an even higher increase in the overall demand for government securities (nearly 10 percent in equilibrium) originating, however, from a massive shift from all assets into CCTs. The demand for CCTs would increase by more than 15 percent after one year and 20 percent in equilibrium, mainly at the expense of BOTs (-10 percent after one year and -14 percent in equilibrium) and postal deposits (-6 and -10 percent, respectively).

Unfortunately, not all results based on the estimated parameters lend themselves to meaningful interpretations. In particular, changes in the rate of return on postal deposits appear to produce quantitatively negligible, albeit qualitatively perverse, responses which deserve further investigation.

Own- and cross-price responses presented in Table 6.6 also imply interesting inflation induced substitution effects. In particular, since changes in the expected inflation rate should affect in principle only the price term of demand deposits and cash, we have shocked this latter in order to achieve a one percent increase in the inflation rate. This leads to a switch from demand deposits and cash (-0.5 percent in equilibrium) to savings deposits (0.8 percent in equilibrium) and to a much lesser extent to BOTs (0.06 percent) and CCTs (0.03 percent). Abstracting from other effects of inflation, it can be noted that these figures do not constitute any substantial evidence against adjusting government deficit for inflation.

Finally, another interesting exercise, motivated by the non-homotheticity of the system, is given by a one percent increase of total short-term assets for given levels of the rental rates. In the short-run, bank deposits absorb a relatively higher proportion of a shock in the level of total assets, as clearly implied by impact elasticities in the neighborhood of 1.3 for M2 money and 0.6 for government securities. One year later the situation is entirely reversed: the scale elasticity of M2 money drops to 0.8 (reaching 0.5 in equilibrium), while the scale elasticity of government securities increases to 1.3 (1.7 in equilibrium).

5   Concluding comments

In this paper we have specified, estimated and tested a utility function approach to the demand for monetary assets and short-term and floating rate government securities on Italian quarterly data referring to the household sector for the period 1977–86. Although much work remains to be done, our results suggest a number of conclusions of both theoretical and empirical interest.

First, from an econometric modeling point of view, the paper has clarified the importance of working with flexible functional forms when estimating systems of asset demand equations characterized, as in the Italian case, by dramatic compositional changes. Rather than invoking structural breaks to make up for functional failures, this approach can interpret substantial data variation while keeping the underlying structure of preferences constant.

Second, from a policy point of view, the empirical results suggest that, in generating liquidity, bank deposits show a sizable degree of substitution with respect to short-term and floating rate government securities. Indeed, the present (end of 1986) level of total financial wealth and the structure of rate of return differentials would imply in the long-run a substitution away from bank deposits, in particular into CCTs, far beyond the one already taking place.

Third, although not negligible, the degree of "moneyness" of short-term and floating rate government debt does not endanger the meaning of traditional monetary aggregates, such as M2 money. At the same time, however, the pattern of substitutions among financial instruments allows to lump together in a single aggregate both short-term and floating rate government securities.

Fourth, it appears that inflation induces asset substitution to a very limited extent and leads to a fall in the demand for M2 money and a marginal rise in the demand for government securities. Portfolio effects of inflation of the kind considered in this paper are not such as to deter inflation adjustment of conventional measures of government deficits.

Finally and more generally, the evidence points to a high degree of responsiveness of households to relative price signals, a conclusion which has important implications in the light of the increasing degree of integration of financial markets, both within and outside the country.

NOTES

* The authors would like to thank I. Angeloni, F. Cesarano, C. Cottarelli, G. Marotta and the participants to the Seminar, especially J. Frankel, G. Galli and A. Giovannini, for many helpful comments and suggestions. Any remaining errors are the authors' responsibility. Any opinions expressed are the authors' own and do not necessarily reflect those of their institutions of affiliation.
1 See Banca d'Italia (1986a) and Commissione per lo Studio della Evoluzione della Ricchezza Finanziaria (1987, Appendix 1.A) where the methodological aspects of the estimation of sectoral wealth are also discussed.

2 Indexed CCTs are debentures whose yield is linked to the BOT rate. Given the present indexation system and the maturity characteristics of the two instruments, they should not necessarily be considered as perfect substitutes.

3 For a complete survey of the main features and causes of financial innovations in Italy during the last decade, see Caranza and Cottarelli (1986).

4 We do not address here the more general, and sometimes neglected, issue of the role of sample vs. prior information in empirical analysis.

5 In a stochastic framework, closed form solutions to the consumer's control problem remain intractable even for very simple representations of preferences like those considered in Poterba and Rotemberg (1986). Therefore, in order to study the effects of changes in, say, interest rates and inflation on consumption and asset holding, they need to revert to a deterministic environment.

6 If direct taxation takes into account all interest income, then

$$v_i = p[(R - r_i)(1 - \tau)]/[1 + R(1 - \tau)]$$

where τ is the marginal income tax rate. Given the present Italian system of taxation, we disregard this correction and consider, in the empirical part of this work, net rates of return.

7 It is worth noticing that in (3) nominal interest rates can be expected to respond to expected inflation rates. In addition, since Jorgensonian user costs for consumer durables do depend inversely upon the expected inflation rate, it follows that expected inflation can influence asset demand through a number of interesting channels.

8 In principle, μ_i can be made dependent on past history in several ways such as a weighted average of all lagged quantities, highest peak attained in the past, and so on. Notice that while the habit formation hypothesis relies on the interpretation of (7) as a model of changing preferences whereby agents gradually learn from past experience, if there exist omitted variables correlated with lagged quantities, the significance of λ_i may indeed reveal misspecification of the original demand system rather than evidence of dynamic adjustment.

9 Although some data were seasonally adjusted, seasonal dummies were included in the regression in order to pick up any residual seasonality.

10 The source for all data used in this paper is Banca d'Italia. The only exception is given by the general (consumer) price index p_t derived from ISTAT, Bollettino Mensile, various issues. (This is the official monthly publication of the Italian statistical office.)

11 Basically this implies computing the return on long-term bonds in R as the nominal one period holding yield plus the ex-post rate of capital gains as proxied by the rate of change of the average bond price (as estimated in Galli 1985).

12 As usual, an additive error term has been appended to the system (8) and has been assumed to be normal i.i.d. with contemporaneous singular covariance matrix, in observance of the adding-up constraint. Estimation and hypothesis testing has been carried out by means of the 4.0 Version of TSP.

13 It is interesting to note that the same evidence can also be inferred from a preliminary analysis of the Banca Nazionale del Lavoro Survey on Households' Finances, based on a sample of its customers. We would like to thank

M. Morciano and G. Raimondi for kindly providing us with the data, which are still unpublished.

14 The quasi-homotheticity hypothesis is relevant for the meaningful construction of monetary aggregates. See Barnett (1980), and Serletis and Robb (1986).

15 Basically, we test whether the quantities

$$(\gamma_{ik} - \beta_i w_k)/(w_i + \beta_i) - (\gamma_{jk} - \beta_j w_k)/(w_j + \beta_j)$$

($\forall i, j \in$ aggregate 1, $\forall k \in$ aggregate 2)

are jointly zero. This corresponds to the well known implication of weak separability, i.e. the ratio of cross-price elasticities of assets i and j with respect to asset k is equal to the ratio of their expenditure elasticities.

16 The choice of computing price elasticities for given total short-term financial wealth has been made mainly to allow comparability with other portfolio studies. Other exercises have been conducted by computing compensated and uncompensated price responses, which are available upon request from the authors. In assessing these figures, the obvious interactions amongst rates of return should be kept in mind (see Banca d'Italia 1986b).

REFERENCES

Anderson, G.J. and G.E. Mizon (1983), "Parameter Constancy Tests: Old and New," (unpublished), Southampton, England: University of Southampton.

Banca d'Italia (1986a), "The Wealth of Italian Households (1975–1985)," *Economic Bulletin*, no. 7, Rome: Banca d'Italia.

——— (1986b), "Modello Trimestrale dell'Economia Italiana," *Temi di discussione* no. 80, Rome: Banca d'Italia.

——— (1987), *Relazione annuale* Rome: Banca d'Italia.

Barnett, W.A. (1978), "The User Cost of Money," *Economics Letters*, Vol. 1.

——— (1980), "Economic Monetary Aggregates: An Application of Index Number and Aggregation Theory," *Journal of Econometrics*, Vol. 14, September.

——— (1981), *Consumer Demand and Labor Supply. Goods, Monetary Assets, and Time*. Amsterdam: North Holland.

Barth, J., A. Kraft, and J. Kraft (1977), "The 'moneyness' of financial assets," *Applied Economics*, Vol. 9, March.

Bollino, C.A. (1987), "GAIDS: A Generalized Version of the Almost Ideal Demand System," *Economics Letters*, Vol. 23.

Caranza, C. and C. Cottarelli (1986), "Financial Innovation in Italy: A Lopsided Process," *Temi di discussione* no. 64, Rome: Banca d'Italia, May.

Caranza, C. and A. Fazio (1983), "Methods of Monetary Control in Italy: 1974–1983," in *The Political Economy of Monetary Policy: National and International Aspects*. Boston: Federal Reserve of Boston.

Commissione per lo studio della evoluzione della ricchezza finanziaria (1987), *Ricchezza finanziaria, debito pubblico e politica monetaria nella prospettiva dell'integrazione internazionale*. Rome: Ministero del Tesoro.

Cotula, F., G. Galli, E. Lecaldano, V. Sannucci and E.A. Zautzik (1984), "Una stima delle funzioni di domanda di attivita' finanziarie," in *Ricerche quantitative per la politica economica*. Rome: Banca d'Italia.

Deaton, A.S. (1976), "A Simple Non-Additive Model of Demand," in *Private and Enlarged Consumption*, edited by L. Solari and J.N. Du Pasquier. Amsterdam: North Holland.

(1986), "Life-Cycle Models of Consumption: Is the Evidence Consistent with the Theory?", Working Paper no. 1910, unpublished. Cambridge, Mass.: National Bureau of Economic Research.

Deaton, A.S. and J. Muellbauer (1980), "An Almost Ideal Demand System," *American Economic Review*, Vol. 70, December.

Diewert, W.E. (1974), "Intertemporal Consumer Theory and the Demand for Durables," *Econometrica*, Vol. 42, May.

Donovan, D.J. (1978), "Modeling the Demand for Liquid Assets: An Application to Canada," *International Monetary Fund Staff Papers*. Washington, D.C. Vol. 25, December.

Ewis, N. and D. Fisher (1984), "The Translog Utility Function and the Demand for Money in the United States," *Journal of Money, Credit, and Banking*, Vol. 16, January.

(1985), "Toward a Consistent Estimate of the Demand for Monies: An Application of the Fourier Flexible Form," *Journal of Macroeconomics*, Vol. 7, Spring.

Feenstra, R.C. (1986), "Functional Equivalence Between Liquidity Costs and the Utility of Money," *Journal of Monetary Economics*, Vol. 17 March.

Forgeaud, C. and A. Nataf (1959), "Consommation en prix et revenues reels et theorie des choix," *Econometrica*, Vol. 27, July.

Frankel, J.A. (1985), "Portfolio Crowding Out, Empirically Estimated," *Quarterly Journal of Economics*, Vol. 100.

Frankel, J.A. and W. Dickens (1983), "Are Assets Demand Functions Determined by CAPM?", Working Paper no. 1113 Cambridge, Mass.: National Bureau of Economic Research.

Friedman, B.M. (1978), "Crowding Out or Crowding In? Economic Consequences of Financing Government Deficits," *Brookings Papers on Economic Activity: 3*, Washington: The Brookings Institution.

(1985), "Crowding Out or Crowding In? Evidence on Debt Equity Substitutability," Working Paper no. 1565 Cambridge, Mass.: National Bureau of Economic Research.

Galli, G. (1985), "Il corso dei titoli a medio e lungo termine: una stima econometrica," *Contributi all'analisi economica*, Rome: Banca d'Italia.

Hansen, L.P. and K. Singleton (1982), "Generalized Instrumental Variables Estimation of Nonlinear Rational Expectations Models," *Econometrica*, Vol. 50, September.

Husted, S. and M. Rush (1984), "On Measuring the Nearness of Near Monies: Revisited," *Journal of Monetary Economics*, Vol. 14, September.

Judd, J.P. and J.L. Scadding (1982), "The Search for a Stable Money Demand Function," *Journal of Economic Literature*, Vol. 20, September.

Meisner, J.F. (1979), "The Sad Fate of the Slutsky Symmetry Test for Large Systems," *Economics Letters*, Vol. 2.

Milbourne, R. (1986), "Financial Innovation and the Demand for Liquid Assets," *Journal of Money, Credit, and Banking*, Vol. 18, November.

Modigliani, F. and F. Cotula (1973), "An Empirical Analysis of the Composition of Financial Wealth in Italy," *Banca Nazionale del Lavoro*, *Quarterly Review*, Rome, Vol. 27, June.

Pollak, R. A. (1970), "Habit Formation and Dynamic Demand Functions," *Journal of Political Economy*, Vol. 78, July–August.

Pollak, R.A. and T.J. Wales (1981), "Specification and Estimation of Dynamic Demand Systems," unpublished, Philadelphia: University of Pennsylvania.

Poterba, J.M. and J.J. Rotemberg (1986), "Money in the Utility Function: An Empirical Implementation," unpublished, Cambridge, Mass.: Massachusetts Institute of Technology.

Pudney, S.E. (1981), "An Empirical Method of Approximating the Separable Structure of Consumer Preferences," *Review of Economic Studies*, Vol. 48, October.

Roley, V.V. (1982), "The Effect of Federal Debt-Management Policy on Corporate Bond and Equity Yields," *Quarterly Journal of Economics*, Vol. 97, November.

Serletis, A. and A.L. Robb (1986), "Divisia Aggregation and Substitutability among Monetary Assets," *Journal of Money, Credit and Banking*, Vol. 18, November.

Discussion

JEFFREY A. FRANKEL

The question that implicitly motivates the Bollino-Rossi paper, within the overall context of the conference, is a macroeconomic one: given the large increase in the supply of short-term Italian debt in recent years, what changes in returns or prices in financial markets have been necessary to induce private investors to absorb this debt willingly? Within the general theoretical framework, in which the demands for various assets depend on the expected returns on the various assets, the natural answer is that an increase in the supply of Treasury bills will drive up the interest rate on Treasury bills, relative to the expected return on other assets.

The authors take a microeconomic approach, and because we are talking about the behavior of individual investors this is quite appropriate. They model a demand system for assets using techniques developed originally to estimate a demand system for consumer durables or other goods. This is an intriguing alternative to the conventional approach to estimating asset demands by assuming optimal portfolio diversification, which has some problems. One advantage of their technique is the "functional flexibility," which avoids the restriction of homogeneity in wealth, for example. The technique also allows the authors, as they say, to avoid the need for structural breaks. But nevertheless I have some doubts about the approach.

My major doubt has to do with their distinction between the two kinds of asset demand: demand for liquidity services and saving demand to transfer wealth into the next period. The conventional approach would be to define money as the only asset that provides liquidity services, and to include income or some other measure of transactions as an explanatory variable along with interest rates. But the authors allow all assets to yield liquidity services, even longer term securities, and they use no transactions variable. The approach used is to assume that, to the extent that some assets pay lower returns than others, they must be yielding

244

services, which are labeled "liquidity services." But if there were in fact only two attributes, liquidity and saving, then one could not explain the demand for five independent assets. Either the prices of the five assets would be fixed, regardless of quantities held, or else three of the assets would be dominated by two others – those two with the best combination of liquidity and return – and would therefore not be held at all. Either way, investors would not have a well-defined portfolio demand for five assets.

It must be that Bollino and Rossi are not thinking of "liquidity services" as a single attribute, but rather as at least four different attributes, that assets can offer besides expected return. Perhaps they are thinking that coins offer liquidity for one kind of transaction (bus tickets, candy machines, etc.), paper currency for another, deposits for a third, etc. Alternatively, they might have motives other than transactions demand in mind. Assets are differentiated by such attributes as default risk, inflation risk, tax treatment, and whether the asset pays a regular coupon.

Leaving aside for the moment the question of the estimation approach, the answers that Bollino and Rossi get are not unreasonable. Their latest parameter estimates in Table 6.6 show a semi-elasticity of the demand for money with respect to its own interest rate of 2.98 as of 1986, and a semi-elasticity with respect to the interest rate on short-term government securities of −4.97. (The coefficients of demand with respect to the other rates of return are much smaller.)

If we multiply the semi-elasticity of 3 by the average level of the interest rate that prevailed in Italy over the sample period, approximately 15 percent, we get an elasticity of .45. This estimate fits well with transactions theories of money demand.

What do such estimates imply about the effects of large shifts in the supplies of assets such as has been experienced by Italy in recent years? The fraction of the portfolio consisting of money (cash and deposits) has declined by about 25 percent between 1980 and 1985, according to Table 6.1, or according to figures provided to the conference by Luigi Spaventa or Marco Pagano. In addition, the supply of short-term Treasury securities roughly doubled as a fraction of the portfolio. The semi-elasticity estimate of 3 implies that a 25 percent reduction in the supply of money would push up the interest rate on short-term government securities, relative to the interest rate on deposits, by 8.33 percentage points. The effect would be even greater if the increase in the supply of Treasury bills is added in. Clearly, no effect this big has shown up in Italian interest rates.

This calculation assumes homogeneity of asset demands with respect to the total size of the portfolio. The authors consider their relaxation of the homogeneity assumption important. They would apparently explain the shift in portfolio demand from money to Treasury bills, not by changes in rates of return, but rather by the fact that there has been a large increase in total wealth: if Treasury bills are a "superior good" and money an "inferior good," then an increase in total wealth could in itself explain the shift in portfolio demand. But such a pattern of demand is not familiar from other countries, and seems implausible. Since the increase in the supply of Treasury bills constituted much of the increase in wealth, the proposed explanation is unpleasantly circular; to caricature, "the demand for Treasury bills went up because the supply of Treasury bills went up."

Obtaining good econometric estimates of portfolio demands is notoriously difficult. Many authors have felt the need to bring more information to bear on the question, to impose *more a priori* constraints than homogeneity and symmetry, rather than fewer. A popular source of *a priori* information is the theory of optimal portfolio diversification.[1] Risk-averse investors are assumed to allocate their portfolio among the available assets so as to maximize a function of the mean and variance of end-of-period wealth.[2] Assuming a constant coefficient of relative risk-aversion ρ, it can be shown that investors will choose portfolio shares, x in vector form, equal to

$$x = A + [\varrho\Omega]^{-1} (r - r^d)$$

where $r - r^d$ is the vector of returns on other assets measured relative to the return on deposits (arbitrarily chosen as the reference asset) and Ω is the variance-covariance matrix of returns. The first term A can be called the minimum-variance portfolio: what investors would hold if they were infinitely risk-averse. The second term can be called the speculative portfolio. In general, if the return is higher on a particular asset, investors will hold more of that asset than the share indicated by A, to an extent limited only by the amount of uncertainty and the degree of risk aversion. This framework gives not only homogeneity and symmetry, but also plausible properties such as the following: if the returns on bills and deposits vary closely together, then these two assets will be close substitutes in investors' portfolios.

The precise parameter estimates within this framework depend on the econometric estimation technique. But the right order of magnitude can be seen from a simple two-asset example, where x is defined as the portfolio share allocated to Treasury bills as opposed to money. If $\varrho = 2$ and the standard deviation of returns is 10 percent per annum (variance

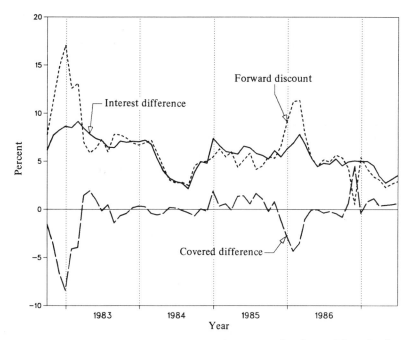

Figure 6.1   Italy: deviations from covered interest parity, 3 month interbank rate versus Euro dollar rate.

= 0.01), then $[\varrho\varOmega]^{-1} = 1/0.02 = 50$. It is a possible advantage of such estimates, within the present Italian context, that an increase in the relative interest rate on Treasury bills of as little as one-half a percentage point per annum could explain a portfolio shift as large as the 25 percent reduction in the share of money. On the other hand, such estimates are not only much bigger than the estimates of Bollino and Rossi, but are also much bigger than seems plausible in other contexts. Portfolio shifts on the scale of the recent Italian numbers are not, after all, a common occurrence.

One possibility is that the existence of capital controls in Italy means that an increase in government debt has a different effect on interest rates than it does in, say, the United States. (Bollino and Rossi do not discuss international considerations.) A common supposition is that when a country has capital markets that are as open as those in the United States, its interest rates are tied closely to world interest rates. But it depends on how we measure interest rates. Even if US interest rates match other countries' rates when both are expressed in dollars, macroeconomic policy can force US *real* interest rates above those of the other countries' to the extent that there is an expectation of future real depreciation of the dollar.

In Italy, capital controls have, at least until recent years, worked to slow the outflow of capital and thus to keep real interest rates from rising more than they have. We can tell this because interest rates in the Euromarket, whether measured as the Eurolira rate or as the Euro-dollar rate covered on the forward market, rose above the comparably short-term interest rate paid in Italy. This is evidence that there were effective barriers discouraging Italian investors from taking their money out of the country; otherwise they would not have settled for the lower domestic rate.[3]

If this were the end of the story, one might conclude that a fuller effect of the Italian debt on interest rates will show up as soon as announced plans to remove capital controls are realized. But in fact the Euro-domestic differential fell to zero in 1983–84 and even reversed sign in much of 1985–87. As Figure 6.1 shows, there is now – as of June 1987 – a small positive differential between the Italian interest rate and the Euromarket rate. This seems to suggest that capital controls are currently working to slow capital *inflow*, if anything, rather than outflow, and that the full upward effect on domestic Italian interest rates is already being felt (at least at the short-term end of the maturity spectrum). Italy is unique among a sample of 24 countries in this respect.[4] The only others that have differentials in this direction are a few, like Germany and Switzerland, that have traditionally had measures in place to discourage capital inflow, but that have also had little need to borrow from abroad on net. (In any case, these countries' differentials are very small: under 50 basis points.) The fact that interest rates are now at least as high on short-term Italian debt as they are in the Euromarket may be precisely the sort of evidence we would expect, evidence of the effect of the increased supply of short-term Italian debt. As with the United States in the 1980s, foreign investors appear eager to help finance the government debt. It is interesting that, according to the evidence of the current lira interest differential, the complete removal of capital controls would under current conditions allow more *inflow*, thereby *dampening* the rise of Italian interest rates, rather than the reverse.

NOTES

1 Frankel (1985), in a study of US portfolio demand, includes many references to the literature and a derivation of the equation to follow.
2 Bollino and Rossi are explicit in their choice to neglect uncertainty in asset

returns. But in their first draft they surprisingly referred to this as "standard practice" (p. 227). At the other extreme, Pagano (1987) says, "In the absence of uncertainty, all types of debt are perfect substitutes" (p. 145).

3 See Giavazzi and Pagano (1985), for the period up to 1983.

4 The statistics are presented in Frankel and MacArthur (1987). The 1987 covered interest differential in favor of Italy appears much greater than the one shown here if a forward lira rate quoted by Barclays Bank is used.

REFERENCES

Bollino, C., Andrea and Nicola Rossi (1987), "Public Debt and Households' Demand for Monetary Assets in Italy: 1970–86," in this volume.

Frankel, J. (1985), "Portfolio Crowding-Out, Empirically Estimated," *Quarterly Journal of Economics*, Vol. 100.

Frankel, J. and A. MacArthur (1987), "Political vs. Currency Premia in International Real Interest Differentials: A Study of Forward Rates for 24 Countries," NBER Working Paper No. 2309. Forthcoming, *European Economic Review*.

Giavazzi, Francisco and Marco Pagano (1985), "Capital Controls and the European Monetary System," in *Capital Controls and Foreign Exchange Legislation*, Occasional Paper, Milan: Euromobiliare.

Pagano, Marco (1987) "The Management of Public Debt and Financial Markets," in this volume.

Discussion

GIAMPAOLO GALLI

The paper of Bollino and Rossi (henceforth BR) is relevant to the theme of this conference; one facet of the problem of how to survive with a high public debt clearly concerns the demand for assets. Will the market continue to buy large amounts of government paper in the future? Will this be possible at going rates of interest or will it be necessary to increase them further?

That a problem exists can hardly be questioned, as appears from the data on deficits, the debt ratio and its growth reported in the introductory chapter in this volume. Further, projections reported in Galli and Masera (1987) show that, holding the ratio of the primary deficit net of seignorage to GDP constant at its 1986 level, the debt can hardly fail to rise by less than 40 percent of GDP; it may even rise by 70 percent if the rate of interest on government paper exceeds the rate of growth by some 2 percentage points, as it mostly did in 1981–86.

The puzzle, which this conference has only partially addressed, is why Italy has not only survived, but managed to perform (in terms of both inflation and growth) no worse than countries like France, which never had a debt problem, and the UK, which no longer has one. Even if one was willing to take this as evidence of Ricardian equivalence, there would still remain an issue of credibility. Since Italy has not fought a war in the recent past, there are no obvious reasons for its running temporary deficits, as should be the case under Lucas-Stockey-Pagano optimal policies. Why, then, should the market believe that the deficits are temporary? In the absence of credible signals of fiscal adjustment, wouldn't households, at some point, start to fear a rerun of the 1970s, when inflation wiped out a considerable portion of their financial wealth?

It is unfortunate that the BR estimates only cover the period after the share of government paper started to soar in 1977, since at least a part of the explanation of this development is to be found in the reasons for its earlier fall. In 1964 the ratio of the financial assets of the private sector, excluding money (in the M2 definition used in the paper) to total financial assets was 0.27; from then on it fell continuously to a low of 0.15 in 1977, then rose very rapidly, passed its 1964 level in 1982 and is now around 0.4. It is worth noting that the main downturns of this ratio occurred in the years immediately following inflationary bursts: 1963, 1969 and 1974. In each of these three episodes the rise in nominal interest rates inflicted losses on the private sector whose holdings were almost exclusively long-term. This pattern was not repeated in 1980–86. By then, long-term fixed interest bonds had become a negligible portion of private sector assets, and the debt was virtually all short-term or linked to short-term rates of interest. Two main innovations had made this possible. First, starting in 1975 the authorities took a number of steps to market Treasury bills with the non-bank private sector. Secondly, in 1977 a new instrument was introduced, the Treasury Credit Certificate, with a coupon linked to the rate on Treasury bills. Some economists have argued that these innovations were more a matter of form than of substance, on the grounds that the degree of moneyness of Treasury bills and Credit Certificates is not much smaller than that of bank deposits.

BR inquire into these issues by estimating a system of demand equations derived from a "flexible" utility function. There are three interesting questions:

Does the model account for the shifts that have taken place since 1977? And if so, how?
Can it help in assessing the degree of moneyness of Treasury bills and Credit Certificates?
What does "flexibility" mean in this context? Which restrictions are imposed and which not?

A satisfactory answer to the first question cannot be given because standard errors (the only measure of goodness of fit which is reported) are not very revealing when significant "dynamic translating" is present in the equation. This procedure is similar to the Brainard-Tobin (1968) procedure of introducing all lagged stocks in each equation; clearly a dynamic simulation of the model is required to assess its performance. In the absence of evidence to the contrary, we can suppose that the model does genuinely capture at least some of the increase in the share of government paper since 1977; the question is how. Interest rates cannot be the answer. It should be remembered that there is no deposit rate regulation in Italy. In 1978 the differential between the average rate on Treasury bills and the average rate on M2 (including non-interest-bearing items) was 4 per cent (the lowest in 5 years); it then rose until

1981 when it reached 10 per cent, but subsequently fell continuously until 1986, by when it was back to its 1978 level. The only other explanation is non-homotheticity, i.e. that the share of government paper rises with the scale of total assets – government paper is a superior good, money is inferior. The message for the future is reassuring: the demand for government debt will naturally continue to grow as long as more is supplied. In the light of the considerations developed above, I find this message unconvincing; at the very least, the hypothesis that money is inferior should be tested on a sample period including a few years before 1977.

As to the second question, I wonder how the degree of liquidity of an asset can be estimated without introducing a proxy for the volume of transactions and, perhaps, for uncertainty about future cash flows. To illustrate the problem, suppose an economist is asked to measure the calorie content of food (rather than the liquidity content of assets). Lacking a direct measure, he assumes that the only characteristic of food people appreciate is the calorie content; under this assumption, relative prices are fixed and are simply proportional to the number of calories contained in each item; it is hence perfectly correct to infer calorie contents from market prices. What is not correct is to let preferences over different types of food be convex: they clearly are not. If our economist nonetheless assumes they are, perhaps to account for the fact that people like to mix different types of food, he undoubtedly adds realism to the model, but relaxes the critical assumption that allows him to measure the number of calories.

The final question is that of flexible functional forms and restrictions. By simple manipulations, the main equation of the model, (equation (8) with equation (10) proxying for V) can be shown to imply the following: (uncommitted) expenditure shares are regressed on a constant – the log of (relative) prices and total (uncommitted) expenditure net of a weighted average of the log prices. This model certainly has more free parameters than a linear expenditure system (which allows only for the first of the above three regressors, the constant) and incorporates the basic idea of flexible functional forms, which consists in allowing at least one free parameter for each effect of interest (see Diewert 1971 and Deaton 1986). Most estimated portfolio models have free parameters for prices (interest rates), but not for total expenditure (total assets); relative to these models, it hence seems that non-homotheticity is the main element of flexibility. In this connection, it would be useful to know what non-homotheticity implies for such utility related issues as risk aversion and the Hicksian marginal utility of money. Likewise, an explanation would be appreciated about the significance, in the present context, of subtracting a weighted average of prices (interest differentials) from total expenditure.

In their preferred estimates, the authors proceed to impose homogeneity and symmetry in prices: these restrictions have a clear meaning in consumer theory, but are somewhat intriguing in the present context. Homogeneity ($\Sigma_j \gamma_{ij} = 0$) relates to the log of *interest differentials* rather than *interest rates*. This implies that shares are unaffected, not when interest rates (on the assets that are endogenous to the model) change by the same amount or in the same proportion, but when they change by *different* amounts consistently with interest differentials changing in the same proportion. This requires that variations of individual rates be inversely related to their levels (i.e. *higher* rates must change by *less*).

Concerning symmetry, it should be noted that it applies to expenditure shares, not to asset shares; hence, when the symmetry restriction is imposed, the response of the demand for asset j to rate i *differs* from that of asset i to rate j.

Unfortunately a restriction that cannot be imposed is that of gross substitutability. On this account the BR model shares the problem reported by Backus, Brainard, Smith and Tobin (1980) and many others, in connection with more traditional portfolio estimates – wrong signs. In the BR model these problems are hard to detect because partial derivatives are non-linear in the variables. The simulations reported in section 4 reveal that not only postal deposits, but also Treasury bills have the wrong sign on their own rate. I can see no other explanation of the fact that a shock to the Treasury Credit Certificates rate alone moves more Treasury bills and credit certificates than a shock to both their rates (Table 6.6).

A final point concerns homogeneity in the *price level*, a restriction that does not seem to be imposed in the present version of the model, though it is certainly compatible with the chosen functional form. There are two separate reasons for this. First, in equation (7) the $\bar{\mu}_j$'s are constant quantities in current lire. Second, the v_j's rise with the price level since they are defined as interest differentials multiplied by the price level (equation 3). Except when $\Sigma_j \gamma_{ij} = 0$, the last term in equation (8) implies that changes in the price level affect expenditure shares.

REFERENCES

Backus, D., W.C. Brainard, G. Smith and J. Tobin (1980), "A Model of US Financial and Non Financial Economic Behavior," *Journal of Money, Credit and Banking*, 2, May.

Brainard, W.C. and J. Tobin (1968), "Pitfalls in Financial Model Building," *American Economic Review* – Papers and Proceedings, May.

Deaton, A. (1986), "Demand Analysis," in *Handbook of Econometrics*, edited by Z. Griliches and M.D. Intriligator, vol. III, North-Holland.

Diewert, W.E. (1971), "An Application of the Shepard Duality Theorem: A Generalized Leontief Production Function," *Journal of Political Economy*, 79.

Galli, G. and R.S. Masera (1987), "Government Deficits and Debts. The Necessity and Cost of Adjustment: The Case of Italy," paper presented at the NEDO Conference on "Keynes's General Theory After 50 Years," London, 15–18 September.

Index

Africa, colonial wars in, 195
Aiyagari, S. R., 114
Alesina, Alberto, 5, 19, 34–79, 130, 167
Anderson, G. J., 234
Andreatta, Beniamino, 97
Argentina, 130
asset markets, "bubble paths," 202–3
assets, menu offered to public, 20
assets demand
  stability of, 17–19
  theories, 228–31
Atkinson, A. B., 182
auction systems, 20, 138

Bachi, R., 192
Backus, D., 253
Baffi, Paolo, 95, 127
balance of payments crises theory, 219
Banca d'Italia, 225, 231
Bank of England, 131
Bank of Italy
  evolution of monetary policy, 90–100
  loss of gold reserves (1927–34), 194–5
  monetary financing by, 7–10
  relations with the Treasury, 10, 90, 96–9
  share of public debt held by, 92–3; see
    also Banca d'Italia
banks, central, representative of the will
  of the people?, 131
Barna, T., 67
Barnett, W. A., 225, 226, 227, 228, 230
Barro, Robert J., 36, 38, 70, 71, 140, 141,
  151, 167, 171
Barth, J., 227
Belgium, ratio of debt to GDP, 3–4
black economy and inflation tax, Italy, 133
black market dollar exchange rate
  (1957–83), 200
Blanchard, O., 38, 57, 71
Bodie, Zvi, 161

Bollino, C. Andrea, 13, 17, 21, 222–43
BOTs, *see* Treasury bills
Brainard, W. C., 251, 253
Brennan, J., 100
Bresciani-Turroni, C., 41, 42, 43, 46, 47,
  48–9
Bretton Woods system, 203; collapse, 199
Britain, *see* United Kingdom
Brumberg, R., 178
Bruni, F., 98, 100
Bryant, J., 103
BTP (fixed-rate debt), 137
Buchanan, J., 100
Buiter, W., 38, 57, 71, 74
Bundesbank, 131
"businessmen," 38–40

Cagan, P., 45
"Caisse d'Amortissement," 55–6
Calvo, Guillermo A., 36, 187, 215
capital controls, 154
  and effect of increase in government
    debt on interest rates, 247–8
  and public finance, Italy, 177–221;
    (1920s) 189–94; (1930s) 194–7;
    (1970s) 15
capital flight, 73
  macroeconomic consequences of, 178,
    181–5
  as tax evasion, 188–97
capital flows, estimates of (1929–36), Italy,
  194–5
capital levy, 29–30, 73, 83, 131, 187
capital mobility, as tax evasion, 178–88
Caporetto, battle of, 58
Caranza, C., 98, 224
Carli, Guido, 94, 98, 127, 128
Cartel des Gauches, 51, 53
Casse di Risparmio, 63
Catholic Party, Italy, 59

255